# Learning Pascal
# Step by Step

# Learning Pascal
# Step by Step

**Vern McDermott**

**Andrew Young**

**Diana Fisher**

Machine Specific for APPLE II Plus • APPLE IIe • IBM PC • TRS-80

COMPUTER SCIENCE PRESS

Copyright © 1985 Computer Science Press, Inc.

Printed in the United States of America.

*Computer Science Press, Inc.*
*1803 Research Blvd.*
*Rockville, Maryland 20850*

1 2 3 4 5 6 Printing                                    Year 90 89 88 87 86 85

**Library of Congress Cataloging in Publication Data**

McDermott, Vern, 1934–
    Learning Pascal step by step.

    1. PASCAL (Computer program language)
I. Fisher, Diana, 1948- . II. Title.
QA76.73.P2M364 1985 001.64'24 84-19869
ISBN 0-88175-045-X {Student Textbook}
ISBN 0-88175-046-8 {Teacher's Edition}

*The cartoon characters were drawn by Laura Bishop.*

*Cover design by Ruth Ramminger.*

# CONTENTS

# PREFACE

While developing a course in Pascal programming, the authors recognized a need for an introductory Pascal textbook that satisfied the following criteria:

The text be written with a style and a reading level that is suitable for high school or junior college students.

The text be suitable for use in an independent study program as well as in a lecture-oriented classroom environment.

The text be complete so it can be used for formal programming classes without supplementing or altering; that is, it contains material that is well organized, and new concepts that are supported by demonstration problems and ample skill development exercises.

Therefore, in developing *Learning Pascal Step by Step* the following features were implemented:

A problem-solving approach that is used throughout the text.

A diagram approach to presenting new concepts that lends itself to easy referencing.

Material that is presented at a pace to encourage progress without frustration.

Ample opportunity for students to become proficient in using the new concepts before moving on to new topics.

Careful organization of new concepts so that no program requires a concept that has not been introduced.

An easy-to-understand format that presents concepts which illustrate strengths of Pascal, such as sets, record structures, type declarations, and passing parameters to procedures.

In order to place maximum emphasis on new concepts being introduced, less emphasis was placed on comments both in the demonstration and skill development programs; however, the use of comments is strongly encouraged in places where they will enhance the clarity and readability of the programs.

# ACKNOWLEDGMENTS

Special thanks go to Mike LaChapelle, Mike Lanzarotta, Tim Carlson, and Gary Schroeder, who, while using the preliminary manuscripts, pointed out many errors and organizational problems.

Andy Young would like to personally thank his grandparents, parents, and friends, Dave and Brian, whose support and encouragement were so greatly appreciated that they could never be repaid.

# INTRODUCTION

Niklaus Wirth designed the language Pascal, which was named after the 17th century mathematician Blaise Pascal. One of the principal reasons for designing the language Pascal was to create a programming language that could be used to teach a well-organized and disciplined approach to programming and problem solving. As a result Pascal has become the major instructional language used in colleges and universities.

Reasons why Pascal is becoming the most popular language in use are:

1. Pascal is widely available on many different types of computers, ranging from large mainframe computers to microcomputers. That is, the different computers have Pascal compilers available that will translate programs written in Pascal into the machine language of the computer being used.

2. Pascal lends itself to good programming techniques. Thus, students of Pascal learn to program effectively.

3. Pascal is a structured programming language. Programs written in Pascal are well-organized and easy to follow.

4. Pascal is an excellent teaching language. Therefore, learning Pascal provides a good background for future studies in computer science.

This book was written for the Apple UCSD Pascal, Radio Shack TRS–80 version of New Classics Pascal–80, and the IBM P–SYSTEM VERSION IV.0.

# GETTING STARTED

In order to complete the problems in this text, the user must become familiar with the computer's Pascal operating system. Abbreviated instructions for using the operating system are located in the appropriate appendix as indicated below.

APPENDIX I

   APPLE Operating System

APPENDIX II

   TRS–80 Operating System

APPENDIX III

   IBM PC Operating System

# Lessons

# Lesson 1
# PASCAL EXPRESSIONS

## 1.1 OBJECTIVES

Objectives: 1. To understand the types of constants, variables, and operations that can be used.
2. To be able to translate expressions from algebra to Pascal.
3. To understand the correct sequence for the order of operations.

## 1.2 CONSTANTS, VARIABLES, AND OPERATIONS

DATA TYPES[1]

| Type | Examples | Description |
|------|----------|-------------|
| INTEGER | 5<br>86<br>0 | Whole numbers (i.e., numbers that do not contain a decimal point). The largest integer allowed is $+32767$ and the smallest is $-32768$. |
| REAL | 5.3<br>18.0<br>0.4<br>6.5E3<br>4.32E-2 | Numbers that involve a decimal. (The decimal must have at least one digit in front of the decimal point and one digit behind the decimal point.)<br><br>$6.5E3 = 6500 \ (6.5 \times 10^3)$<br>$4.32E-2 = 0.0432 \ (4.32 \times 10^{-2})$ |

VARIABLES (IDENTIFIERS)

*Examples:*

N
Sum
Average1
Average2
AppliedToPrin

*Rules for Identifiers*

1. They contain a sequence of the letters (A–Z) or a combination of the letters (A–Z) and the digits (0–9).
2. They must begin with one of the letters.
3. They cannot contain symbols such as /,*,–,&,$,%, or blanks.

PROBLEM IDENTIFIERS

Summation1
Summation2

*Problem*

Even if there is no specified limit to the number of digits that a variable can contain, it is common that only the first eight are actually used. Therefore, the two identifiers to the left will be treated as the same variable by some compilers.

---

[1] Other types such as STRING, BOOLEAN, and CHAR will be presented in later lessons.

## ILLEGAL IDENTIFIERS

| ILLEGAL IDENTIFIERS | *Reason* |
|---|---|
| Miles/Gal | Only the characters (A–Z) are allowed; symbols like "/" are illegal. |
| 3rdGroup | A variable must start with one of the letters (A–Z). |
| Net Salary | Blanks are not allowed. |
| Real | Reserved words cannot be used as variables. (REAL, END, PROGRAM, INTEGER, DIV are examples.) |

## OPERATIONS

| OPERATIONS | *Meaning* |
|---|---|
| + | Addition |
| − | Subtraction |
| * | Multiplication |
| / | Division (Real type) |
| DIV | Division (Integer type) |
| MOD | Remainder Division (See explanation below.) |

Note: Problems involving exponents must be treated like multiplication problems until the proper functions are presented in a later lesson. Example: $X^2$ must be written as $(X*X)$.

## ORDER OF EXECUTION

Rules for the order of execution of operations are the same as the rules in algebra.

| First | Exponents and parentheses |
|---|---|
| Second | *, /, DIV, and MOD from left to right |
| Third | + and − from left to right |

## ASSIGNMENT STATEMENT EXAMPLES

| ASSIGNMENT STATEMENT EXAMPLES | EXPLANATION |
|---|---|
| Y:= A + B | The value of A + B is assigned to Y. |
| Ave:= (Item1 + Item2) / 2 | The numbers stored in Item1 and Item2 are added together, the sum is divided by two, and the result is assigned to Ave. Item1 and Item2 may be real or integer type numbers. |
| IntQuot:= Num DIV Den | The number stored in Num is divided by the number stored in Den and the integer part of the result is assigned to IntQuot. For example:    25 DIV 4 = 6    −14 DIV 3 = −4 |
| RealQuot:= Num / Den | Same as above only the real result is assigned to RealQuot. For example:    25 / 4 = 6.25    −14 / 5 = −2.8 |

```
Rem: = Num1 MOD Num2
```

The value stored in Num1 will be divided by the value stored in Num2 and the remainder will be assigned to Rem.

For example:
```
     6 MOD 2  = 0
    10 MOD 3  = 1
   -15 MOD 4  = 3
     4 MOD (-15)= 4[1]
```

## 1.3 DEMONSTRATION PROBLEMS

Changing algebraic expressions to Pascal expressions:

| *Algebraic Expression* | *Equivalent Pascal Expression* |
|---|---|
| 1. $8X+3$ | 8*X + 3 |
| 2. $5(X+6)$ | 5*(X + 6) |
| 3. $\dfrac{A+B}{2C}$ | (A + B) / (2*C) |
| 4. $A^2 + B^2$ | A*A + B*B (temporary solution[2]) |
| 5. $\dfrac{XY}{Z+10}$ | X*Y / (Z + 10) or (X*Y) / (Z + 10) |

Note: In the above examples the identifiers were chosen as they would be in algebra. When used in programs, the identifiers should be chosen so that they are as descriptive as possible. For example, averaging three numbers in Pascal may look like this: (Item1 + Item2 + Item3) / HowMany.

Evaluating Pascal expressions:

| *Pascal Expression* | *Value* |
|---|---|
| 6. 8*5 + 3 | 43 |
| 7. 6 + 4*2 - 3 | 11 |
| 8. 15 DIV 2 | 7 |
| 9. 0.5 * 8.0 + 1.6 * 1.2 | 5.92 |
| 10. 50.0 / 2.5 * (4.2 + 1.8) | 120 |
| 11. 25 MOD 8 | 1 |

---

[1] On some compilers the parentheses are not necessary. However, it is recommended they be used in order to make the programs more universally accepted.

[2] This is a temporary solution until the proper functions are introduced in a later lesson.

If X: = 5, Y: = 2, and Z: = 7, then the value assigned to A in each of the following problems is:

| *Pascal Statement* | *Value of* A |
|---|---|
| 12. A: = X*X − Y | 23 |
| 13. A: = Y DIV X*Z | 0 |
| 14. A: = 3*Y + Z*Z DIV Y + 4 | 34 |
| 15. A: = X*Y + Z MOD X | 12 |

If Num1 = 4.9, Num2 = 0.7, and Cost = 5.30, find the value assigned to Answer.

| *Pascal Statement* | *Value assigned to* Answer |
|---|---|
| 16. Answer: = Num1 / Num2 * Cost | 37.1 |
| 17. Answer: = (Num1+Num2 / 2.0)* Cost | 27.825 |

If A = 3.2E2, B = −4.6E3, and C = 5.5E-2, find the value assigned to Result. (To make the calculations easier, change all numbers to decimal form before completing the arithmetic operations.)

| *Pascal Statement* | *Value assigned to* Result |
|---|---|
| 18. Result: = (A + B) / 2.0 | −2.14E3 |
| 19. Result: = C*100.0 + A*10.0 | 3.2055E3 |

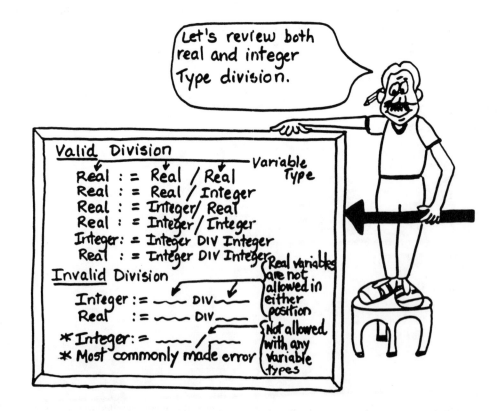

## 1.4 SKILL DEVELOPMENT EXERCISES

Indicate whether or not the following are valid variables (identifiers):

1. A5

2. Sum

3. A4-B

4. 5X

5. FinalResultOf2

6. $5.80

7. Div

Write these algebraic expressions in their equivalent Pascal form:

8. $\dfrac{3A - B}{3}$

9. $B(A + B)$

10. $\left(\dfrac{A}{B + C}\right)\left(\dfrac{C}{D}\right)$

If $X = 2$, $Y = 4$, and $Z = 3$, find the value assigned to A in each of the Pascal statements:

11. A: = X + Y + Z*3

12. A: = (2*X + 2*Y) DIV 3

13. A: = Z*Y − 4*X

14. A: = 5*Y DIV X*Z DIV (5*X)

15. A: = (Y*Z) MOD 4

If Case1 = 1.23, Case2 = 0.831, Alpha = 8.15E-2, and Beta = −1.6E3, find the value assigned to CalVal in each of the following Pascal statements:

16. CalVal: = Case2 / 3 * 0.05

17. CalVal: = Alpha * 2 + 6.21E-2

18. CalVal: = Case1 / 0.5 * Case2 / 0.2

19. CalVal: = Alpha * 1.0E5 + Beta

# Lesson 2
# INTRODUCTION TO PROGRAMMING

## 2.1 OBJECTIVES

Objectives: 1. To write a simple Pascal program.
2. To be able to type a program into the computer and get an answer displayed.

## 2.2 ASSIGNMENT, WRITE, DECLARATIONS, BEGIN, and END

| PARTS OF A PASCAL PROGRAM | EXPLANATION |
|---|---|
| `PROGRAM Payroll;` | Every program must have a name that is declared in the first statement. The name must be followed by a semicolon. |
| `VAR X, Y, Count: INTEGER;`<br>`  Ave, Percent: REAL;` | The declaration section of the program must include a declaration of each variable in the program as to its type. (Each declaration must be followed by a semicolon.) |
| `BEGIN`<br><br>`END.` | The body of the program begins with the BEGIN statement and ends with the END statement. The working statements of the program are between the BEGIN and END statements. |

Note: In a Pascal program, a semicolon is used following each statement to separate that statement from the next statement. No semicolon is used after BEGIN and is optional following the statement just before the END.

BEGINNING PROGRAM STRUCTURE (summary)

```
PROGRAM Inventory;
VAR N,C: INTEGER;
    Average: REAL;
BEGIN
    _____;  ⎫
    _____;  ⎬ Program
    _____;  ⎪ statements
    _____;  ⎭
END.
```

The program Inventory will use two variables, N and C, that are integers, and one variable, Average, that is a real. The execution of the calculations and the display of the results will be done between the BEGIN and END statements. A " ; " must follow each statement except the BEGIN and END statements. The semicolon is optional following the statement before the END statement; however, to prevent potential errors, it is recommended that the semicolon also be included. The END statement is following by a period.

Note: Indentation is used to make the program more readable. It is recommended that it be used from the first program on so that it becomes a natural programming procedure. As the programs become more difficult, indentation becomes increasingly important.

PASCAL STATEMENTS

    X:= -10;

    Y:= X*5 + 3;


    WRITELN(X);

    WRITELN(X,Y);

Display Sample
```
 -10
 -10-47

```

    WRITELN(X,'     ',Y);

Display Sample
```
 -10    -47

```

EXPLANATION

The : = is used to assign a number to the variable or the identifier to the left of the assignment symbol. Any valid Pascal expression or constant can be used to the right of the symbol.

The WRITELN statement causes the numbers assigned to the variable(s) to be displayed. On most computers there will be no spaces between the numbers of the display. Variables are separated by commas and the list is enclosed in parentheses. After the information is printed, the WRITELN statement automatically executes a return and line feed.

When spaces are not left after each variable, the spaces between the single-quote marks in the WRITELN statement provide the desired spaces between the numbers.

Note:  In all dialog and demonstration problems from this point on, it will be assumed that spaces are not left after variables in the display. If the system used does provide such spaces, then the quotation marks ( '    ' )  are  not  necessary.

## 2.3 DEMONSTRATION PROBLEMS

1. Write a computer program to calculate and display the values of $X$ and $Y$ when $Y = \dfrac{X^2 + 5}{X - 3}$ and $X = 8$.

```
PROGRAM Algebra;
   VAR X: INTEGER;
       Y: REAL;
BEGIN
   X:= 8;
   Y:= (X*X + 5)/(X–3);
   WRITELN(X,'    ',Y);
END.
```

Display Sample

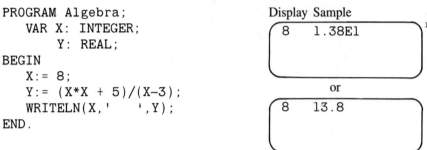

```
8    1.38E1          [1]
```

or

```
8    13.8
```

2. Write a computer program to compute the increase in pay for a 40-hour week if the hourly wage was changed from $3.50 to $3.75.

```
PROGRAM Wages;
   VAR W1,W2,I: REAL;
BEGIN
   W1:= 40*3.50;
   W2:= 40*3.75;
   I:= W2–W1;
   WRITELN(I);
END.
```

Display Sample

```
1.00000E1          [1]
```

or

```
10
```

3. Use the computer to find the average of the areas of three circles with radii of 3.2 inches, 4.6 inches, and 5.8 inches respectively.

```
PROGRAM CArea;
   VAR P,A1,A2,A3,Average: REAL;
BEGIN
   P:= 3.14159;
   A1:= P*3.2*3.2;
   A2:= P*4.6*4.6;
   A3:= P*5.8*5.8;
   Average:= (A1 + A2 + A3)/3;
   WRITELN(Average);
END.
```

Display Sample

```
6.81097E1          [1]
```

or

```
68.1096712
```

## 2.4 SKILL DEVELOPMENT EXERCISES

1. Trace through the logic of this program and indicate what the computer will display.

```
PROGRAM Trace;
   VAR A,B,C: REAL;
BEGIN
   A:= 3.5;
   B:= 6*A –1;
   WRITELN(B);
   C:= A + B/5;
   WRITELN(C);
END.
```

Display Sample

---

[1] The technique for obtaining a display of a real number in the normal decimal form rather than in exponential form will be presented in later lessons.

2. Given a salary of $4.85 per hour, use the computer to determine the wage for a 40-hour week.

   Answer: $194

3. The charges for gas, water, and electricity are $24.80, $10.52, and $15.42 respectively. Use the computer to determine the total charges for that particular month.

   Answer: $50.74

4. Given that the length and width of a rectangle are 10.5 inches and 8.3 inches respectively, make the computer calculate and print out the area and perimeter of the rectangle. $(A = lw, P = 2l + 2w.)$

   Answer: 87.15 and 37.6

*Skill Development Exercises are continued on next page.*

5. Given 54 half dollars, 128 quarters, 112 dimes, 181 nickels, and 351 pennies, have the computer calculate and print out the total value of the coins.

   Answer: $82.76

6. Determine the value of $Y$ in the expression $Y = 3X^2 + 2X - 8$ when $X = 5.3$.

   Answer: 86.87

7. If the radius of a sphere increases from 1.3652 feet to 2.8971 feet, determine the increase in volume.

   $$V = \frac{4}{3} \pi r^3 \qquad \pi = 3.14159$$

Answer: 91.1961

# Lesson 3
# WRITE and WRITELN

## 3.1 OBJECTIVES

Objectives: 1. To know the general strategy for developing a program.
2. To use headings in output displays both on the monitor and the printer.
3. To introduce the concept of formatting output.

## 3.2 PROGRAMMING STRATEGY AND FORMATTING DISPLAYS

*Programming a Problem*

1. Define the problem.
   a. Know what data is involved.
   b. Know how to work the problem out longhand (with paper and pencil).
   c. Know what is to be displayed.
2. Determine the sequence of steps that must be used to construct the program.
3. Write the program code.

*More about* WRITE *and* WRITELN

PASCAL STATEMENT                                   EXPLANATION

⌐Characters to be displayed

WRITELN('TOTAL DUE');                              Displays the letters, numbers, or characters that are
                                                   between quotation marks exactly as they appear in
Display Sample                                     the statement.

```
TOTAL DUE
```

⌐First item to be displayed
 ⌐Field width for first item
  ⌐Second item to be displayed
   ⌐Field width for second item

WRITELN('LENGTH':8,'WIDTH':8);                     The word "LENGTH" will be displayed to the
                                                   right side of the specified field of eight spaces
Display Sample                                     (right justified). The word "WIDTH" will be dis-
```
 1   3      8            16                         played to the right side of the second field of eight
      LENGTH       WIDTH                            spaces. The left-hand portion of the field spaces
                                                   will remain blank. If the item to be displayed
                                                   requires more spaces than the specified field con-
                                                   tains, it will be truncated on the right.
```

11

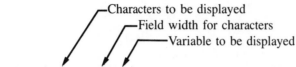

```
WRITELN('X= ':10,X);
```

Displays "X=    " in the columns 8 through 10. The value of X (in this case 45) is then printed.

Display Sample

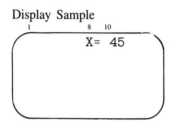

```
WRITE(X);
WRITELN('     ',Y);
```

The WRITE statement tells the computer to print the indicated item and stay on the same line. This allows for a subsequent WRITE or WRITELN statement to display another item on the same line. The example to the left only illustrates how the WRITE statement works; the statements could be replaced by WRITELN(X'     ',Y) if both values for *X* and *Y* are available (in this case *X* = -10 and *Y* = -47).

Display Sample

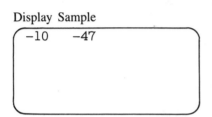

Note: On some computers the numbers will be displayed with spaces and the statement WRITELN(Y) would replace WRITELN('     ',Y).

```
WRITELN('X');
WRITELN;
WRITELN(X);
```

A WRITELN with no arguments[1] will result in a skipped line on the display.

Display Sample

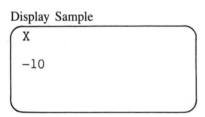

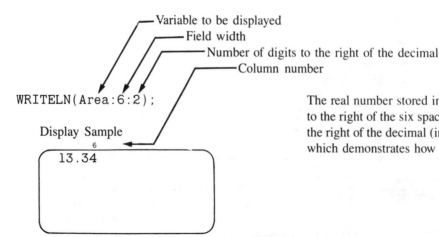

```
WRITELN(Area:6:2);
```

The real number stored in Area will be displayed to the right of the six space field with two places to the right of the decimal (in this case *X* = 13.3418, which demonstrates how the .0018 is truncated).

Display Sample

---

[1] An argument is the information between parentheses.

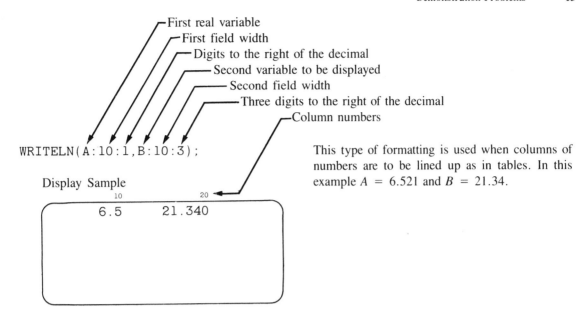

First real variable
First field width
Digits to the right of the decimal
Second variable to be displayed
Second field width
Three digits to the right of the decimal
Column numbers

```
WRITELN(A:10:1,B:10:3);
```

Display Sample

```
        10            20
     6.5      21.340
```

This type of formatting is used when columns of numbers are to be lined up as in tables. In this example $A = 6.521$ and $B = 21.34$.

## 3.3 DEMONSTRATION PROBLEMS

1. Trace through the logic of this program and indicate what the computer will display.

```
PROGRAM Trace;
  VAR A: INTEGER;
BEGIN
  WRITELN ('HELLO','      ','THERE');
  WRITELN ('HOW AR':7,'E YOU');
  A:= 100;
  WRITE ('I HOPE YOU MAKE ':17,A);
  WRITELN (' PERCENT');
  WRITELN ('ON THIS QUESTION');
END.
```

Display Sample

```
HELLO      THERE
 HOW ARE YOU
 I HOPE YOU MAKE  100 PERCENT
ON THIS QUESTION
```

2. Write a computer program to calculate and display the values of $X$ and $Y$ as shown in the display sample when $Y = \dfrac{X+5}{X-2}$ and $X = 8$.

```
PROGRAM L3Demo2;
VAR  X: INTEGER;
     Y: REAL;
BEGIN
  X:= 8;
  Y:= (X + 5)/(X - 2);
  WRITELN('IF X = ',X);
  WRITELN('THEN Y = ',Y:5:2);
END.
```

Display Sample

```
IF X = 8
THEN Y =  2.17
```

3. Given the radii for three circles, 7.5 cm, 3.2 cm, and 12 cm, write a program to calculate the areas and print the answers as shown in the display sample. (Area = $\pi r^2$.)

```
PROGRAM L3Demo3;
    VAR Area1,Area2,Area3,Total,Pi:REAL;
BEGIN
    WRITELN ('AREA 1':10,'AREA 2':10,'AREA 3':10);
    WRITELN;
    Pi:= 3.14159;
    Area1:= Pi * 7.5 * 7.5;
    Area2:= Pi * 3.2 * 3.2;
    Area3:= Pi * 12 *12;
    WRITELN (Area1:10:2,Area2:10:2,Area3:10:2);
    WRITELN;
    Total:= Area1 + Area2 + Area3;
    WRITELN ('TOTAL AREA = ',Total:6:2);
END.
```

Display Sample

```
     AREA 1    AREA 2    AREA 3

     176.71     32.17    452.39

TOTAL AREA = 661.27
```

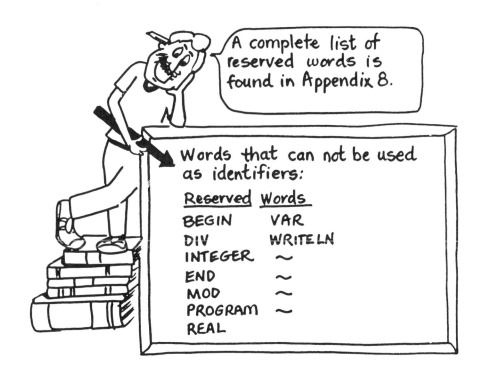

## 3.4 SKILL DEVELOPMENT EXERCISES

1. Trace through the logic of this program and indicate what the computer will display.

```
PROGRAM L3P1;
  VAR Cost, Mark, Price: REAL;
BEGIN
  Cost:= 175.50;
  Mark:= 52.65;
  Price:= Cost + Mark;
  WRITELN('COST           $', Cost:7:2);
  WRITELN('MARKUP         $', Mark:7:2);
  WRITELN('SELLING PRICE $', Price:7:2);
END.
```

2. Given the yearly cost of three utilities (heating = $1140.82, water = $420.50, and electricity = $562.82), calculate and display the average monthly cost of each of the utilities and the total of the monthly averages.

   Display Sample

   ```
        YEARLY COST
   HEATING    WATER    ELECT
   1140.82    420.50   562.82


         MONTHLY AVERAGE
    95.07     35.04     46.90


   TOTAL MONTHLY AVE =    177.01
   ```

3. Write a program to determine the total for a monthly budget that will be spent on rent, utilities, food, and miscellaneous items. The rent is $150 per month, the utilities average 35% of the rent, and food averages $70 per week (consider a month to consist of 4½ weeks). Miscellaneous items are usually 60% of the cost of the food.

   Display Sample

   ```
      MONTHLY BUDGET

   RENT        = $ 150.00
   UTILITIES   = $  52.50
   FOOD        = $ 315.00
   MISC        = $ 189.00

   TOTAL       = $ 706.50
   ```

---

[1] When the Display Sample is enclosed in a box as shown above, the printout should have a similar appearance. That is, it should have the same spacing, headings, and word descriptions.

# Lesson 4
# LOOPING

## 4.1 OBJECTIVES

Objectives: 1. To become familiar with relations and Boolean expressions.
2. To use READLN statements for keying in data.
3. To learn to use comments in programs.
4. To learn to use stopping signals in loop control.
5. To display results in table form.

## 4.2 READLN, BOOLEAN EXPRESSIONS, AND WHILE–DO

RELATIONS                                EXPLANATION

$<$                                      Is less than
$<=$                                     Is less than or equal to
$>$                                      Is greater than
$>=$                                     Is greater than or equal to
$=$                                      Is equal to
$<>$                                     Is not equal to

BOOLEAN EXPRESSIONS                      EXPLANATION

$X = Y$                                  A Boolean expression is evaluated as either true or
                                         false. The variables or numbers on either side of
Payment $>=$ Bal $+$ Int                 the relation are called operands.

Total $< 5$

INPUT STATEMENTS                         EXPLANATION

Variable list

READLN (___,___);

All data that is keyed in before a ⟨return⟩ will be
assigned to the respective variables. For example,
when the READLN statement given below is executed and the user keys in the data as shown in the
display sample, the indicated assignments will be
made:

READLN(Num,Total);     Display Sample

5   8   ⟨return⟩ [1]

Assignments   { Num:= 5
              { Total:= 8

---

[1] On some computers the numbers may be separated by commas; in more technical terms, a comma may be
used as a delimiter. In this example a space is the delimiter.

READLN(A,B,C);

Display Sample

```
┌─────────────────┐
│ 6.3   ⟨return⟩   │
│ 9     ⟨return⟩   │
│ 62    ⟨return⟩   │
└─────────────────┘
```

Assignments

$$\begin{cases} A := 6.3 \\ B := 9 \\ C := 62 \end{cases}$$

## COMMENT STATEMENTS

(*ANY COMMENT*)

(*CALCULATES NET WAGES*)

## EXPLANATION

The characters enclosed by the symbols (* and *) are comments. They are ignored by the compiler when executing the program but are listed with the program statements to aid the programmer in documenting the program.  Some computers may use { }.

```
(****************************************)
(* Author: Andrea Brady                 *)
(* Date written: 01-02-85               *)
(*                                      *)
(* Purpose: To determine the percentage *)
(* of employees that have a retirement  *)
(* fund established.                    *)
(****************************************)
```

Every program should be documented with comment statements containing the author's name and a brief description of what the program is to accomplish.

## LOOP CONTROL STATEMENTS

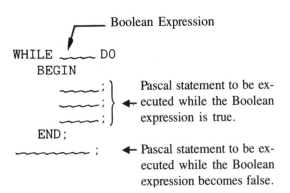

Boolean Expression

WHILE ﹏ DO
    BEGIN
      ﹏ ;
      ﹏ ;  ← Pascal statement to be executed while the Boolean expression is true.
      ﹏ ;
    END;
﹏ ;  ← Pascal statement to be executed while the Boolean expression becomes false.

## EXPLANATION

The WHILE ﹏ DO statement has a looping effect since the execution keeps cycling between the BEGIN and END statements until the Boolean expression becomes false. No semicolon follows the word DO.

STOPPING SIGNAL WITH LOOP CONTROL

EXPLANATION

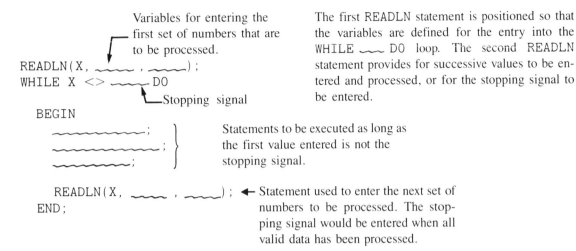

Variables for entering the
first set of numbers that are
to be processed.

```
READLN(X, _____ , _____);
WHILE X <> _____ DO
```
Stopping signal

```
   BEGIN
      _____;  ⎫
      _____;  ⎬
      _____;  ⎭
```
Statements to be executed as long as
the first value entered is not the
stopping signal.

```
      READLN(X, _____ , _____);
   END;
```
← Statement used to enter the next set of
numbers to be processed. The stopping signal would be entered when all
valid data has been processed.

The first READLN statement is positioned so that
the variables are defined for the entry into the
WHILE ⌣ DO loop. The second READLN
statement provides for successive values to be entered and processed, or for the stopping signal to
be entered.

## 4.3 DEMONSTRATION PROBLEMS

1. Write a program that provides for entering temperatures in degrees Fahrenheit and converts them to
degrees Celsius. Display both the Fahrenheit and Celsius temperatures with appropriate column headings
as shown in the Display Sample. Use a temperature of −999 as a stopping signal. When the stopping
signal is entered, have the computer display "TABLE COMPLETE".

Note: C = (F − 32)5/9

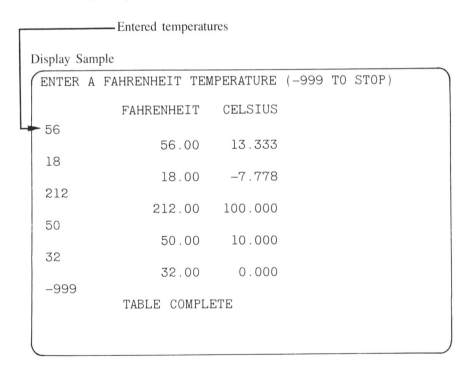

Entered temperatures

Display Sample

```
ENTER A FAHRENHEIT TEMPERATURE (-999 TO STOP)

          FAHRENHEIT   CELSIUS
56
              56.00    13.333
18
              18.00    -7.778
212
             212.00   100.000
50
              50.00    10.000
32
              32.00     0.000
-999
        TABLE COMPLETE
```

```
PROGRAM FahCel;
  VAR Fah, Cel: REAL;
BEGIN
  WRITELN ('ENTER A FAHRENHEIT TEMPERATURE (-999 TO STOP)');
  WRITELN;
  WRITELN ('FAHRENHEIT':20,'CELSIUS':10);
  READLN (Fah);                          (*ENTER FIRST TEMP.*)
  WHILE Fah <> -999 DO
    BEGIN
      Cel:= (Fah - 32)*(5 / 9);
      WRITELN (Fah:20:2,Cel:10:3);
      READLN (Fah);              (* ENTER SUCCESSIVE TEMP OR *)
    END;                         (* -999 AS A STOPPING SIGNAL *)
  WRITELN ('TABLE COMPLETE':25);
END.
```

2. Write a program that will accept values for the length and width of a rectangle, and calculate the area and perimeter. Use a negative length to terminate the execution of the program and display the results as shown in the display sample.

Display Sample

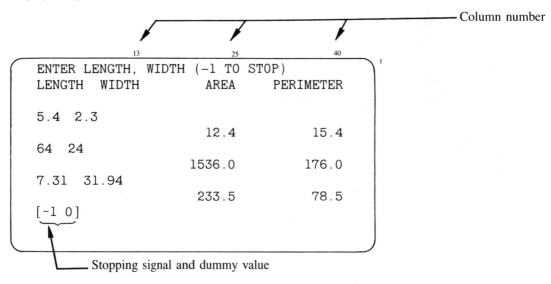

— Stopping signal and dummy value

```
PROGRAM L4Demo2;
  VAR L,W,Area,Per: REAL;
BEGIN
  WRITELN ('ENTER LENGTH, WIDTH (-1 TO STOP)');
```

---

[1] The READLN statement will not display a "?" as a prompt on some computers (APPLE, for example). On the TRS-80, a READLN statement will produce a "?" as a prompt.

Requires 13 spaces

Field of 12 spaces

```
WRITELN ('LENGTH WIDTH','AREA':12,'PERIMETER':15);
WRITELN;                           (* DISPLAYS A BLANK LINE*)
READLN (L,W);                      (*FIRST NO. TO BE PRINTED*)
WHILE L > 0 DO
  BEGIN
    Area:= L*W;
    Per:= 2*L + 2*W;
    WRITELN (Area:25:1,Per:15:1);
    READLN (L,W);                  (*ENTERS NEXT NO.*)
  END;                             (*TO BE PROCESSED*)
END.
```

The heading requires 13 + 12 spaces. Therefore, a field of 25 spaces is necessary to properly position the result stored in Area.

## 4.4 SKILL DEVELOPMENT EXERCISES

1. What will the computer display when the following program is executed using the following data:

| Employee # | 1000 | Sales: | $9500 |
|---|---|---|---|
| # | 1020 | | $12,400 |
| # | 1035 | | $10,200 |
| # | 2000 | | $15,500 |

Use a negative ID number as a stopping signal.

```
PROGRAM L4P1;
  VAR ID: INTEGER;
      Sales, Salary: REAL;
BEGIN
  WRITELN ('ENTER ID - SALES (-1 0 TO STOP)');
  WRITELN;
  WRITELN ('ID  SALES','SALARY':20);
  WRITELN;
  READLN (ID, Sales);
  WHILE ID > 0 DO
    BEGIN
      Salary:= Sales*0.20 + 400;
      WRITELN (Salary:29:2);
      READLN (ID, Sales);
    END;
  WRITELN ('LIST COMPLETE');
END.
```

2. Write a program for computing the value for $Y$ in the equation $Y = (X + 2)(X - 5)$ when $X$ is 3, 4, −8, 23.56, and −2.43. Display both the value of $X$ and the corresponding value of $Y$ in table form. Print an appropriate heading and use an input of −999 as a stopping signal.

Display Sample

```
ENTER X VALUES (-999 TO STOP)

                     X         Y
3
                   3.00    -10.00
4
                   4.00     -6.00
-8
                  -8.00     78.00
23.56
                  23.56    474.39
-2.43
                  -2.43      3.19
-999

```

3. Given the following combination of coins, write a program that will accept as input the number of coins of each denomination and will calculate and display the dollar value.

   a. 52 half dollars, 128 quarters, 112 dimes, 181 nickels, 351 pennies.
   b. 64 half dollars,  82 quarters, 345 dimes,  86 nickels, 482 pennies.
   c. 19 half dollars, 245 quarters,  98 dimes, 324 nickels, 567 pennies.
   d. 56 half dollars, 198 quarters, 576 dimes,  90 nickels, 369 pennies.

Display Sample

```
ENTER NUMBER OF
HALF DOLLARS - QUARTERS - DIMES - NICKELS - PENNIES
(-1 0 0 0 0 TO STOP)

52 128 112 181 351
                          $   81.76
64 82 345 86 482
                          $   96.12
19 245 98 324 567
                        $ 102.42
56 198 576 90 369
                        $ 143.29
-1 0 0 0 0
```

# Lesson 5
# USING A PRINTER

## 5.1 OBJECTIVES

Objectives: 1. To be able to use a printer.
2. To gain more practice in using the WRITE and WRITELN statements.
3. To be able to calculate fielding numbers for printing headings and columns of numbers.

## 5.2 TEXT VARIABLE, REWRITE STATEMENT

**APPLE    IBM PC**

PASCAL STATEMENT                                   EXPLANATION

┌─Output variable (any valid variable name)

      ┌─Declaration

_(1)_ : TEXT;                                       In order to understand the use of the text declaration, files would have to be presented. This material is too confusing at this level of programming and will be left for later lessons.

┌── Same variable as in the declaration
    ┌── Specifies printer

REWRITE ( _(1)_ , 'PRINTER:');                      This statement associates the output variable with the printer. The output variable used must have been previously declared as a TEXT variable.

┌─Same output variable
    ┌──Variables to be printed

WRITELN ( _(1)_ , ‿‿‿,‿‿,‿‿‿ );                    This statement will send the values stored in the variables to the printer. A REWRITE statement must have been previously executed.

24

—Same output variable

WRITELN(  (1)  );

If only the output variable is within the parentheses the statement will send only a return and line feed to the printer. If the print head is at the left then a blank line will be the result. If the print head is in the middle of a line then the print head will be placed at the beginning of the next line. No blank line will be created.

*Summary* (Printing results in table form)

EXAMPLE (APPLE & IBM only):
```
PROGRAM ⌇⌇⌇⌇⌇⌇;
   VAR⌇⌇,⌇⌇,⌇⌇:⌇⌇;
        Outfile : TEXT;  ←    Declares (Outfile)
BEGIN
 ¹REWRITE(Outfile,'PRINTER:');  ←  Associates Outfile with the printer
```

—Displays first item of heading
—Displays second item of heading

```
   WRITELN(Outfile,'1ST NUM':12,'2ND NUM':12);
   WRITELN(Outfile);   ←——  Displays blank line
   ⌇⌇⌇⌇;
   ⌇⌇⌇⌇;
   WRITELN(Outfile,First,Second);   } Controlled loop
   ⌇⌇⌇⌇⌇;
   ⌇⌇⌇⌇⌇;
END.
```

—Second variable to be printed
—First variable to be printed

Note: If an APPLE or IBM is being used and access to a printer is limited, Appendix VI demonstrates a technique to use TEXT files to store the printed text until it can be transferred to the printer.

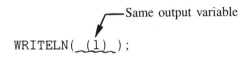

**TRS-80**

PASCAL STATEMENT                           EXPLANATION

—Specifies the printer
—Variable list to be printed

WRITELN(LP,⌇⌇,⌇⌇,⌇⌇);

This statement will send the numbers stored in the variables listed in the printer.

---

¹ While the program is being debugged and tested, the REWRITE statement can be replaced with REWRITE (Outfile,'CONSOLE:') and the output will go to the monitor. Changing the one statement back to REWRITE (Outfile,'PRINTER:') will cause the same information to be printed on the printer.

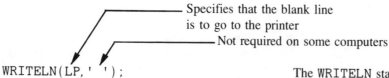

Specifies that the blank line
is to go to the printer

Not required on some computers

WRITELN(LP,' ');

The WRITELN statement with only the letters LP
and a ' ' in the variable list will cause a blank
line to be printed. If the print head is not at the left
margin, the WRITELN statement will cause the
print head to be returned and not leave a blank line.

*Calculating Field Numbers*

When writing a program that will be displaying columns of values with appropriate headings, a method must
be developed to calculate the numbers needed to field (position) each column heading and values under each
column heading. A trial and error method to position the values is completely unsatisfactory and should
never be used.

The following illustrates a method for determining the numbers used in the WRITELN statements. The
solution is broken down into three steps. After the three steps are explained, a summary shows what would
actually be written when using the described method.

The variables to be printed, the maximum number of spaces provided for each value, and a print sample are
shown below.

ID (4 spaces maximum (____))
PreBal (8 spaces maximum (_____.__))
SerChar (5 spaces maximum (__.__))
NewBal (8 spaces maximum (_____.__))

Print Sample

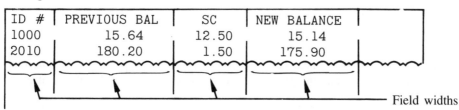

Centering the column headings

*1st Step*

Determine the field widths. They may be equal in width or determined by the number of spaces the heading or numbers require.

| 6 | 15 | 10 | 12 | ← Chosen field widths

*2nd Step*

Determine the spaces needed to center the heading in each field.

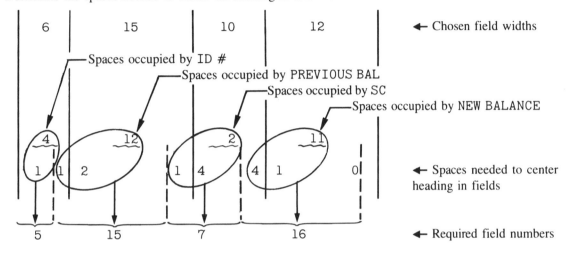

All numbers needed to complete the WRITELN statement for the heading are now known. Each column heading will be right justified in the specified field.

```
WRITELN('ID #':5, 'PREVIOUS BAL':15, 'SC':7, 'NEW BALANCE':16);
```

The following calculations were used to determine required field numbers:

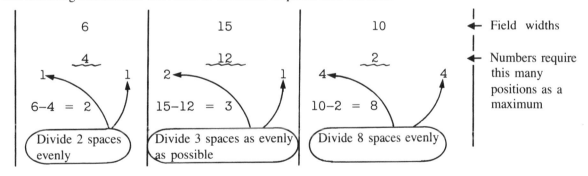

Centering the column values:

*3rd Step*

To determine the spaces needed to center the column values in each of the fields follow the same procedure used in Step 2.

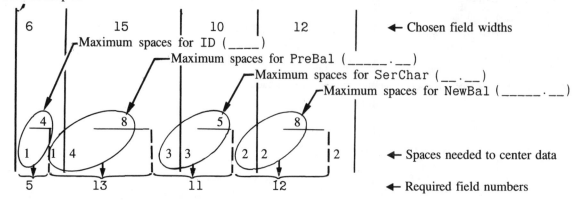

All numbers are now known to complete the WRITELN statement for printing the values. Each number will be right justified in the specified field.

```
WRITELN(ID:5,PreBal:13:2,SerChar:11:2,NewBal:12:2);
```

*Summary*

When the actual calculations are done for a program all of the above sketches would be reduced to the following:

Print Sample

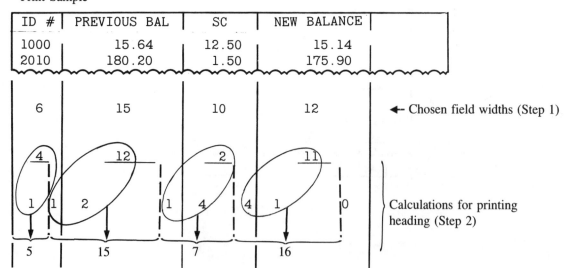

```
WRITELN('ID #':5,'PREVIOUS BAL':15,'SC':7,'NEW BALANCE':16);
```
↖——Prints heading

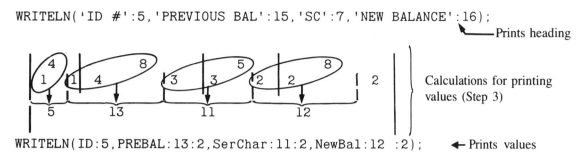

Calculations for printing values (Step 3)

```
WRITELN(ID:5,PREBAL:13:2,SerChar:11:2,NewBal:12 :2);
```
← Prints values

The method shown above is only a suggestion. Other methods may be preferred by the programmer; however, trial and error is not an acceptable method to be used to calculate field numbers.

## 5.3 DEMONSTRATION PROBLEM

1. Write a program that will accept input from the operator that contains the quantity of motorcycles on hand, the size in cubic centimeters, and the price of each. The program should calculate the total amount invested in each size of cycle.

Data Sample

11   50CC cycles at $795.00 each
3   250CC cycles at $1295.50 each
2   750CC cycles at $1895.00 each
1   1100CC cycles at $2195.98 each

Print Sample

```
QUANTITY    CC      PRICE      TOTAL AMOUNT
      11      50     795.00         8745.00
       3     250    1295.50         3886.50
       2     750    1895.00         3790.00
       1    1100    2195.98         2195.98
```

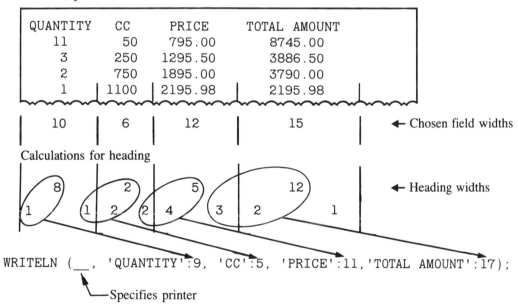

Calculations for heading

```
WRITELN ( __, 'QUANTITY':9, 'CC':5, 'PRICE':11,'TOTAL AMOUNT':17);
```
↖——Specifies printer

Determine maximum size of each variable value
Quan (2 spaces maximum)
Size (4 spaces maximum)
Price (8 spaces maximum)
TotalAmt (9 spaces maximum)

Calculations for data fields

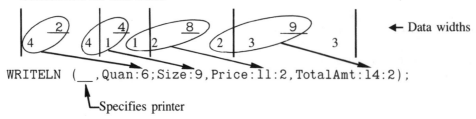

```
WRITELN (__,Quan:6;Size:9,Price:11:2,TotalAmt:14:2);
```

└─Specifies printer

### APPLE IBM PC

```
PROGRAM L5Demo1;
   VAR Quan,Size: INTEGER;
       Price,TotalAmt: REAL;
       Table: TEXT;
BEGIN
  ¹REWRITE (Table,'PRINTER:');
   WRITELN (Table,'QUANTITY':9,'CC':5,'PRICE':11,'TOTAL AMOUNT':17);
   READLN (Quan,Size,Price);
   WHILE Quan > 0 DO
     BEGIN
       TotalAmt:= Quan*Price;
       WRITELN (Table,Quan:6,Size:9,Price:11:2,TotalAmt:14:2);
       READLN (Quan,Size,Price);
     END;
END.
```

### TRS-80

```
PROGRAM L5Demo1;
   VAR Quan,Size: INTEGER;
       Price,TotalAmt: REAL;
BEGIN
   WRITELN (LP,'QUANTITY':9'CC':5,'PRICE':11,'TOTAL AMOUNT':17);
   READLN (Quan,Size,Price);
   WHILE Quan > 0 DO
     BEGIN
       TotalAmt:= Quan * Price;
       WRITELN (LP,Quan:6,Size:9,Price:11:2,TotalAmt:14:2);
       READLN (Quan,Size,Price);
     END;
END.
```

---

[1] While the program is being debugged and tested, the REWRITE statement can be replaced with REWRITE (Table,'CONSOLE:') and the output will go to the monitor. Changing the one statement back to REWRITE (Table,'PRINTER:') will cause the same information to be printed on the printer.

## 5.4 SKILL DEVELOPMENT EXERCISES

Note:  (APPLE and IBM PC) Reading data from the keyboard, as illustrated in the demonstration problems of this lesson, leaves much to be desired. After several Skill Development Exercise problems have been completed using the illustrated method and the technique is understood, the instructor may permit the use of Data Files. Data Files are explained in Appendix V and when used the process of entering data becomes much more efficient.

When running a program that has output to a printer, the most convenient method is to write the output to the console as shown on page 25 until a printer is available. However, the output can be sent to a text file and the file transferred to a printer when one is available. The technique to complete this operation is explained in Appendix VI.

1.  Write a program to enter data consisting of a lot number, dimensions (in feet), and market value per acre, and calculate the acreage and taxable value of the land. Format the printout using field widths as shown in the Print Sample below. Center heading and printed data in each field.

Note:  1.  One acre equals 43560 square feet.
       2.  Each acre has a taxable value equal to 60% of its market value.

Data Sample

Lot 10, dimensions 200 ft. by 400 ft., market value $10000 per acre.[1]
Lot 20, dimensions 75 ft. by 75 ft., market value $25800 per acre.
Lot 30, dimensions 500 ft. by 1000 ft., market value $15000 per acre.
Lot 40, dimensions 150 ft. by 200 ft., market value $22600 per acre.

Print Sample

| LOT | ACRES | TAXABLE VALUE |
|-----|-------|---------------|
| 10  | 1.84  | 11019.3[1]    |
| 20  | 0.13  | 1998.97       |
| 30  | 11.48 | 103306.[1]    |
| 40  | 0.69  | 9338.84       |
| 8   | 10    | 15            |

← Field widths

---

[1] The largest integer allowed is 32767. Because $200 \times 400 = 80000$, the declaration of the length and width as integers will produce incorrect results for Lot 10 and Lot 30. Declaring the variables as reals will eliminate the problem.

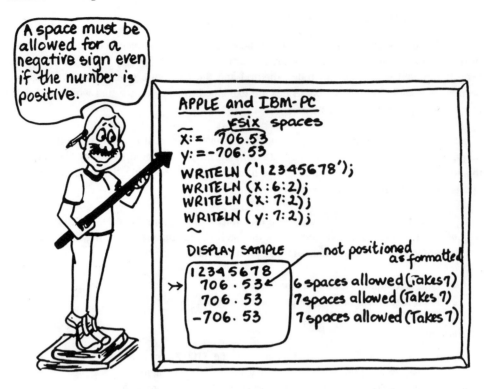

2. Determine the net pay after the deductions are made from the gross salary. Print the information as shown in the Print Sample using field widths of 9, 12, and 10 respectively.

Data Sample

| Gross Salary | Social Security | % State Tax | % Federal Tax |
|--------------|-----------------|-------------|---------------|
| $480.50 | $29.43 | 2% | 12% |
| 1080.40 | 66.17 | 3 | 20 |
| 810.20 | 49.62 | 3 | 16 |
| 342.50 | 20.98 | 2 | 10 |

Print Sample

```
  GROSS    TOTAL DED     NET
  480.50      96.70    383.80
 1080.40     314.66    765.74
  810.20     203.56    606.64
  342.50      62.08    280.42
```

3. Find the cost and total due for the following stock purchases and print as shown in the print sample.

   Note: 1. Cost = number of shares times the price per share.
         2. Commission = 3% of cost + $2 per share.
         3. Total due = cost + commission.

Data Sample

```
 5 shares Avon     at $ 46.50 per share.
25 shares Burrghs  at $181.00 per share.
14 shares Exxon    at $ 81.50 per share.
20 shares NwstAirl at $ 20.25 per share.
```

Print Sample

```
NO.  SHARES   PRICE      COST    TOTAL DUE
        5      46.50    232.50      249.48
       25     181.00   4525.00     4710.75
       14      81.50   1141.00     1203.23
       20      20.25    405.00      457.15
```

4. Write a program where a series of integers can be entered and the computer will calculate and print a running average for pairs of numbers (that is, average the first and second, second and third, third and fourth, etc). By using a stopping signal of $-999$, the program will accommodate any number of averages. Each number is to be entered only once.

Display sample

```
ENTER INTEGERS
(-999 TO STOP)

8
15
4
36
18
64
17
3
-999
```

or

```
ENTER INTEGERS
(-999 TO STOP)

8    15
4
36
18
64
17
3
-999
```

Print Sample

```
THE AVERAGE OF    8 AND   15 IS  11.5
THE AVERAGE OF   15 AND    4 IS   9.5
THE AVERAGE OF    4 AND   36 IS  20.0
THE AVERAGE OF   36 AND   18 IS  27.0
THE AVERAGE OF   18 AND   64 IS  41.0
THE AVERAGE OF   64 AND   17 IS  40.5
THE AVERAGE OF   17 AND    3 IS  10.0
```

# Lesson 6
# CONDITIONAL BRANCHING AND FLOWCHARTS

## 6.1 OBJECTIVES

Objectives: 1. To understand and be able to use the conditional branching statement.
2. To understand single and double alternative statements.
3. To work with relations.

## 6.2 IF-THEN, ELSE, Flowcharts

PASCAL STATEMENT                                    EXPLANATION

Boolean expression
Statement to be executed only when the Boolean expression is true.

IF____THEN____;
_____;

The statement between the THEN and the semicolon will be executed only when the Boolean expression is evaluated as true. The statement following the semicolon of the IF−THEN statement is then executed. That is, both statements will be executed if the Boolean expression is true; and only the statement following the first semicolon will be executed if the Boolean expression is false.

Statement to be executed on both true and false evaluations of the Boolean expression.

Boolean expression

Statement to be executed only when the Boolean expression is true.

IF_____THEN
_____;
_____;

The statement on the left is treated exactly the same as the statement in the previous example. The semicolon determines the end of the statement so the number of lines that it takes to state the IF−THEN statement is immaterial.

Statement to be executed on both true and false evaluations of the Boolean expression.

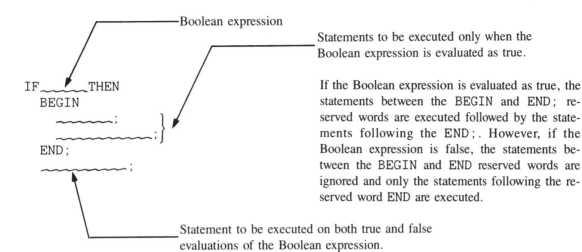

Boolean expression

Statements to be executed only when the Boolean expression is evaluated as true.

If the Boolean expression is evaluated as true, the statements between the BEGIN and END; reserved words are executed followed by the statements following the END;. However, if the Boolean expression is false, the statements between the BEGIN and END reserved words are ignored and only the statements following the reserved word END are executed.

Statement to be executed on both true and false evaluations of the Boolean expression.

Note: All three forms of the previous IF—THEN statements are *single* alternative decision statements.

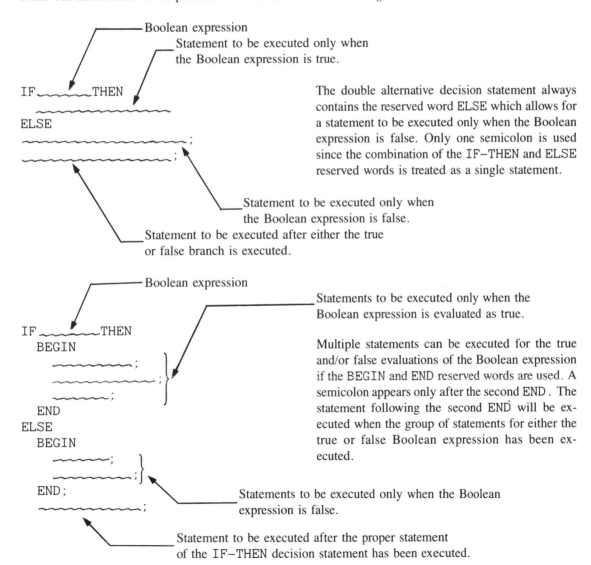

Boolean expression
Statement to be executed only when the Boolean expression is true.

The double alternative decision statement always contains the reserved word ELSE which allows for a statement to be executed only when the Boolean expression is false. Only one semicolon is used since the combination of the IF—THEN and ELSE reserved words is treated as a single statement.

Statement to be executed only when the Boolean expression is false.

Statement to be executed after either the true or false branch is executed.

Boolean expression

Statements to be executed only when the Boolean expression is evaluated as true.

Multiple statements can be executed for the true and/or false evaluations of the Boolean expression if the BEGIN and END reserved words are used. A semicolon appears only after the second END. The statement following the second END will be executed when the group of statements for either the true or false Boolean expression has been executed.

Statements to be executed only when the Boolean expression is false.

Statement to be executed after the proper statement of the IF—THEN decision statement has been executed.

Note: The previous two forms of the IF—THEN—ELSE statement are double alternative decisions.

## 6.3. DEMONSTRATION PROBLEMS

1. The policy of a retail store is to charge a $5.00 service charge on all accounts in which the previous month's balance is not paid in full each month. Write a program to enter the previous month's balance, payments made during the month, and charges made during the month, and display the new balance. A negative previous balance is to be used as a stopping signal.

New balance = previous balance − payments + charges + service charge (if any)

Display Sample

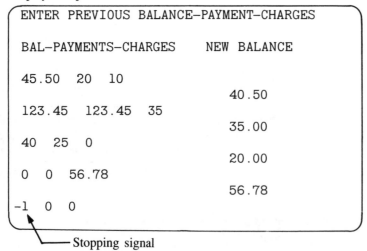

— Stopping signal

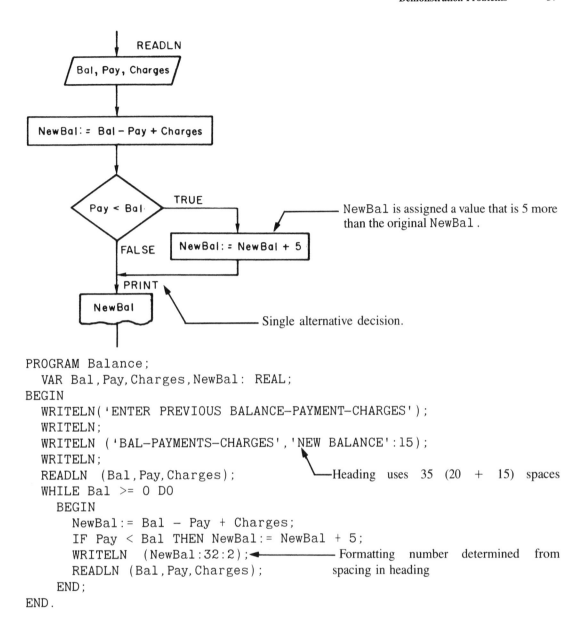

NewBal is assigned a value that is 5 more than the original NewBal.

Single alternative decision.

```
PROGRAM Balance;
  VAR Bal,Pay,Charges,NewBal: REAL;
BEGIN
  WRITELN('ENTER PREVIOUS BALANCE-PAYMENT-CHARGES');
  WRITELN;
  WRITELN ('BAL-PAYMENTS-CHARGES','NEW BALANCE':15);
  WRITELN;
  READLN (Bal,Pay,Charges);
  WHILE Bal >= 0 DO
    BEGIN
      NewBal:= Bal - Pay + Charges;
      IF Pay < Bal THEN NewBal:= NewBal + 5;
      WRITELN (NewBal:32:2);
      READLN (Bal,Pay,Charges);
    END;
END.
```

Heading uses 35 (20 + 15) spaces

Formatting number determined from spacing in heading

2. A construction firm lets out subcontracts on a cost + 20% basis. However, if the subcontractor completes the job at a cost of less than 5% above the estimated cost, he is given a $500 bonus. In other words, the amount due to the subcontractor is the actual cost plus 20% of the cost. If the actual cost is less than 5% above the estimated cost, an additional $500 (bonus) is added to the amount due.

Write a program such that the estimated cost and actual cost can be entered, and the computer will display the amount due to the subcontractor. Use a negative estimated cost as a stopping signal.

Display Sample

```
ENTER  EST  COST  &  ACT  COST
EST  COST  &  ACT  COST                    BONUS        AMOUNT DUE

12500    19500
                                            0.00         23400.00
10400    9050
                                          500.00         11360.00
3200    3450
                                            0.00          4140.00
-1   0
```

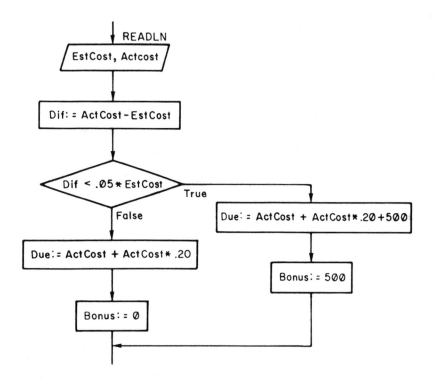

```
PROGRAM L6Demo2;
  VAR EstCost,ActCost,Dif,Due,Bonus: REAL;
BEGIN
  WRITELN ('ENTER EST COST & ACT COST');
  WRITELN;
  WRITELN ('EST COST & ACT COST','BONUS':15,'AMOUNT DUE':14);
  WRITELN;
  READLN (EstCost,ActCost);
  WHILE EstCost > 0 DO
  BEGIN
    Dif:= ActCost - EstCost;
    IF Dif < 0.05 * EstCost THEN
      BEGIN
        Due:= ActCost + ActCost * 0.20 + 500;
        Bonus:= 500;
      END
    ELSE
      BEGIN
        Due:= ActCost + ActCost * 0.20;
        Bonus:= 0;
      END;
    WRITELN (Bonus:34:2,Due:13:2);
    READLN (EstCost,ActCost);
  END;
END.
```

## 6.4 SKILL DEVELOPMENT EXERCISES

1. Write a program that will print out the ordered pairs of numbers (X,Y) where $Y = X^3 - 4X^2 + 5X + 10$ and $Y$ is not to exceed 100. If the formula produces a value of Y which is greater than or equal to 100, a value of 100 is to be printed. The values to be used for $X$ are 5, 5.3, 5.7, 5.9, 5.8, 5.83, 5.81. When the stopping signal ($-999$) is entered, the words "DATA COMPLETE" will be printed.

Print Sample

| X | Y |
|---|---|
| 5.000 | 60.000 |
| 5.300 | 73.017 |
| 5.700 | 93.733 |
| 5.900 | 100.000 |
| 5.800 | 99.552 |
| 5.830 | 100.000 |
| 5.810 | 100.000 |
| DATA COMPLETE | |

2. A simplified method for calculating the yearly premiums for automobile insurance is as follows:

Primary driver's age (25 and over)

Collision = 2.1% of original cost
Comprehensive = .3% of original cost + $80
Liability = $67.50

Primary driver's age (16–24)

Collision = 3.56% of original cost
Comprehensive = 1% of original cost + $150
Liability = $128

Total Premium = Collision + Comprehensive + Liability

Write a program that allows the operator to enter the insured person's ID number, age, and the original cost of the automobile. The program should then calculate the premiums for collision, comprehension, and liability, and the total premium according to the above information. Study the Print Sample for further clarification.

Display Sample

```
ENTER ID,AGE,ORIGINAL COST (-999 0 0 TO STOP)
1000  18  8500
2070  42  11000
3054  50  9400
3080  21  10500
-999  0   0
```

Print Sample

| ID | COLLISION | COMPREHENSIVE | LIABILITY | TOTAL PREMIUM |
|------|-----------|---------------|-----------|---------------|
| 1000 | 302.60 | 235.00 | 128.00 | 665.60 |
| 2070 | 231.00 | 113.00 | 67.50 | 411.50 |
| 3054 | 197.40 | 108.20 | 67.50 | 373.10 |
| 3080 | 373.80 | 255.00 | 128.00 | 756.80 |

# Lesson 7
# COUNTERS AND ACCUMULATORS

## 7.1 OBJECTIVES

Objectives: 1. To understand and be able to use counters.
2. To understand and be able to use accumulators (summation).
3. To learn another method of controlling loops.
4. To learn the purpose of initializing variables.

## 7.2 COUNTERS AND ACCUMULATORS IN LOOP CONTROL

COUNTERS

Using counters to control loops:

Study the program segment below and determine why it makes 30 loops.

```
Count := 1;
WHILE Count <= 30 DO
  BEGIN
    ~~~~~~;
    ~~~~~~~~~~;          Statements that are to
    ~~~~~~~;             be executed 30 times.
    Count := Count + 1;
  END;
```

Using counters to generate numbers:

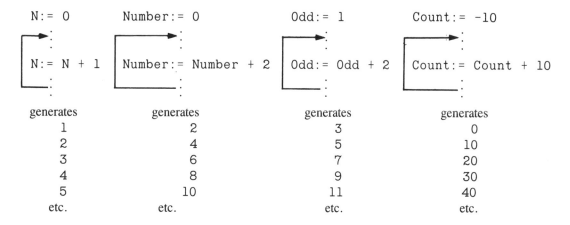

| generates | generates | generates | generates |
|:---:|:---:|:---:|:---:|
| 1 | 2 | 3 | 0 |
| 2 | 4 | 5 | 10 |
| 3 | 6 | 7 | 20 |
| 4 | 8 | 9 | 30 |
| 5 | 10 | 11 | 40 |
| etc. | etc. | etc. | etc. |

## ACCUMULATORS (SUMMATION)

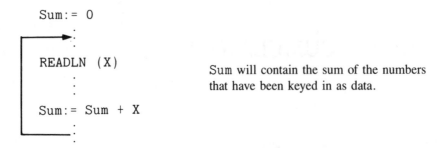

```
Sum:= 0
       .
       .
READLN (X)
       .
       .
Sum:= Sum + X
       .
       .
```

Sum will contain the sum of the numbers
that have been keyed in as data.

Note:  All counters are accumulators. The main difference is that in a counter the same number is added each
time while in an accumulator a different number is usually added each time.

## COMBINING COUNTERS AND ACCUMULATORS

```
NumOfTimes:= 1; Total:= 0;
WHILE NumOfTimes <= 5 DO
  BEGIN
    READLN (Num);
    Total:= Total + Num;            Accumulator (Sum of entered
    NumOfTimes:= NumOfTimes + 1;                    numbers, Num)
  END;                              Counter (Counts for 5 loops)
```

## 7.3 DEMONSTRATION PROBLEMS

1.  Write a program such that the operator can key in six numbers one at a time and the computer will print
the six numbers on a line along with the sum and average. See the Print Sample below.

Display Sample

```
20.2
31
16
5.3
18.6
25
```

Print Sample

```
 20.20 31.00 16.00  5.30 18.60 25.00
SUM =  116.10
AVERAGE =  19.35
```

### ALGORITHM

1. Initialize counter and accumulator
2. Loop while counter <= 6
   2.1 Read data
   2.2 Accumulate data
   2.3 Print data
   2.4 Increment counter
3. Calculate average
4. Print sum and average

### EXPLANATION

An algorithm is a step by step outline of how a
problem is to be solved. The purpose of an algorithm is to set up the general logic of the program that will follow.

**APPLE        IBM PC**

```
PROGRAM L7Demol;
  VAR Count:INTEGER:
      X,Sum,Average:REAL;
      Output:TEXT;
BEGIN
  Count:= 1;
  Sum:= 0;
  REWRITE(Output,'PRINTER:');
  WHILE Count <= 6 DO)
    BEGIN
      READLN(X);
      WRITE(Output,X:6:2);
      Sum:= Sum + X;
      Count:= Count + 1;
    END;
  WRITELN(Output);
  Average:= Sum / 6;
  WRITELN(Output,'SUM = ',Sum:6:2);
  WRITELN(Output,'AVERAGE = ',Average:6:2)
END.
```

**TRS-80**

```
PROGRAM L7Demol;
  VAR Count: INTEGER;
      X,Sum,Average: REAL;
BEGIN
  Count:= 1;
  Sum:= 0;
  WHILE Count <=6 DO
    BEGIN
      READLN(X);
      WRITE(LP,X:6:2);
      Sum:= Sum + X;
      Count:= Count + 1;
    END;
  WRITELN(LP,' ');
  Average:= Sum / 6;
  WRITELN(LP,'SUM = ',Sum:6:2);
  WRITELN(LP,'AVERAGE = ',Average:6:2)
END.
```

2. Write a program that displays the sum of the squares of the integers from 1 to 25.

ALGORITHM

1. Initialize counter and accumulator
2. Loop while counter <= 25
   2.1 Square the counter
   2.2 Accumulate the square of the counter
   2.3 Increment the counter
3. Display answer

```
PROGRAM L7Demo2;
   VAR Count, Square, Sum: INTEGER;
BEGIN
   Count:= 1;
   Sum:= 0;
   WHILE Count <= 25 DO
     BEGIN
       Square:= Count * Count;
       Sum:= Sum + Square;
       Count:= Count + 1;
     END;
   WRITELN(Sum);
END.
```

Display Sample

```
5525
```

## 7.4 SKILL DEVELOPMENT EXERCISES

1. What will be displayed when the following program is executed?

```
PROGRAM Trace;
  VAR Even, Sum : INTEGER;
BEGIN
  Even:= 2;
  Sum:= 0;
  WHILE Even <= 20 DO
    BEGIN
      Sum:= Sum + Even;
      Even:= Even + 2;
    END;
  WRITELN (Sum: 6);
END.
```

2. Write a program to compute and display the sum of the odd integers from 1 to 150. (A READLN statement should not be used in this program.)

   Answer: 5625

3. Assume that a person wants to determine the speed of his car using the mile markers on the highway. He will time how long it takes him to travel from one marker to the next (in seconds). Since the distance is one mile, the formula for determining the speed of the car (rate) in miles per hour is:

   $R = 3600/S$     where $R$ = rate in miles per hour
   $S$ = seconds to travel one mile

   Write a program that will print out a chart showing the rate of the car for different time intervals. Start the chart at 50 seconds and terminate at 80 seconds.

   Print Sample

   | SECONDS | MILES/HOUR |
   |---------|------------|
   | 50 | 72.0 |
   | 51 | 70.6 |
   | 52 | 69.2 |
   | 53 | 67.9 |
   | 54 | 66.7 |
   | : | : |
   | : | : |
   | 76 | 47.4 |
   | 77 | 46.8 |
   | 78 | 46.2 |
   | 79 | 45.6 |
   | 80 | 45.0 |

4. Mileage records were obtained on five automobiles, as shown below:

| Model # | Miles | Gallons Consumed |
|---|---|---|
| 2011 | 302 | 21.3 |
| 3081 | 418 | 25.3 |
| 6658 | 192 | 15.1 |
| 7211 | 225 | 14.8 |
| 9843 | 295 | 14.1 |

Write a program that will:

a. Calculate each car's average miles per gallon.
b. Calculate the total miles driven and the total gallons consumed.
c. Calculate the average miles per gallon using the total miles and total gallons for all five cars.

Print Sample

```
   MODEL  #     MILES/GAL
    2011         14.2
    3081         16.5
    6658         12.7
    7211         15.2
    9843         20.9

TOTAL MILES DRIVEN       =   1432.0
TOTAL GALLONS CONSUMED   =     90.6
AVERAGE MILES/GALLON     =     15.8
```

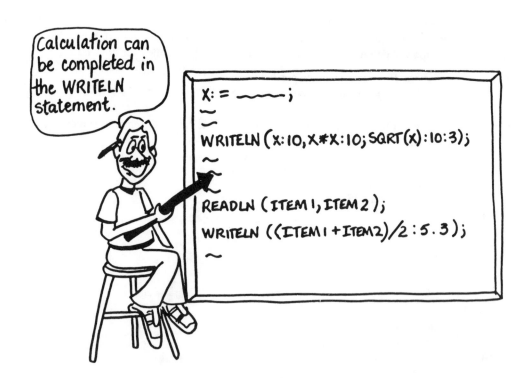

5. The data contains the ID number and hours worked for the employees of a certain company. The rate paid by the employer is $5.40 per hour with 1½ times this rate for all hours over forty.

Data Sample

| ID # | Hours Worked |
|------|--------------|
| 1001 | 40 |
| 1002 | 42 |
| 1003 | 36 |

Write a program that will:
a. Print out the employee's ID number, hours worked, and the wages.
b. Print out the total wages paid by the company for the week.
c. Terminate the run when a zero value is read for the ID Number.

Print Sample

```
 ID    HOURS    WAGES
1001    40     216.00
1002    42     232.20
1003    36     194.40

TOTAL WAGES  =      642.60
```

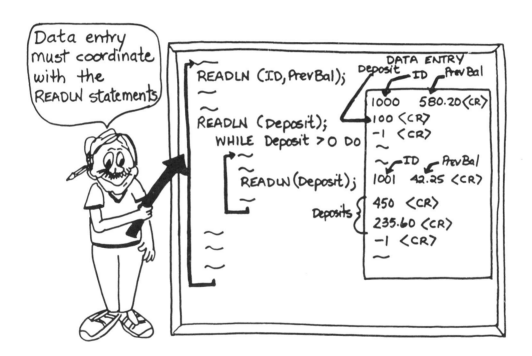

6. (Checking Account Problem) Write a program that determines the total of the deposits, total of the drafts, and the new balance for each of four accounts at a bank. Print the information as shown in the Print Sample. The data contains the person's ID number, previous balance, a variable number of deposits followed by a signal, and a variable number of drafts followed by a signal. Study the Data Sample and Print Sample to clarify the problem.

Data Sample

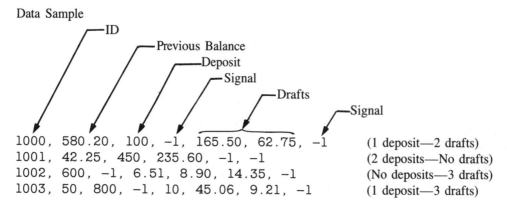

```
1000, 580.20, 100, -1, 165.50, 62.75, -1        (1 deposit—2 drafts)
1001, 42.25, 450, 235.60, -1, -1                (2 deposits—No drafts)
1002, 600, -1, 6.51, 8.90, 14.35, -1            (No deposits—3 drafts)
1003, 50, 800, -1, 10, 45.06, 9.21, -1          (1 deposit—3 drafts)
```

Print Sample

| ID | PREV BAL | DEPOSITS | DRAFTS | NEW BAL |
|-----|-----|-----|-----|-----|
| 1000 | 580.20 | 100.00 | 228.25 | 451.95 |
| 1001 | 42.25 | 685.60 | 0.00 | 727.85 |
| 1002 | 600.00 | 0.00 | 29.76 | 570.24 |
| 1003 | 50.00 | 800.00 | 64.27 | 785.73 |

# Lesson 8
# PREDEFINED FUNCTIONS

## 8.1 OBJECTIVES

Objectives: 1. To understand and be able to use predefined functions.
2. To use predefined functions to (a) Test for divisibility and (b) round off numbers.

## 8.2 PREDEFINED FUNCTIONS, DIVISIBILITY, AND ROUNDING NUMBERS

*Frequently Used Predefined Functions:*

PREDEFINED FUNCTION AND EXAMPLE        EXPLANATION

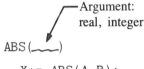

ABS(＿＿)

   X:= ABS(A−B);

A positive number will be assigned to X. (A−B) and (B−A) would assign the same positive number to X.

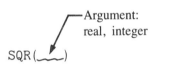

SQR(＿＿)

   SumSq:= SQR(A) + SQR(B);

The value of $A^2 + B^2$ is calculated and the result assigned to SumSq.

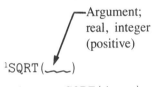

¹SQRT(＿＿)

   Len:= SQRT(Area);

The positive square root of the value stored in Area will be assigned to Len.

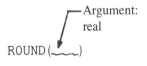

ROUND(＿＿)

   Approx:= ROUND(X);

X is rounded-off to the nearest integer and the result assigned to Approx.
   Examples:
   If X = 12.3 then Approx = 12.
   If X = 6.8 then Approx = 7.
   If X = −2.53 then Approx = −3.
   If X = 2.5 then Approx = 3.
   If X = −2.5 then Approx = −3.

---

¹ Apple Pascal includes a collection of mathematical functions in a special unit called TRANSCEND. TRANSCEND is supplied with Apple Pascal and saved in the file SYSTEM.LIBRARY on the APPLE1 diskette. In order to use any of these functions, TRANSCEND must be included in a USES declaration block which must appear before the VAR declaration. See the Demonstration Problems in this lesson for further clarification.

Argument:
real

TRUNC(____)

Whole:= TRUNC(X);

The decimal part of X is discarded and the resulting integer is assigned to Whole.

Example:

If X = 1.31 then Whole = 1.

If X = .021 then Whole = 0.

If X = −8.32 then Whole = −8.

If X = 2.75 then Whole = 2.

Note: The argument of a predefined function must be placed in parentheses and can be any valid arithmetic expression. A predefined function can also appear in an arithmetic expression.

*Examples:* Distance:= SQRT(SQR(X2−X1) + SQR(Y2−Y1));
        Remainder:= Number − TRUNC(Number * Divisor);

*Other Predefined Functions:*

PREDEFINED FUNCTION AND EXAMPLE          EXPLANATION

Argument:
real, integer

[1]EXP(____)

Power:= EXP(X);

POWER is assigned the value of $e^x$. That is: Power = 2.71828 raised to the X power.

Argument:
real, integer
(positive)

[1]LN(____)

NatLog:= LN(X);

The natural logarithm of X is assigned to NatLog.

Argument:
real, integer
(positive)

[1]LOG(____)
(Not on all computers)

ComLog:= LOG(X);

The common logarithm of X is assigned to ComLog.

Argument

PWROFTEN(____)
(Not on all computers)

SciNot:= Num * PWROFTEN(X);

Ten is raised to the power X and the result is multiplied by Num. That is: SciNot = Num * $(10^x)$.

---

[1] Apple Pascal includes a collection of mathematical functions in a special unit called TRANSCEND. TRANSCEND is supplied with Apple Pascal and saved in the file SYSTEM.LIBRARY on the APPLE1 diskette. In order to use any of these functions, TRANSCEND must be included in a USES declaration block which must appear before the VAR declaration. See the Demonstration Problems in this lesson for further clarification.

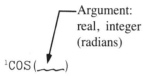

ATAN-Argument:
real, integer

¹ATAN(    )    (APPLE & IBM)
ARCTAN(    ) (TRS-80)

The arctangent of X is assigned to `Radians`.

```
Radians:= ATAN(X);    (* APPLE & IBM *)
Radians:= ARCTAN(X); (* TRS-80 *)
```

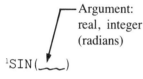

Argument:
real, integer
(radians)

¹COS(    )

The degrees will be converted to radians and the cosine of the resulting radians will be assigned to `Ratio`.

```
Ratio:= COS(Deg*3.14159/180);
```

Argument:
real, integer
(radians)

¹SIN(    )

```
XComp:= R * SIN(Alph);
```

The value of `SIN(Alph)`, where `Alph` is in radians, is multiplied by R and the result is assigned to `XComp`.

## USING PREDEFINED FUNCTIONS

*Divisibility Check*

```
IF Num / Den = TRUNC(Num / Den) THEN
```
⟵————————— Statement executed when `Num` is divisible by `Den`.
```
ELSE            ;
```
————— Statement executed when `Num` is not divisible by `Den` (The ELSE is optional)

A divisibility check can also be accomplished by using the `MOD` operation. That is:

```
IF Num MOD Den = 0 THEN
```
⟵————————— Statement executed when `Num` is divisible by `Den`.
```
ELSE            ;
```
————— Statement executed when `Num` is not divisible by `Den` (The ELSE is optional)

---

[1] Apple Pascal includes a collection of mathematical functions in a special unit called `TRANSCEND`. `TRANSCEND` is supplied with Apple Pascal and saved in the file `SYSTEM.LIBRARY` on the APPLE1 diskette. In order to use any of these functions, `TRANSCEND` must be included in a USES declaration block which must appear before the VAR declaration. See the Demonstration Problems in this lesson for further clarification.

*Round Off*

The following statements will round off the value of X to the nearest hundredth and assign the result to `DollarVal`.

```
DollarVal:= ROUND(X*100)/100
        or
DollarVal:= TRUNC(X*100 + 0.5)/100
```

If each 100 is changed to 10, or 1000, etc., the value of X will be rounded off to the nearest tenth, or thousandths position, etc., respectively.

*Exponents*

There is no exponential function in Pascal. For example, $B^x$ for any real values of B and X cannot be calculated directly. The calculations can be completed by using the EXP and LN functions. For example, the statement, `Y:= EXP(X*LN(B))`, will raise B to the Xth power and assign the result to Y. The statement equivalent to $Y = 7^{12}$ would be `Y:= EXP(12 * LN(7))` in Pascal.

## 8.3 DEMONSTRATION PROBLEMS

1. What will the computer display when the following program is executed with the input values of 5.218, 2.74, −7.5, 9, −.29, 999.

Note:  The calculations using the predefined functions could have been completed and displayed by a single WRITELN statement but are calculated in several statements in order to illustrate the use of the WRITE statement. The program as shown also illustrates predefined functions being used both inside and outside of the WRITELN and WRITE statement.

**APPLE　IBM PC**

```
PROGRAM L8Demol;
  USES TRANSCEND; (*Apple only*)
  VAR X, Ab, Sq, SRoot: REAL;
BEGIN
  WRITELN ('ENTER X (999 TO STOP)');
  WRITELN ('X  ':16,'ABS':7,'SQR':8,'SQRT':9,'TRUNC':8,'ROUND':8);
  READLN (X);
  WHILE X<>999 DO
    BEGIN
      Ab:= ABS (X);
      Sq:= SQR (X);
      SRoot:= SQRT (ABS(X));
      WRITE (X:16:3,Ab:8:3,Sq:8:3,SRoot:8:3);
      WRITELN (TRUNC (X):6,ROUND (X):8);
      READLN (X);
    END;
END.
```

**TRS–80**

```
PROGRAM L8Demol;
  VAR X, Ab, Sq, SRoot: REAL;
BEGIN
  WRITELN ('ENTER X (999 TO STOP)');
  WRITELN ('X  ':16,'ABS':7,'SQR':8,'SQRT';9,'TRUNC':8,'ROUND':8);
  READLN (X);
  WHILE X<>999 DO
    BEGIN
      Ab:= ABS (X);
      Sq:= SQR (X);
      SRoot:= SQRT (ABS (X));
      WRITE (X:16:3,Ab:8:3,Sq:8:3,SRoot:8:3);
      WRITELN (TRUNC (X):6,ROUND (X):8);
      READLN (X);
    END;
END.
```

Display Sample

```
ENTER X (999 TO STOP)
          X      ABS      SQR     SQRT    TRUNC   ROUND
 5.21800
          5.218    5.218   27.228    2.284      5       5
 2.74000
          2.740    2.740    7.508    1.655      2       3
-7.50000
         -7.500    7.500   56.250    2.739     -7      -8
 9.00000
          9.000    9.000   81.000    3.000      9       9
-2.90000E-1
         -0.290    0.290    0.084    0.539      0       0
 999
```

2. Write a program that will request that positive integers be keyed in and have the computer calculate their square root, rounding off the root to the nearest thousandth. The program should print the number, the square root rounded off, and display a "YES" or "NO" to indicate if the integer is a perfect square. Use a negative number as a stopping signal.

Display Sample

```
ENTER POSITIVE INTEGER (-1 TO STOP)
5
18
36
24
100
-1
```

Print Sample

```
   NUMBER        SQR RT       PERFECT SQUARE
      5           2.236            NO
     18           4.243            NO
     36           6.000            YES
     24           4.899            NO
    100          10.000            YES
```

ALGORITHM

1. Read number
2. While number is > 0
   2.1 Calculate square root
   2.2 Check if square root is an integer
       2.2.1 Print numbers and appropriate message
   2.3 Read additional numbers
3. End

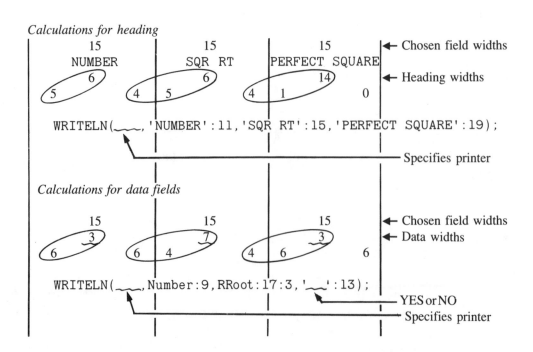

*Calculations for heading*

WRITELN(____,'NUMBER':11,'SQR RT':15,'PERFECT SQUARE':19);

*Calculations for data fields*

WRITELN(____,Number:9,RRoot:17:3,'____':13);

**APPLE IBM PC**

```
PROGRAM L8Demo2;
  USES TRANSCEND; (*APPLE ONLY*)
  VAR Number: INTEGER;
      SRoot, RRoot: REAL;
      Table: TEXT;
BEGIN
  REWRITE (Table,'PRINTER:');
  WRITELN (Table,'NUMBER':11,'SQR RT':15,'PERFECT SQUARE':19);
  READLN (Number);
  WHILE Number >= 0 DO
    BEGIN
      SRoot:= SQRT (Number);
      RRoot:= ROUND (SRoot * 1000) / 1000;
      IF RRoot = TRUNC (RRoot) THEN
        WRITELN (Table,Number:9,RRoot:17:3,'YES':13)
      ELSE
        WRITELN (Table,Number:9,RRoot:17:3,'NO':13);
      READLN (Number);
    END;
END.
```

**TRS-80**

```
PROGRAM L8Demo2;
  VAR Number: INTEGER;
      SRoot, RRoot: REAL;
BEGIN
  WRITELN (LP,'NUMBER':11,'SQR RT':15,'PERFECT SQUARE':19);
  READLN (Number);
  WHILE Number >= 0 DO
    BEGIN
      SRoot:= SQRT (Number);
      RRoot:= ROUND (SRoot * 1000) / 1000;
      IF RRoot = TRUNC (RRoot) THEN
        WRITELN (LP,Number:9,RRoot:17:3,'YES':13)
      ELSE
        WRITELN (LP,Number:9,RRoot:17:3,'NO':13);
      READLN (Number);
    END;
END.
```

3. Write a program that determines and displays the number of one dollar bills and the number of coins necessary to add up to a value of \$18.64 (then \$186.25, \$15.93, and \$8.90). Use the least possible number of coins.

Display Sample

```
 ENTER DOLLAR VALUE (0 TO STOP)
          D     H    Q     D    N    P
 18.64
          18    1    0     1    0    4
 186.25
          186   0    1     0    0    0
 15.93
          15    1    1     1    1    3
 8.90
          8     1    1     1    1    0
 0
```

```
PROGRAM L8Demo3;
  VAR DollarV,Remainder:REAL;
      Dollars,Halves,Quarters,Dimes,Nickels,Pennies:INTEGER;
BEGIN
  WRITELN('D':10,'H':5,'Q':5,'D':5,'N':5,'P':5);
  READLN(DollarV);
  WHILE DollarV > 0 DO
    BEGIN
      WRITELN ('ENTER DOLLAR VALUE (0 TO STOP)');
      Dollars:= TRUNC(DollarV);
      Remainder:= DollarV - Dollars;
     ¹Remainder:=Remainder + 0.0001;
      Halves:= TRUNC(Remainder / 0.50);
      Remainder:= Remainder - Halves * 0.50;
      Quarters:= TRUNC(Remainder / 0.25);
      Remainder:= Remainder - Quarters * 0.25;
      Dimes:= TRUNC(Remainder / 0.10);
      Remainder:= Remainder - Dimes *0.10;
      Nickels:= TRUNC(Remainder / 0.05);
      Remainder:= Remainder - Nickels * 0.05;
      Pennies:= TRUNC(Remainder * 100);
      WRITELN(Dollars:10,Halves:5,Quarters:
              5,Dimes:5,Nickels:5,Pennies:5);
      READLN(DollarV);
    END;
END.
```

---

[1] The statement `Remainder:= Remainder + 0.0001` should not be necessary in order for the program to follow correct logic. However, because the computer must store all numbers in binary code, numbers like 8.90 may be stored as 8.899999. The number of coins would then be calculated using .89 instead of .90 introducing error in both the number of nickels and pennies. By adding the 0.0001 to `Remainder` the problem with storing the numbers does not affect the final result.

## 8.4 SKILL DEVELOPMENT EXERCISES

1. What will be displayed when the following program is executed? Use appropriate headings to coordinate with the information that is to be printed.

```
PROGRAM L8P1;
  VAR X,X2,X3,X4: INTEGER;
BEGIN
  WRITELN ('X':10,'_____':10,'_____':8,'_____':11);
  X:= 1;
  WHILE X<=5 DO
    BEGIN
      X2:= SQR (X);
      X3:= SQR (X) * X;
      X4:= SQR (SQR (X));
      WRITELN (X:10,X2:7,X3:10,X4:9);
      X:= X+1;
    END;
END.
```

2. Write a program to test your computer to see if the formatting of the print out will round off numbers according to the round off rule. That is, the table will be printed using a statement similar to WRITELN(Number:10,Number:12:2,RnOff:13:2,Trun:10:2) where RnOff contains Number rounded off to the nearest hundredth using the ROUND function and Trun contains Number rounded off to the nearest hundredth using the TRUNC function (see page 52).

Display Sample

```
ENTER 999 TO STOP
1.028
5.961
-7.756
-4.032
7.985
999
```

Print Sample

| NUMBER | FORMAT ONLY | ROUND OFF | TRUNCATE |
|--------|-------------|-----------|----------|
| 1.02800 | ~~~~~ | ~~~~~ | ~~~~~ |
| 5.96100 | ~~~~~ | ~~~~~ | ~~~~~ |
| -7.75600 | ~~~~~ | ~~~~~ | ~~~~~ |
| -4.03200 | ~~~~~ | ~~~~~ | ~~~~~ |
| 7.98500 | ~~~~~ | ~~~~~ | ~~~~~ |

Use the printout of the program above to answer these questions:

1. When printing with formatting only (for example WRITELN (__:8:2)) does the computer truncate the digits past the second place or does it use the normal round off rule before truncating?
2. When the TRUNC function is applied to a positive number, is the resulting integer smaller or larger than the original number?
3. When the TRUNC function is applied to a negative number, is the resulting integer smaller or larger than the original number?

3. Write a program to key in two positive integers (the larger first), then determine if the first is divisible by the second.

Display Sample

```
ENTER TWO NUMBERS
(0 0 TO STOP)
20 4
      20 IS DIVISIBLE BY 4
35 3
      35 IS NOT DIVISIBLE BY 3
104 8
      104 IS DIVISIBLE BY 8

etc.
```

4. An equation of the form $Ax^2 + Bx + C = 0$, where A, B, and C are real numbers, has two solutions (or roots) that can be found by using the following two formulas.

$$X1 = \frac{-B + \sqrt{B^2 - 4AC}}{2A} \qquad X2 = \frac{-B - \sqrt{B^2 - 4AC}}{2A}$$

Use the computer to determine the two solutions (roots) for each of the following equations:

1. $x^2 + 3x - 4 = 0$
2. $2x^2 + 7x + 6 = 0$
3. $x^2 - 6x - 3 = 0$

When writing the program code, store the value of $\sqrt{B^2 - 4AC}$ in location `Discrim` and use `Discrim` in writing the formulas for X1 and X2.

Answer: 1.   1, −4    2.   −1.5, −2    3.   6.4641, − .464102

5. Write a program to convert measurements from feet and inches to meters and centimeters. The results should be printed out on the same line with the given numbers.

Note: 1 inch = 2.54 centimeters
      1 meter = 100 centimeters

Display Sample

```
ENTER INCHES, FEET (-999 0 TO STOP)
4   7.5
5   0
27  8
0   4
12  1
-999  0
```

Print Sample

| FEET | INCHES | METERS | CENTIMETERS |
|------|--------|--------|-------------|
| 4    | 7.5    | 1      | 40.97       |
| 5    | 0.0    | 1      | 52.40       |
| 27   | 8.0    | 8      | 43.28       |
| 0    | 4.0    | 0      | 10.16       |
| 12   | 1.0    | 3      | 68.30       |

6. A certain flooring store sells square carpets with sides measured in whole numbers of yards (for example, 5 yds. × 5 yrds., 3 yds. × 3 yds., etc.). Given the dimensions of a rectangular room (in feet) and the price per square yard of carpet, use the computer to determine:

   a. The area of the room in square yards.
   b. The dimensions of the square carpet that must be purchased to be sure the floor will be covered. Assume the square carpet will be cut and the pieces rearranged and sewn to fit the room if enough carpet is purchased.
   c  The cost of the carpet purchased.

   Data Sample

   Room 1 is 20 ft. by 22 ft., carpet costs $8.90/sq. yd.
   Room 2 is 15.5 ft. by 10 ft., carpet costs $16.45/sq. yd.
   Room 3 is 23.6 ft. by 21.5 ft., carpet costs $7.50/sq. yd.
   Room 4 is 32 ft. by 18 ft., carpet costs $10.40/sq. yd.

   Print Sample

   | ROOM | (SQ YD) | PURCHASE DIM | COST |
   |------|---------|--------------|--------|
   | 1 | 48.89 | 7 X 7 | 436.10 |
   | 2 | 17.22 | 5 X 5 | 411.25 |
   | 3 | 56.38 | 8 X 8 | 480.00 |
   | 4 | 64.00 | 8 X 8 | 665.60 |

7. Write a program that requests a series of two-digit numbers to be keyed in, and the computer will print out the numbers with the digits interchanged. Study the following Display and Print Samples for further clarification.

   Display Sample

   ```
   ENTER A TWO-DIGIT NUMBER
   (-999 TO STOP)
   16
   45
   32
   66
   -999
   ```

   Print Sample

   | NUMBER | INTERCHANGE |
   |--------|-------------|
   | 16 | 61 |
   | 45 | 54 |
   | 32 | 23 |
   | 66 | 66 |

8. Check all the integers from 10 to 30 for divisibility by 2, 3, and 5, and print according to the following Print Sample. Do not use a READLN statement in the program. Blank lines will be permitted but be creative and try to avoid them.

Print Sample

| DIV BY 2 | DIV BY 3 | DIV BY 5 |
|----------|----------|----------|
| 10       |          | 10       |
| 12       | 12       |          |
| 14       |          |          |
|          | 15       | 15       |
| 16       |          |          |
| 18       | 18       |          |
| 20       |          | 20       |
|          | 21       |          |
| 22       |          |          |
| 24       | 24       |          |
|          |          | 25       |
| 26       |          |          |
|          | 27       |          |
| 28       |          |          |
| 30       | 30       | 30       |

9. Assume that $80 per month is paid on a $1,000 loan. The simple interest is 18%. Write a program that will print out: (a) the monthly payment schedule in a table, and (b) the total interest paid on the loan. See the Print Sample below. Be sure to round out all answers to the nearest cent.

Note: The last payment may be less than $80.

Print Sample

| PAYMENT NUMBER | MONTHLY PAYMENT | APPLIED TO INTEREST | APPLIED TO PRINCIPAL | PRINCIPAL BALANCE |
|--------|--------|--------|--------|--------|
| 1  | 80.00 | 15.00 | 65.00 | 935.00 |
| 2  | 80.00 | 14.03 | 65.97 | 869.03 |
| 3  | 80.00 | 13.04 | 66.96 | 802.07 |
| 4  | 80.00 | 12.03 | 67.97 | 734.10 |
| 5  | 80.00 | 11.01 | 68.99 | 665.11 |
| 6  | 80.00 | 9.98  | 70.02 | 595.09 |
| 7  | 80.00 | 8.93  | 71.07 | 524.02 |
| 8  | 80.00 | 7.86  | 72.14 | 451.88 |
| 9  | 80.00 | 6.78  | 73.22 | 378.66 |
| 10 | 80.00 | 5.68  | 74.32 | 304.34 |
| 11 | 80.00 | 4.57  | 75.43 | 228.91 |
| 12 | 80.00 | 3.43  | 76.57 | 152.34 |
| 13 | 80.00 | 2.29  | 77.71 | 74.63 |
| 14 | 75.75 | 1.12  | 74.63 | 0.00 |

TOTAL INTEREST =     115.75

# Lesson 9
# MORE ABOUT CONDITIONAL BRANCHING

## 9.1 OBJECTIVES

Objectives: 1. To learn how to structure nested IF–THEN statements.
2. To be able to declare and use constants.
3. To be able to declare and use Boolean variable types.

## 9.2 NESTED IF-THEN, CONSTANT, AND BOOLEAN VARIABLE TYPES

BOOLEAN TYPE VARIABLE

EXPLANATION

A boolean variable can be designated as either TRUE or FALSE. No other characters or numbers can be placed in a boolean variable. A boolean variable cannot be used in a READ or WRITE statement. Boolean is of the ordinal type with TRUE the successor of FALSE.

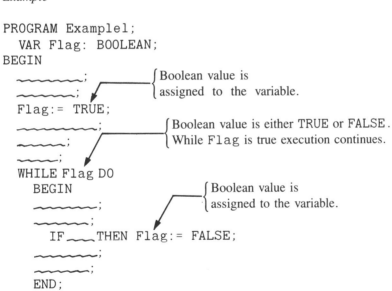

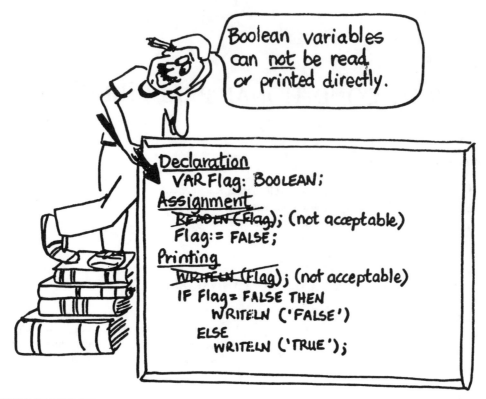

CONSTANT IDENTIFIER                              EXPLANATION

*Declaration*

```
                   Identifier
                           Constant to be assigned

   CONST _____ = _____ ;
```

The specified value is assigned to the identifier. The value in that identifier cannot be changed by any subsequent program statement. The CONST declaration must be placed before the VAR declaration.

*Example*

```
PROGRAM Example2;
   CONST Pi = 3.14159;
        Rate = .0932;
   VAR Area,Interest: REAL;
BEGIN
   _____;                3.14159 will be used for Pi
   _____;
   Area:= Pi * _____;
   _____;
   _____;                .0932 will be used for Rate
   Interest:= _____ *Rate *_____;
   _____;
   _____;
END.
```

## NESTED IF—THEN STATEMENTS

*First Format*

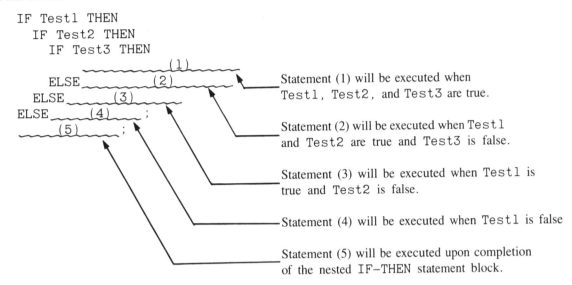

```
IF Testl THEN
   IF Test2 THEN
      IF Test3 THEN
                      (1)
         ELSE         (2)
      ELSE        (3)
   ELSE     (4)    ;
          (5)      ;
```

Statement (1) will be executed when `Testl`, `Test2`, and `Test3` are true.

Statement (2) will be executed when `Testl` and `Test2` are true and `Test3` is false.

Statement (3) will be executed when `Testl` is true and `Test2` is false.

Statement (4) will be executed when `Testl` is false

Statement (5) will be executed upon completion of the nested IF—THEN statement block.

Note: In the nested IF—THEN block a semicolon is placed only after the statement following the last ELSE.

*Summary*

| True | False | Executed Statements |
|---|---|---|
| Test1, Test2, Test3 | ——— | (1) (5) |
| Test1, Test2 | Test3 | (2) (5) |
| Test1 | Test2 | (3) (5) |
| ——— | Test1 | (4) (5) |

*Second Format*

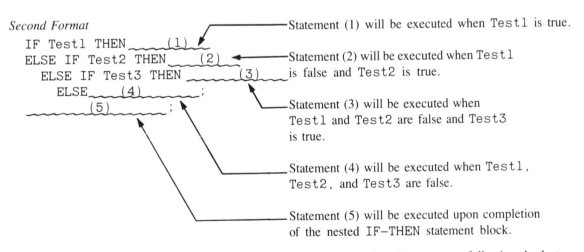

```
IF Testl THEN ____ (1)
ELSE IF Test2 THEN    (2)
   ELSE IF Test3 THEN       (3)
      ELSE    (4)    ;
             (5)     ;
```

Statement (1) will be executed when `Testl` is true.

Statement (2) will be executed when `Testl` is false and `Test2` is true.

Statement (3) will be executed when `Testl` and `Test2` are false and `Test3` is true.

Statement (4) will be executed when `Testl`, `Test2`, and `Test3` are false.

Statement (5) will be executed upon completion of the nested IF—THEN statement block.

Note: In the nested IF—THEN block, a semicolon is placed only after the statement following the last ELSE.

*Summary*

| False | True | Executed Statements |
|---|---|---|
| Test1, Test2, Test3 | ——— | (4) (5) |
| Test1, Test2 | Test3 | (3) (5) |
| Test1 | Test2 | (2) (5) |
| ——— | Test1 | (1) (5) |

Getting confused with what comes first in the program structure? Here is where the CONST goes.

```
PROGRAM ——;
   USES ——;
   CONST —— = ——;
   VAR —— : ——;
BEGIN
   ——
   ——
   ——

END.
```

## 9.3 DEMONSTRATION PROBLEMS

1. Write a program that will request a customer's bank account number, account balance, and number of checks written, and will calculate the service charge in the following way:

| Account Balance | Service Charge |
|---|---|
| 0 – $300 | $2.50 + 10¢ per check |
| Over $300 | No Service Charge |

Use a Boolean variable in conjunction with a (–999) as a bank account number to terminate the program.

Display Sample

```
ENTER ACCOUNT NUMBER, BALANCE, AND NUMBER OF CHECKS
ENTER -999 0 0 TO STOP

ACCOUNT#-BALANCE-#CHECKS        ACCOUNT#      NEW BALANCE
1200   156.80   21
                                  1200          152.20
2030   452.80   12
                                  2030          452.80
-999   0   0
```

ALGORITHM

1. Print prompts
2. Print heading
3. Initialize Boolean variable to TRUE
4. While Boolean is TRUE do
   4.1 Read data.
   4.2 Check Balance
       4.2.1 If <=300 Then NewBal= Balance − 2.50 − .10 * #Checks
       4.2.2 Else NewBal= Balance
   4.3 Check acct #
       4.3.1 If −999 then Boolean = FALSE
       4.3.2 Else Print Acct + NewBal

```
PROGRAM L9Demol;
  VAR Bal, NewBal: REAL;
      AccNo, Checks: INTEGER;
      Continue: BOOLEAN;
BEGIN
  WRITELN ('ENTER ACCOUNT NUMBER, BALANCE, AND NUMBER OF CHECKS');
  WRITELN ('ENTER -999 0 0 TO STOP');
  WRITELN;
  WRITELN ('ACCOUNT#-BALANCE-#CHECKS','ACCOUNT#':15,'NEW BALANCE':14);
  WRITELN;
  Continue:= TRUE;
    WHILE Continue DO
      BEGIN
        READLN (AccNo,Bal,Checks);
        IF Bal > 300 THEN NewBal:= Bal
          ELSE NewBal:= Bal - Checks * 0.10 - 2.50;
        IF AccNo= -999 THEN Continue:= FALSE
          ELSE WRITELN (AccNo:37,NewBal:15:2);
      END;
END.
```

2. Salesmen for a certain company receive commissions on their monthly sales according to the following scale:

| Monthly Sales | Commission |
|---|---|
| 0 – $ 5000 | 10% of sales |
| $ 5000+ – $15000 | $ 500 + 6% of sales |
| $15000+ – $20000 | $1100 + 4% of sales |
| over $20000 | $1300 + 2% of sales |

Also a base salary of $400 is given to each salesman each month.

Write a program that allows the user to key in the salesmen's ID numbers and monthly sales and obtain a printed table of the ID number, sales, and commission for each salesman. Declare the base salary as a constant in the program.

Display Sample

```
ENTER ID AND SALES
ENTER A NEGATIVE ID TO STOP
1000   3495
1050   9900
1200   16450
-1   0
```

Print Sample

```
ID       SALES      COMMISSION
1000      3495         749.50
1050      9900        1494.00
1200     16450        2158.00
```

ALGORITHM

1. Print prompts
2. Print heading
3. Read ID
4. While ID > 0
    4.1 Check sales
        4.1.1 <= 5000 Commission= Sales * .10
        4.1.2 > 5000 and <= 15000 Commission= Sales * .06 + 500
        4.1.3 > 15000 and <= 20000 Commission= Sales * .04 + 1100
        4.1.4 > 20000 Commission= Sales * .02 + 1300
    4.2 Add base pay
    4.3 Write ID, Sales, and Commission
    4.4 Read ID

```
PROGRAM L9Demo2;
  CONST Base = 400;
  VAR Id, Sales: INTEGER;
      Commission: REAL;
      LP: TEXT;
BEGIN
  REWRITE (LP,'PRINTER:');
  WRITELN ('ENTER ID AND SALES');
  WRITELN ('ENTER A NEGATIVE ID TO STOP');
  WRITELN (LP,'ID':4,'SALES':9,'COMMISSION':15);
  READLN (Id, Sales);
  WHILE Id > 0 DO
    BEGIN
      IF Sales > 5000 THEN
        IF Sales > 15000 THEN
          IF Sales > 20000 THEN
            Commission:= 1300 + Sales * 0.02
          ELSE Commission:= 1100 + Sales * 0.04
        ELSE Commission:= 500 + Sales * 0.06
      ELSE Commission:= Sales * 0.10;
      Commission:= Commission + Base;
      WRITELN (LP,Id:5,Sales:8,Commission:14:2);
      READLN (Id, Sales);
    END;
END.
```

## 9.4 SKILL DEVELOPMENT EXERCISES

1. The Energy Plus Coal Company sells coal at the following rates:

| Orders for | Cost |
|---|---|
| 0   to 35 TONS | $72/TON |
| 35 + to 50 TONS | $65/TON |
| Over 50 TONS | $59/TON |

The present tax is $8.31 per ton but is subject to change. Therefore, the tax per ton should be assigned as a constant at the beginning of the program to allow the tax to be changed without searching the complete program in order to change all statements involving the levied tax.

Write a program that will accept the number of tons sold as input and will print the number of tons sold and the cost. The cost includes the levied tax on the purchased coal.

Display Sample

```
ENTER TONS
(0 TO STOP)
27
42
98
0
```

Print Sample

| TONS | COST |
|---|---|
| 27 | 2168.37 |
| 42 | 3079.02 |
| 98 | 6596.38 |

2. A factory is using a computer to print labels that are to be placed on steel drive shafts as they come off the assembly line. The factory uses a computerized meter system that displays the serial number and the difference of each shaft's measurements from the perfect size. The shafts are to be labeled with a grade and price which will be determined by the scale shown below:

| Size Difference | Grade | % of Premium Price |
|---|---|---|
| 0 − .02mm | Premium | 100% |
| .02+ − .05mm | Quality | 90% |
| .05+ − .13mm | Average | 75% |
| over .13mm | Poor | 50% |

Write a program in which a worker can key in the Serial # and Size Difference of a shaft and the computer will print out a label with the serial number, grade, price, and percent deviation for each shaft. The perfect size and price for those shafts that are true-to-size should be declared as constants. See Data and Print Sample below for further clarification.

Label Price = Premium Price * % of Premium Price
% Deviation = Size Difference / Perfect Size * 100

Constant Values

Premium Price = 120.13
Perfect Size = 250.8

| Serial # | Size Difference |
|---|---|
| 1035 | .15mm |
| 1036 | .052mm |
| 1037 | .003mm |
| 1038 | .032mm |

Print Sample

| SERIAL NO | GRADE | PRICE | % DEVIATION |
|---|---|---|---|
| 1035 | POOR | 60.07 | 0.060 |
| SERIAL NO. | GRADE | PRICE | % DEVIATION |
| 1036 | AVERAGE | 90.10 | 0.021 |
| SERIAL NO. | GRADE | PRICE | % DEVIATION |
| 1037 | PREMIUM | 120.13 | 0.001 |
| SERIAL NO. | GRADE | PRICE | % DEVIATION |
| 1038 | QUALITY | 108.12 | 0.013 |

# Lesson 10
# PROGRAM STRUCTURE USING PROCEDURES

## 10.1 OBJECTIVES

Objectives: 1. To learn how to use Stepwise Refinement in developing programs.
2. To learn to use procedures to simplify or shorten programs (or both).
3. To understand the scope of variables in procedures and the main program.
4. To be able to use both value and VARiable parameters.

## 10.2 PROCEDURES AND STEPWISE REFINEMENT

*Stepwise Refinement*

As a program becomes more complex, a systematic way of developing the structure to be used when coding a program is necessary. Stepwise Refinement is the process of dividing a complex problem into two or more less complex sub-problems. In some cases these sub-problems may still be too complex. In this case the sub-problem is divided into a third level of sub-problems. These sub-problems may then be divided again and again until all parts of the main problem are simple enough to be written as an algorithm which can then be coded into Pascal. See the following illustrations for clarification.

Some of the advantages of using Stepwise Refinement in developing programs are:

1. The original problem appears much less complex.
2. The Pascal instructions used to code the sub-problem are easy to follow and understand.
3. Programs using the concept of sub-problems are more easily modified.

If a problem lends itself to only one level of subdividing, an illustration of how it might be divided is shown below:

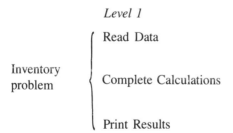

If each of the three sub-problems are relatively simple, the program would basically contain three independent blocks of instructions.

If a problem lends itself to more than one level of subdividing, an illustration of how one is divided is shown below:

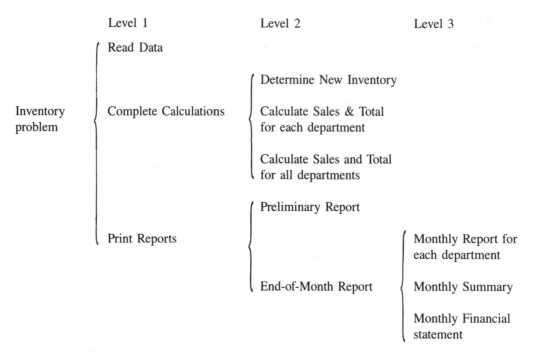

| | Level 1 | Level 2 | Level 3 |

Inventory problem

Read Data

Complete Calculations
- Determine New Inventory
- Calculate Sales & Total for each department
- Calculate Sales and Total for all departments

Print Reports
- Preliminary Report
- End-of-Month Report
  - Monthly Report for each department
  - Monthly Summary
  - Monthly Financial statement

Notice that the "lowest" most refined level may not be the same for all parts of the program. (Read Data) is refined enough in level 1. (Complete Calculations) is completed at level 2 and (Print Reports) needs to extend to level 3.

*Procedures*

The structure of a procedure is very similar to the structure of earlier programs.

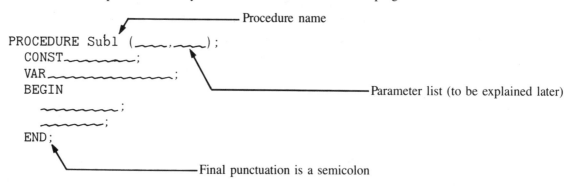

```
                                    ──────── Procedure name
PROCEDURE Sub1 (──,──);
   CONST────;
   VAR────;
   BEGIN
                                    ──────Parameter list (to be explained later)
   ────;
   ────;
   END;
                    ──────Final punctuation is a semicolon
```

Note: 1. A procedure is a smaller program that is being used by the main program.
2. All variable and constant names should be listed within the CONST, VAR, or parameter list[1] of the procedure in order to keep it as independent of the main program as possible. These variables are called Local variables as opposed to Global variables which are declared in the main program. More explanation follows in the section on Scope.
3. The sub-programs that result from using the stepwise refinement concept will indicate which procedures will be needed.

---

[1]An explanation of the function of a parameter list is given later in this lesson.

The procedures are placed after the VAR declaration part and before the BEGIN and END part of the main program. To execute a procedure the name of the procedure, with its parameter list[1], is placed in the main program between the BEGIN—END, wherever it is to be executed. Placing the name of the procedure in the body of the main program (or another procedure) is designated as a procedure call.

*Program Structure Using Procedures*

*Program name*

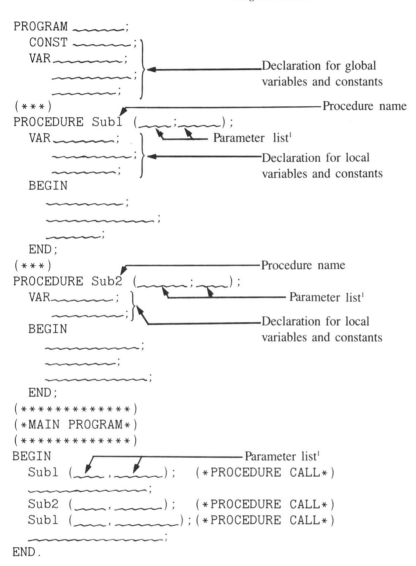

END.

Note: 1. A procedure may be called as many times as needed.
   2. A procedure is usually called from the main program but can be called from another procedure. The program code for the procedure being called must be placed before the procedure from which it is called.
   3. After a procedure action is complete, the execution moves to the statement that follows the procedure call.

---

[1]Parameter list will be explained later in this lesson.

*Scope*

The following illustration indicates which variable names are recognized within a program or procedure. This is referred to as the scope of the variable name. It is important to understand which names can be legally used in each part of the program; however, even though a variable name may be legal to use, it may not be desirable to use it in certain parts of the program. Prime examples are the variables L, W, and Average in the following illustration.

VARIABLE AND CONSTANT DECLARATION          EXPLANATION

```
PROGRAM_____;
   CONST Pi = 3.14159;
   VAR Count: INTEGER;
       L,W,Average: REAL;
(***)
PROCEDURE SubOne;
   VAR X1,X2,Root: REAL;
   BEGIN
       _____;    ⎫
       _____     ⎬
       _____     ⎭
   END;
(***)
PROCEDURE SubTwo;
   VAR Count; INTEGER;
       Y1,Y2,Root: REAL;
   BEGIN
       _____;     ⎫
       _____;     ⎪
       _____;     ⎬
       _____;     ⎪
       _____;     ⎭
   END;
(************)
(*MAIN PROGRAM*)
(************)
BEGIN
       _____;     ⎫
       _____;     ⎬
       _____;     ⎭
END.
```

The variables L, W, and Average are declared as global variables and if used in a procedure will cause the procedure to no longer be independent of the main program. Procedures that are independent of the main program are one of the most outstanding strengths of Pascal.

Variables and Constants that can be used:
   Global—Pi, Count, L, W, Average
   Local—X1, X2, Root

Variables and Constants that can be used:
   Global— Pi, L, W, Average
   Local—Count, Y1, Y2, Root

Variables and constants that can be used:
   Global—Pi, Count, L, W, Average

Note: 1. The constant Pi is assigned a value in the example. It is declared as a global constant and the value assigned to Pi can be used throughout the program.
   2. The variable Root is declared in both procedures SubOne and SubTwo as a local variable. The variable Root is used locally in each procedure and will not pass information from one procedure to the other nor will they be related to or conflict with each other.
   3. The variable Count in procedure SubTwo is declared as a local variable in SubTwo as well as a global variable in the main program. Therefore, while SubTwo is being executed Count is treated as a different variable than the global Count. While SubTwo is being executed any number assigned to the local variable Count will not affect the global variable Count.

Three ways of passing information to procedures are:

1. Using no parameters
2. Using value parameters
3. Using VARiable parameters

*Technique 1*

One type of procedure that requires no parameter list is one that displays instructions and needs no information passed to or from the main program.

*Example*

```
PROCEDURE Help1;
  BEGIN
    WRITELN ('REMEMBER TO PRESS "ESC" TO EXIT');
    WRITELN ('THE "D" KEY DRAWS A LINE');
    WRITELN ('THE "F" KEY SPECIFIES COLOR');
  END;
(************)
(*MAIN PROGRAM*)
(************)
BEGIN
  ~~~~~;
  ~~~~~~~~;
  Help1;      (*PROCEDURE CALL*)
  ~~~~~~;
END.
```

Another type of procedure that requires no parameter list is one that passes information to or from the main program in global variables (see Scope, page 72). This type of procedure is not independent of the main program, therefore, it is not emphasized.

```
PROGRAM Example;
  VAR Sum: REAL;
      Number: INTEGER;
(***)
PROCEDURE Average;
  BEGIN
    Sum:= Sum / Number;
    WRITELN ('THE AVERAGE OF THE NUMBERS IS:', Sum);
    WRITELN;
  END;
(************)
(*MAIN PROGRAM*)
(************)
BEGIN
  ~~~~~~~;
  ~~~~~~~~~;
  Average; (*PROCEDURE CALL*)
  ~~~~~~~;
  ~~~~~~~~;
  ~~~~~~~;
END.
```

*Technique 2* (Using Value Parameters)

The technique of using value parameters is used when the main program must pass information to a procedure but the procedure does not have to pass any information back to the main program.

```
                                                        ──── Value variable names
                                                        ──── Type declaration

   PROCEDURE PrintTotals (GrossTot,NetTot: REAL);
     BEGIN
       WRITELN ('THE TOTAL GROSS WAGE IS', GrossTot);
       WRITELN ('THE TOTAL NET WAGE IS',NetTot);
     END;
   (************)
   (*MAIN PROGRAM*)
   (************)
   BEGIN
       ~~~~~~~~~~;
       ~~~~~~~~~~;
       PrintTotals (Gross,Net);      (*PROCEDURE CALL*)

       ~~~~~~~~~~;
       ~~~~~~~~~~;
   END.
```

Note: 1. The parameter list in the procedure call must be of the same *type*, but not necessarily the same name, as those used in the procedure parameter list.
2. The variables used in the procedure call parameter list must be variables that have been defined in the main program.
3. The variables used in the procedure call parameter list must be of the same type and in the same order as those used in the procedure parameter list.
4. The parameter list can contain more than one type of value parameter and any number of each type.

*Example*

```
PROCEDURE PrintOut (Gross,Net,Rate: REAL; Hours: INTEGER);
                                         ──Semicolon is used between the types.
```

Using value parameters does not alter the contents of the variable in the original program. The contents will be passed to the procedure but any changes made in the procedure will not be sent back even if the same name is used in both the main program and the procedure.

*Example*

```
PROGRAM ValuePar;
  VAR Gross,Ded: REAL;
(***)
PROCEDURE PrintOut (Gross, Ded: REAL);
  BEGIN
    Gross:= Gross - Ded;
    WRITELN ('PROCEDURE GROSS = ',Gross:8:2);
  END;
(*************)
(*MAIN PROGRAM*)
(*************)
BEGIN
  Gross:= 1000;
  Ded:= 200;
  PrintOut (Gross,Ded);   (*PROCEDURE CALL*)
  WRITELN ('MAIN PROGRAM GROSS = ',Gross:8:2);
END.
```

The above program would result in the following Display Sample.

Display Sample

```
 PROCEDURE GROSS =     800.00
 MAIN PROGRAM GROSS =   1000.00
```

The main program assigns values to Gross and Ded as shown below:

← Main program
   locations

Then, when the procedure is called, two new locations are set up and copies of the numbers are transferred to these locations.

← Procedure
   locations

These new locations are now dominate and the first two locations are dormant until the procedure ends. When the procedure ends, the two procedure locations are destroyed and the main program locations are active again.

Unlike the previous example, the following example uses value parameters where the corresponding names are not the same.

*Example*

```
PROGRAM Different;
  VAR PreviousBal,SerCharge: REAL;
(***)
PROCEDURE Print (PrevBal,Charge: REAL);
  VAR NewBal: REAL;
  BEGIN
    NewBal:= PrevBal - Charge;
    WRITELN ('PREVIOUS BALANCE = ',PrevBal:8:2);
    WRITELN ('SERVICE CHARGE = ',Charge:8:2);
    WRITELN ('NEW BALANCE = ',NewBal:8:2);
  END;
(*************)
(*MAIN PROGRAM*)
(*************)
BEGIN
  PreviousBal:= 600;
  SerCharge:= 3.50;
  Print (PreviousBal,SerCharge); (*PROCEDURE CALL*)
END.
```

Display Sample

```
PREVIOUS BALANCE =     600.00
SERVICE CHARGE =         3.50
NEW BALANCE =      596.50
```

*Technique 3* (Using VARiable parameters)

The technique of using VARiable parameters is used when information needs to either be passed from a procedure or passed both to and from a procedure.

*Example*

```
PROGRAM VarParameters;
  VAR Time: INTEGER;
      PayRate,Grossl: REAL;
(***)
PROCEDURE CalWages (VAR Hours: INTEGER; VAR Rate,Gross:REAL);
  BEGIN
    Gross:= Hours * Rate;
    Hours:= Hours - 1;
  END;
(*************)
(*MAIN PROGRAM*)
(*************)
BEGIN
  Time:= 40;
  PayRate:= 7.25;
  CalWages (Time,PayRate,Grossl); (*PROCEDURE CALL*)
  WRITELN (Time:10,PayRate:10:2,Grossl:10:2);
END.
```

The addition of the VAR distinguishes these parameters as VARiable parameters rather than value parameters.

Grossl is placed here to receive information from procedure (it need not be loaded with a number before procedure is executed).

Note: The variables `Time`, `PayRate`, and `Grossl` of the main program must be of the same type and in corresponding positions as `Hours`, `Rate`, and `Gross` of the procedure in order for the program to compile and pass information.

To understand VARiable parameters it is best to think about what is happening in memory as illustrated below.

In the previously stated example when the main program is executed, three locations are in existence with the following contents:

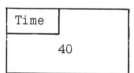 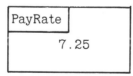 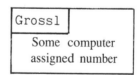

When the procedure is called, new locations are *not* created. The three storage locations above can be thought of as having double names, the ones from the main program and the ones from the procedure.

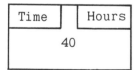 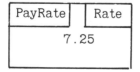 

Assume the procedure changes `Hours` to 39, `Rate` to 7.25, and `Gross` to 290; the contents of `Time`, `PayRate`, and `Grossl` would then be:

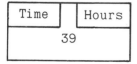  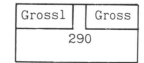

After execution of the procedure, the second names for the variables will be eliminated and any changes of the contents will be in the variables in the main program.

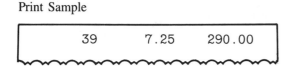

The program would then print:

Print Sample

```
        39       7.25     290.00
```

Note: Both value and VARiable parameters may occur in the same parameter list.

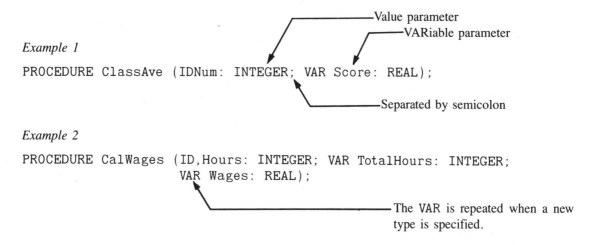

*Example 1*

```
PROCEDURE ClassAve (IDNum: INTEGER; VAR Score: REAL);
```

*Example 2*

```
PROCEDURE CalWages (ID,Hours: INTEGER; VAR TotalHours: INTEGER;
                    VAR Wages: REAL);
```

The VAR is repeated when a new type is specified.

## 10.3 DEMONSTRATION PROBLEM

1. A business firm pays its employees in two ways. The group with ID numbers from 1000 to 1999 are on an hourly wage. The group with ID numbers from 2000 to 2999 are paid for piece work at $1.60 for each item they produce. Social security at 6¼% of the gross salary, and insurance at $9.85 per week are deducted from each gross salary to determine the net salary. All employees with ID# 1000–1999 working more than 40 hours in a given week are paid 1½ times the hourly rate for all hours over 40.

   The data sample shows ID #, rate of pay, and hours worked for all employees with ID numbers from 1000 to 1999. It shows ID# and number of items produced for all employees with ID numbers from 2000 to 2999.

   Write a program that will print the desired information as shown in the print sample. Subdivide the problem where convenient so that it lends itself to using procedures.

Data Sample
1000, 8.80, 40

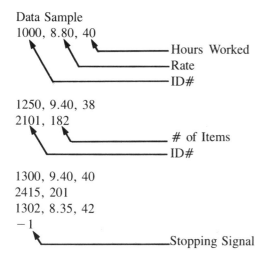

Hours Worked
Rate
ID#

1250, 9.40, 38
2101, 182

# of Items
ID#

1300, 9.40, 40
2415, 201
1302, 8.35, 42
−1

Stopping Signal

Print Sample

| ID | HOURS | #ITEMS | GROSS | NET W |
|------|-------|--------|--------|--------|
| 1000 | 40.0 | | 352.00 | 320.15 |
| 1250 | 38.0 | | 357.20 | 325.02 |
| 2101 | | 182 | 291.20 | 263.15 |
| 1300 | 40.0 | | 376.00 | 342.65 |
| 2415 | | 201 | 321.60 | 291.65 |
| 1302 | 42.0 | | 375.75 | 342.42 |

```
TOTAL SOCIAL SECURITY =    129.61
TOTAL INSURANCE       =     59.10
TOTAL NET WAGES       =   1885.04
```

*Level 1*

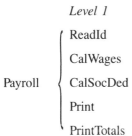

Payroll

ReadId

CalWages

CalSocDed

Print

PrintTotals

Only level 1 subdividing is necessary. The sub-problems that result from the subdividing lead to the following procedures:

ReadId
  Reads ID.

CalWages
  Reads rate and hours or number of pieces and calculates wages using appropriate formulas.

CalSocDed
  Calculates social security, deductions, net wages, and all totals.

Print
  Prints line of information.

PrintTotals
  Prints summary totals.

In an algorithm of a procedure:

1. ↑ indicates a VARiable parameter where no valid information is received from the main program but information will be passed from the procedure to the main program.
2. ↑↓ indicates a VARiable parameter where valid information is received from the main program, altered, and new information is passed back to the main program.
3. ↓ indicates a value parameter where information is only passed from the main program to the procedure.

ALGORITHM (Procedures)

1. ReadID (Group ↑, ID ↑)
    1.1 Prompt and read ID
2. CalWages (Group ↓, Hours ↑↓, Number ↑↓, Wages ↑)
    2.1 If ID < 2000
            2.1.1 If overtime use overtime formulas
            2.1.2 If no overtime use Hours * Rate(constant)
    2.2 If ID >= 2000
            2.2.1 Use number * PieceRate(constant)
3. CalSocDed (Wages ↓,NetWages ↑,TotalSoc ↑, TotalInsur ↑, TotalNet ↑)
    3.1 SocialSec:= Wages * SocPercent(constant)
    3.2 Deduction:= SocialSec + Insurance(constant)
    3.3 NetWages:= Wages - Deduction
    3.4 Total SocialSec
    3.5 Total Insurance
    3.6 Total NetWages
4. Print (Group ↓, ID ↓, Number ↓, Hours ↓, Wages ↓, NetWages ↓)
    4.1 If ID < 2000 print ID, hours, wages, and net wages
    4.2 If ID >= 2000 print ID, number, wages, and net wages
5. PrintTotals (TotalSoc ↓, TotalInsur ↓, TotalNet ↓)
    5.1 Print total social security
    5.2 Print total insurance
    5.3 Print total net wages

```
PROGRAM L1ODemo1;
  VAR ID,Number: INTEGER;
      Hours,Wages,NetWages,TotalSoc,TotalInsur,TotalNet: REAL;
      Lp: TEXT; (*APPLE & IBM*)
(***)
PROCEDURE ReadID (VAR ID: INTEGER);
  BEGIN
    WRITELN ('ID');
    READLN (ID);
  END;
```

```
(***)
PROCEDURE CalWages (ID: INTEGER; VAR Wages,Hours: REAL;
                         VAR Number: INTEGER);
  CONST PieceRate = 1.60;
  VAR Rate: REAL;
  BEGIN
    IF ID < 2000 THEN
      BEGIN
        WRITELN ('RATE        HOURS');
        READLN (Rate,Hours);
        IF Hours > 40 THEN
            Wages:= Rate * Hours + Rate * (Hours - 40) * 1.5
          ELSE
            Wages:= Rate * Hours;
      END
    ELSE
      BEGIN
        WRITELN ('PIECES');
        READLN (Number);
        Wages:= Number * PieceRate;
      END;
END;
(***)
PROCEDURE CalSocDed (Wages: REAL; VAR NetWages,TotalSoc,TotalInsur,
                         TotalNet: REAL);
  CONST SocPercent = 0.0625;
        Insurance = 9.85;
  VAR SocialSec,Deduction: REAL;
  BEGIN
    SocialSec:= Wages * SocPercent;
    Deduction:= SocialSec + Insurance;
    NetWages:= Wages - Deduction;
    TotalSoc:= TotalSoc + SocialSec;
    TotalInsur:= TotalInsur + Insurance;
    TotalNet:= TotalNet + NetWages;
  END;
(***)
PROCEDURE Print (ID,Number: INTEGER; Hours,Wages,NetWages: REAL);
  BEGIN
    IF ID < 2000 THEN
        WRITELN (Lp,ID:6,Hours:8:1,'  ':7,Wages:11:2,NetWages:10:2)
      ELSE
        WRITELN (Lp,ID:6,'   ':8,Number:7,Wages:11:2,NetWages:10:2);
  END;
(***)
PROCEDURE PrintTotals (TotalSoc,TotalInsur,TotalNet: REAL);
  BEGIN
    WRITELN (Lp);
    WRITELN (Lp,'TOTAL SOCIAL SECURITY = ',TotalSoc:8:2);
    WRITELN (Lp,'TOTAL INSURANCE       = ',TotalInsur:8:2);
    WRITELN (Lp,'TOTAL NET WAGES       = ',TotalNet:8:2);
  END;
(*************)
(*MAIN PROGRAM*)
(*************)
```

```
BEGIN
  REWRITE(Lp,'PRINTER:');      (*APPLE & IBM*)
  TotalSoc:= 0.0; TotalInsur:= 0.0; TotalNet:= 0.0;
  WRITELN (Lp,'ID':5,'HOURS':10,'#ITEM':8,'GROSS':9,'NET W':10);
  ReadID (ID);    (*PROCEDURE CALL*)
  WHILE ID > 0 DO
    BEGIN
      CalWages (ID,Wages,Hours,Number);              (*PROCEDURE CALL*)
      CalSocDed (Wages,NetWages,TotalSoc,
                 TotalInsur,TotalNet);               (*PROCEDURE CALL*)
      Print (ID,Number,Hours,Wages,NetWages);        (*PROCEDURE CALL*)
      ReadID (ID);                                   (*PROCEDURE CALL*)
    END;
  PrintTotals (TotalSoc,TotalInsur,TotalNet);        (*PROCEDURE CALL*)
END.
```

## 10.4 SKILL DEVELOPMENT EXERCISES

1. The data to be processed for a department store consists of a customer's ID number, previous balance, purchases, payments, and the value of any merchandise returned. The problem is to write a program which processes the data by determining both the total due and the service charge, and prints out a billing statement. If the total due is negative a check is to be printed that will set the account balance to zero. Because names are not provided with the data, the print out will have to identify the customer by an ID number only (the name can be typed in by a clerk at a later time). A summary representing the total amount due for all customers and total of all the checks is to be printed when a negative ID stopping signal is encountered. Write a program that uses the given algorithm and suggested procedures to complete the project. Study the following information for further clarification:

Service Charge = (Prev. Bal - Payments - Returns) * .18 / 12

Total Due = Prev. Bal + Purchases - Payments - Returns + Service Charge
(Billing Statement)

Total Due = Prev. Bal + Purchases - Payments - Returns (Checks)

Data Sample

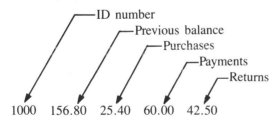

```
    1000   156.80   25.40   60.00   42.50
```

Print Sample (Billing statement)

```
ID # 1000 Name _____
PREVIOUS BALANCE      156.80
PURCHASES              25.40
PAYMENTS               60.00
RETURNS                42.50
SERVICE CHARGE          0.81
BALANCE DUE            80.51
```

Print Sample (Checks)

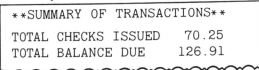

```
PAY TO THE ORDER OF _____
ID # 1999
THE AMOUNT OF $    5.05 _____
```

Print Sample (Summary)

```
**SUMMARY OF TRANSACTIONS**

TOTAL CHECKS ISSUED   70.25
TOTAL BALANCE DUE    126.91
```

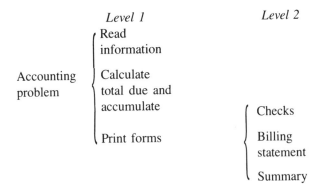

|  | *Level 1* | *Level 2* |
|---|---|---|
| Accounting problem | Read information | |
| | Calculate total due and accumulate | |
| | | Checks |
| | | Billing statement |
| | Print forms | Summary |

## PROCEDURES

PrintChecks
When the total due is negative, a check will be printed to reduce the balance to zero.

PrintBills
When the total due is positive, the billing statement is printed.

PrintSummary
Print the total of the amount due for all customers with positive balances and the total of all checks written.

## ALGORITHM (Main Program)

1. Read information (ID, previous balance, purchases, payments)
2. While ID > 0
    2.1 If total due < 0
        2.1.1 Print check (ID,BalDue)
        2.1.2 Accumulate total checks
    2.2 If total due >= 0
        2.2.1 Calculate service charge
        2.2.2 Print billing statement (full parameter list)
        2.2.3 Accumulate total due
3. Print summary (TotalChecks,TotlBalDue)

Display Sample

```
1000  156.80  25.40  60.00  42.50
1035  40  5.80  0  0
1082  14.50  20.30  100  0
1999  24.95  0  30.00  0
```

Print Sample

```
ID # 1000 NAME _____
PREVIOUS BALANCE    156.80
PURCHASES            25.40
PAYMENTS             60.00
RETURNS              42.50
SERVICE CHARGE        0.81
BALANCE DUE          80.51
— — — — — — — — — — — — — — — — —
ID # 1035 NAME _____
PREVIOUS BALANCE     40.00
PURCHASES             5.80
PAYMENTS              0.00
RETURNS               0.00
SERVICE CHARGE        0.60
BALANCE DUE          46.40
— — — — — — — — — — — — — — — — —
PAY TO THE ORDER OF _____
ID # 1082
THE AMOUNT OF  $ 65.20
— — — — — — — — — — — — — — — — —
PAY TO THE ORDER OF _____
ID # 1999
THE AMOUNT OF  $ 5.05
— — — — — — — — — — — — — — — — —
**SUMMARY OF TRANSACTIONS**
TOTAL CHECKS ISSUED  70.25
TOTAL BALANCE DUE   126.91
```

2. Use Stepwise Refinement in developing a program that uses procedures when convenient to read the measures of two angles in degrees-minutes-seconds form and prints out the measure of:

   a. Each angle.
   b. The sum of the two angles.
   c. The first angle doubled.
   d. The second angle tripled.

Print all answers in reduced form.

Note: 60 Sec = 1 min
      60 min = 1 degree

Data Sample

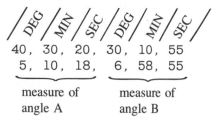

```
40, 30, 20,  30, 10, 55
 5, 10, 18,   6, 58, 55
```

measure of     measure of
angle A        angle B

Print Sample

```
MEAS. A          = 40 DEG 30 MIN  20 SEC
MEAS. B          = 30 DEG 10 MIN  55 SEC
MS.A + MS.B      = 70 DEG 41 MIN  15 SEC
2 MS. A          = 81 DEG  0 MIN  40 SEC
3 MS. B          = 90 DEG 32 MIN  45 SEC

MEAS. A          =  5 DEG 10 MIN  18 SEC
MEAS. B          =  6 DEG 58 MIN  55 SEC
MS.A + MS.B      = 12 DEG  9 MIN  13 SEC
2 MS. A          = 10 DEG 20 MIN  36 SEC
3 MS. B          = 20 DEG 56 MIN  45 SEC
```

# Lesson 11
# FOR LOOPS

## 11.1 OBJECTIVES

Objectives: 1. To be able to declare and use CHARacter variable types.
2. To understand and be able to use looping with automatic counters (FOR—TO and FOR—DOWNTO loops).
3. To learn a second method of controlling loops.
4. To learn to use the READ statement.

## 11.2 FOR—TO, FOR—DOWN TO, AND LOOP CONTROL

CHAR VARIABLE TYPE                    EXPLANATION

CHAR variable declaration:

*Example 1*

```
VAR Alphabet,CharSet: CHAR;
```

CHAR variable assignment:

The CHAR variable type allows for variables to contain a single character. The character can be a symbol, number, or letter. The CHAR variable can be used in all Pascal expressions except where mathematical calculations are completed.

*Example 2*

```
Alphabet:= 'C';
```

```
CharSet:= Alphabet;
```

CharSet contains the letter C.

READLN and WRITELN with CHAR variables:

*Example 3*

```
PROGRAM Example3;
  VAR FirstLetter,SecondLetter,ThirdLetter: CHAR;
BEGIN
  WRITE ('ENTER 1ST LETTER: ');
    READLN (FirstLetter);
  WRITE ('ENTER 2ND LETTER: ');
    READLN (SecondLetter);
  ThirdLetter:= FirstLetter;
  WRITELN (FirstLetter:3,SecondLetter:3,ThirdLetter:3);
END.
```

Display Sample

```
ENTER 1ST LETTER: T
ENTER 2ND LETTER: Y
   T  Y  T
```

FOR-TO LOOPS

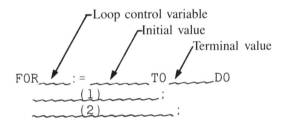

EXPLANATION

The loop variable must be of the ordinal type (i.e., an ordered range of values). The standard ordinal types are INTEGER, CHAR, and BOOLEAN. A variable of the REAL type cannot be used as the loop control variable.

When a FOR-TO loop is entered, the loop control variable is set equal to the initial value and incremented by one or advances to the next letter each time the statement following the DO is executed. When the loop control variable equals the terminal value it will execute statement (1) one last time and then control goes to statement (2).

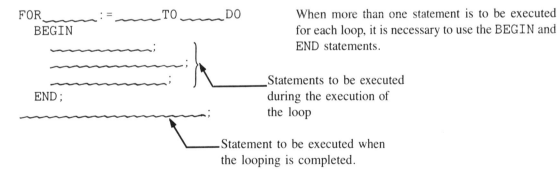

When more than one statement is to be executed for each loop, it is necessary to use the BEGIN and END statements.

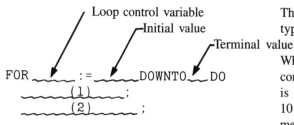

The loop control variable must be of the ordinal type (not of the REAL type).

When a FOR–DOWNTO loop is entered, the loop control variable is set equal to the initial value and is decremented to its predecessor value (i.e., 10,9,8,..., or N,M,L,K,J,...) each time the statement following the DO is executed. When the loop control variable equals the terminal value, it will execute statement (1) one last time and then control goes to statement (2).

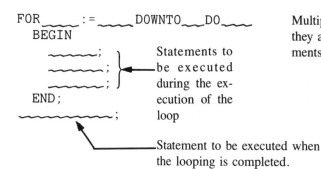

Multiple statements may be used within a loop if they are bracketed by the BEGIN and END statements.

Statement to be executed when the looping is completed.

READ STATEMENT

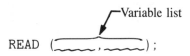

EXPLANATION

The difference between the READ and READLN statements is that the READLN only reads the information needed, any information on the line that is not needed is ignored. The next information would be read starting at the beginning of the next line. The READ statement would not ignore the rest of the information on the line but would read it on the next loop.

The following program segments accomplish exactly the same task:

Example (READ Statement)

```
FOR Loop := 1 TO 5 DO
   READ (Number);
```

*Example* (READLN Statement)

```
FOR Loop := 1 TO 5 DO
   READLN (Number);
```

Display Sample (READ statement)

```
45 34 93 67 12
```

Display Sample (READLN statement)

```
45
34
93
67
12
```

## 11.3 DEMONSTRATION PROBLEMS

1. Write a program that displays the integers from 10 to 20 vertically on the screen.

```
PROGRAM DemoL11P1;
   VAR Count: INTEGER;
BEGIN
   FOR Count:= 10 TO 20 DO
      WRITELN(Count);
END.
```

Display Sample
```
10
11
12
13
14
15
16
17
18
19
20
```

2. Write a program that displays the letters of the alphabet from A to M horizontally and, on the line below, displays the letters Z to N with the letter Z appearing first. Have two spaces between each character.

Display Sample
```
A  B  C  D  E  F  G  H  I  J  K  L  M
Z  Y  X  W  V  U  T  S  R  Q  P  O  N
```

```
PROGRAM L11P2Demo;
   VAR Alph, Reverse: CHAR;
BEGIN
   FOR Alph:= 'A' TO 'M' DO
      WRITE (Alph:3);
   WRITELN;
   FOR Reverse:= 'Z' DOWNTO 'N' DO
      WRITE (Reverse:3);
   WRITELN;
END.
```

3. Write a program that will determine and display the average of groups of eight numbers. Use a READ statement so the numbers can be entered on a single line.

Display Sample
```
16  32  4  21  81  67  82  31

     41.75
ANOTHER AVERAGE Y-YES, N-NO
Y
56  78  14  31  75  60  25  30
etc.
```

ALGORITHM

1. Set Continue to True (Boolean)
2. While Continue = True
    2.1 Set Sum to 0
    2.2 For Count = 1 to 8
        2.2.1 Read X
        2.2.2 Accumulate X in Sum
    2.3 Calculate and display answer
    2.4 Prompt and enter stopping signal
    2.5 If Continue = False then terminate

```
PROGRAM L11P4Demo;
   VAR Continue: BOOLEAN;
       Signal: CHAR;
       Count: INTEGER;
       X,Sum,Ave: REAL;
BEGIN
   Continue:= TRUE;
   WHILE Continue DO
     BEGIN
       Sum:= 0.0;
       FOR Count:= 1 TO 8 DO
         BEGIN
           READ(X);
           Sum:= Sum + X;
         END;
       Ave:= Sum / 8.0;
     ¹ READLN (Signal);
       WRITELN;
       WRITELN(Ave:10:2);
       WRITELN;
       WRITELN('ANOTHER AVERAGE Y-YES, N-NO');
       READLN(Signal);
       IF Signal = 'N' THEN Continue:= FALSE;
     END;
END.
```

---

¹ APPLE and IBM
When a character is to be entered after a series of numbers have been entered using a READ statement, it is necessary to execute a READLN statement using a CHAR type variable to process the return (EOL) character.

When used in a program, the following procedure will read eight numbers and send the average of those numbers back to the main program for further processing. This procedure uses Technique 3 (of Lesson 10) where information is sent back to the main program.

————VARiable parameter

```
PROCEDURE Average (VAR Ave: REAL);
   VAR Count: INTEGER;
        X, Sum: REAL;
        Return: CHAR;
   BEGIN
     Sum:= 0.0;
     FOR Count:= 1 TO 8 DO
       BEGIN
          READ (X);
          Sum:= Sum + X;
       END;
     Ave:= Sum / 8.0;
     READLN (Return);
   END;
```

## 11.4 SKILL DEVELOPMENT EXERCISES

1. What will be displayed when the following program is executed?

```
PROGRAM Stars;
   VAR Asterisk: CHAR;
        Number: INTEGER;
BEGIN
   Asterisk:= '*';
   FOR Number:= 6 DOWNTO 1 DO
     WRITE(Asterisk);
   WRITELN;
   WRITELN('PATTERN COMPLETE');
END.
```

2. Write a program that will convert and print each degree, 1 to 20, in Fahrenheit and in its equivalent Celsius temperature. Use an appropriate heading. Create the numbers 1 to 20 with a FOR—TO statement.

Note: $C = (F - 32)\dfrac{5}{9}$

Print Sample

```
     FAHRENHEIT          CELSIUS
          1             -17.222
          2             -16.667
          3             -16.111
          4             -15.556
          5             -15.000
          .
          .
          .
         18              -7.778
         19              -7.222
         20              -6.667
```

3. Write a program to print out a multiplication table for the numbers from 1 to 9. Generate all the numbers needed in a FOR—TO statement and print the table as shown in the Print Sample.

Print Sample

```
1 ⅹ  2 =   2
2 ⅹ  3 =   6
3 ⅹ  4 =  12
4 ⅹ  5 =  20
5 ⅹ  6 =  30
6 ⅹ  7 =  42
7 ⅹ  8 =  56
8 ⅹ  9 =  72
9 ⅹ 10 =  90
```

4. Write a program that will print out a table of decimal equivalents for the fractions from 1/10 to 1/2. Generate the denominators using a FOR—DOWNTO statement.

Print Sample

```
1/10 = 0.10000
1/ 9 = 0.11111
1/ 8 = 0.12500
1/ 7 = 0.14286
1/ 6 = 0.16667
1/ 5 = 0.20000
1/ 4 = 0.25000
1/ 3 = 0.33333
1/ 2 = 0.50000
```

# Lesson 12
# FOR STATEMENTS WITH VARIABLE CONTROLS

## 12.1 OBJECTIVES

Objectives: 1. To use variables and algebraic expressions in FOR—TO statements.
2. To handle problems requiring decisions in FOR—TO statements.

## 12.2 VARIABLES, ALGEBRAIC EXPRESSIONS IN A FOR LOOP

USING VARIABLES IN FOR—TO STATEMENTS          EXPLANATION

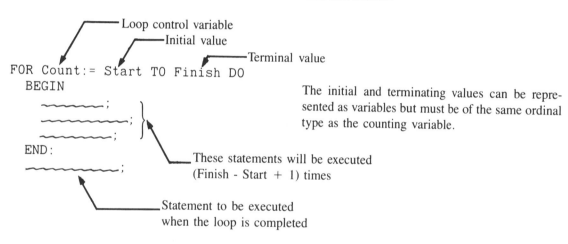

The initial and terminating values can be represented as variables but must be of the same ordinal type as the counting variable.

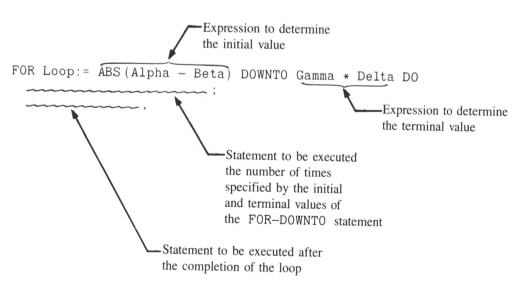

The rules for FOR—TO or FOR—DOWNTO statements are given below. However, they should be reviewed *after* the reader has studied the demonstration problems and has acquired a good understanding of the new looping statements.

- The loop control variable, initial value, and terminal value must all be of the same ordinal type (INTEGER, CHAR, or BOOLEAN).
- The loop control variable must be locally declared.
- The loop control variable should not be changed within the loop. Its value may be used but not changed other than by the normal incrementing process. For example, in the loop

    Count:= Start TO Finish DO

  a statement such as

    Count:= ⎽⎽⎽⎽⎽⎽⎽⎽⎽⎽;

  would not be allowed.
- The expressions that give the initial and terminating values for the loop control variables are evaluated when the FOR—TO or FOR—DOWNTO loop is entered.
- The value of the loop control variable is undefined immediately after the loop is completed.
- The loop control variable is automatically incremented to its successor (in a FOR—TO statement) or predecessor (in a FOR—DOWNTO statement). If a larger increment is needed, a WHILE—DO or RE-PEAT—UNTIL statement should be used instead of the FOR statement.
- If the initial value of the loop counter is equal to the terminating value, the statement(s) in the loop will be executed once. If the initial value of the loop is greater than the final value, the statement(s) in the loop will not be executed.

## 12.3 DEMONSTRATION PROBLEMS

1. Write a program to generate an answer sheet where the questions are labeled alphabetically. Have a prompt request for the beginning and terminating letters. See Display and Print Sample for further clarification.

Display Sample

```
BEGINNING LETTER? C
TERMINATING LETTER? G
```

Print Sample

```
C. _____

D. _____

E. _____

F. _____

G. _____
```

ALGORITHM

1. Set up for printer (APPLE & IBM)
2. Prompt and read BLetter and TLetter
3. FOR Count = BLetter TO TLetter
   3.1 Print blank line
   3.2 Print Count, ".", and line

```pascal
PROGRAM L12Demo1;
  VAR Count,BLetter,TLetter: CHAR;
  Lp: TEXT;                       (*APPLE & IBM*)
BEGIN
  REWRITE(Lp,'PRINTER:');         (*APPLE & IBM*)
  WRITE('BEGINNING LETTER? ');
  READLN(BLetter);
  WRITE('TERMINATING LETTER? ');
  READLN(TLetter);
  FOR Count:= BLetter TO TLetter DO
    BEGIN
      WRITELN(Lp);
      WRITELN(Lp,Count,'. _____');
    END;
END.
```

The following procedure, when used in a program, will prompt the user to enter beginning and terminating letters and print lines as shown in the Print Sample. This procedure uses Technique 1 (of Lesson 10) which does not pass any information to or from the main program.

```
PROCEDURE L12Demo1;
  VAR Count, BLetter, TLetter: CHAR;
      Lp: TEST;                        (*APPLE & IBM*)
  BEGIN
    REWRITE (Lp,'PRINTER:');          (*APPLE & IBM*)
    WRITE ('BEGINNING LETTER? ');
    READLN (BLetter);
    WRITE ('TERMINATING LETTER? ');
    READLN (TLetter);
    FOR Count:= BLetter TO TLetter DO
      BEGIN
        WRITELN (Lp);
        WRITELN (Lp,Count,'. _____');
      END;
  END;
```

2. Write a Pascal program to compute and print the greatest common divisor (GCD) and the least common multiple (LCM) of two integers M and N. Run the program using the numbers 200 and 125; 45 and 60; 12 and 8; and 120 and 180.

Note: $LCM = \dfrac{M*N}{GCD}$

Display Sample

```
ENTER -1  0 TO STOP
ENTER TWO INTEGERS 200   125
ENTER TWO INTEGERS 45   60
ENTER TWO INTEGERS 12   8
ENTER TWO INTEGERS 120   180
ENTER TWO INTEGERS -1   0
```

Print Sample

| M | N | GCD | LCM |
|-----|-----|-----|------|
| 200 | 125 | 25 | 1000 |
| 45 | 60 | 15 | 180 |
| 12 | 8 | 4 | 24 |
| 120 | 180 | 60 | 360 |

ALGORITHM

1. Set up for printer (APPLE & IBM)
2. Heading
3. Prompt and read Num1 and Num2
4. While Num1 > 0
    4.1 FOR Divisor = 1 to Num1
        4.1.1 If Num1 and Num2 divisible
              by Divisor then Gcd = Divisor
    4.2 Print line of information
    4.3 Read new Num1 and Num2

```
PROGRAM Ll2Demo2;
  VAR Num1,Num2,Divisor,Gcd,Lcm: INTEGER;
      Lp: TEXT;                              (*APPLE & IBM*)
BEGIN
  REWRITE(Lp,'PRINTER:');                    (*APPLE & IBM*)
  WRITELN(Lp,'M':4,'N':6,'GCD':7,'LCM':6);
  WRITELN ('ENTER -1  0 TO STOP');
  WRITE('ENTER TWO INTEGERS ');
  READLN(Num1,Num2);
  WHILE Num1 > 0 DO
    BEGIN
      FOR Divisor:= 1 TO Num1 DO
        BEGIN
          IF Num1 MOD Divisor = 0 THEN
            IF Num2 MOD Divisor = 0 THEN
              Gcd:= Divisor;
        END;
      Lcm:= Num1 * Num2 DIV Gcd;
      WRITELN(Lp,Num1:5,Num2:6,Gcd:6,Lcm:6);
      WRITE('ENTER TWO INTEGERS ');
      READLN(Num1,Num2);
    END;
END.
```

The following procedure, when used in a program, receives two numbers from the main program, finds the GCM and LCM of the two and returns the GCM and LCM to the main program. Both Techniques 2 and 3 are being used. Technique 2 is used when information is being passed only from the main program in Num1 and Num2, and Technique 3 when information is being passed to the main program in Gcd and Lcm.

```
                              ──────Value  parameter
                                              ──────VARiable  parameter

PROCEDURE Ll2Demo2 (Num1, Num2: INTEGER; VAR Gcd, Lcm: INTEGER);
  VAR Divisor: INTEGER;
  BEGIN
    FOR Divisor:= 1 TO Num1 DO
      BEGIN
        IF Num1 MOD Divisor = 0 THEN
          IF Num2 MOD Divisor = 0 THEN
            Gcd:= Divisor;
      END;
    Lcm:= Num1 * Num2 DIV Gcd;
  END;
```

3. Write a procedure that will print a double line of dashes if the Boolean variable Divider is true, and a single line of dashes if the variable Divider is false.

```
Procedure BTest (Divider: BOOLEAN);
  VAR Binary: BOOLEAN;
  BEGIN
    FOR Binary:= False TO Divider DO
      WRITELN ('------------------------------');
  END;
```

A program to check the procedure BTest is shown below:

```
PROGRAM L11P3Demo;
  VAR Divider: BOOLEAN;
(***)                                          ——— Value parameter
Procedure BTest (Divider: BOOLEAN);
  VAR Binary: BOOLEAN;
BEGIN
  FOR Binary:= False TO Divider DO
    WRITELN('——————————————————————————————');
END;
(*************)
(*MAIN PROGRAM*)
(*************)
BEGIN
  Divider:= False;◀——————— Note: False is not a variable. Divider could be
  BTest (Divider);                 assigned the value of either True or False.
END.                               (True is the successor of False.)
```

## 12.4 SKILL DEVELOPMENT EXERCISES

1. Write a program to find the sum of the reciprocals of the First $K$ positive integers.

   That is:  $\dfrac{1}{1} + \dfrac{1}{2} + \dfrac{1}{3} + \dfrac{1}{4} + \cdots + \dfrac{1}{K}$

   Input $K$ as 2, then 10, 100, 200, 1000.

   Display Sample

   ```
   VALUE FOR K ?2
   VALUE FOR K ?10
   VALUE FOR K ?100
   VALUE FOR K ?1000
   VALUE FOR K ?-1
   ```

   Print Sample

   ```
   SUM OF THE FIRST    2 RECIPROCALS = 1.50000
   SUM OF THE FIRST   10 RECIPROCALS = 2.92897
   SUM OF THE FIRST  100 RECIPROCALS = 5.18738
   SUM OF THE FIRST 1000 RECIPROCALS = 7.48547
   ```

2. Write a program that processes numbers by printing out the factorial of that number and its value, as shown in the Print Sample below.

   Note: n! = (n)(n-1)(n-2) ...(3)(2)(1), where n is a positive integer.

   Data Sample 5, 11, 7, 3                                    Will not be condensed
                                                              on computer printout

   Print Sample (TRS–80)

   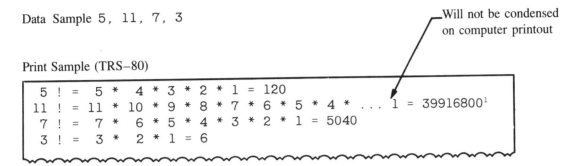

   ```
    5 ! =  5 *  4 * 3 * 2 * 1 = 120
   11 ! = 11 * 10 * 9 * 8 * 7 * 6 * 5 * 4 * ... 1 = 39916800[1]
    7 ! =  7 *  6 * 5 * 4 * 3 * 2 * 1 = 5040
    3 ! =  3 *  2 * 1 = 6
   ```

                                                              Will not be condensed
                                                              on computer printout

   Print Sample (APPLE and IBM PC)

   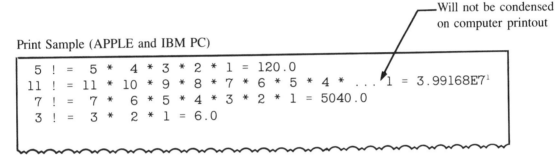

   ```
    5 ! =  5 *  4 * 3 * 2 * 1 = 120.0
   11 ! = 11 * 10 * 9 * 8 * 7 * 6 * 5 * 4 * ... 1 = 3.99168E7[1]
    7 ! =  7 *  6 * 5 * 4 * 3 * 2 * 1 = 5040.0
    3 ! =  3 *  2 * 1 = 6.0
   ```

3. Write a program that asks for a positive integer and then displays whether or not the integer is prime.

   Display Sample

   ```
   ENTER -1 TO STOP
   POSITIVE INTEGER?13
   POSITIVE INTEGER?20
   POSITIVE INTEGER?189
   POSITIVE INTEGER?-1
   ```

   Print Sample

   ```
   13 IS PRIME
   20 IS NOT PRIME
   189 IS NOT PRIME
   ```

---

[1] Because this number is greater than the maximum integer, a real variable must be used.

4. Write a program that:

   a. Accepts an input for the number of tests required.
   b. Accepts input values containing the student's Id number, number of tests taken, and the test grades.
   c. Averages the test grades and rounds off the average to the nearest tenth.
   d. Uses the following grade range to determine letter grade assignments:

| | |
|---|---|
| 90 to 100 | A |
| 80 to 89.9 | B |
| 70 to 79.9 | C |
| 60 to 69.9 | D |
| 0 to 59.9 | F |

Data Sample

```
1000, 6, 96, 90, 86, 100, 90, 92
1001, 3, 34, 54, 20
1002, 6, 45, 76, 50, 60, 51, 49
1003, 5, 75, 84, 96, 74, 81
1004, 6, 90, 82, 65, 78, 89, 93
1005, 6, 75, 79, 82, 64, 70, 79
1006, 6, 52, 69, 67, 68, 63, 66
```

Display Sample

```
TESTS REQUIRED? 6
ID AND NUMBER OF TESTS? 1000 6
96
90
86
100
90
92
ID AND NUMBER OF TESTS? 1001 3
34
54
20
etc.
```

These numbers would all be on the same line if a READ is used in place of a READLN

Print Sample

| ID | AVERAGE | GRADE |
|---|---|---|
| 1000 | 92.3 | A |
| 1001 | 36.0 | INC |
| 1002 | 55.2 | F |
| 1003 | 82.0 | INC |
| 1004 | 82.8 | B |
| 1005 | 74.8 | C |
| 1006 | 64.2 | D |

# Lesson 13
## NESTED LOOPS

### 13.1 OBJECTIVE

Objective:  To use nested FOR–TO loops.

### 13.2 NESTED FOR–TO LOOPS

PASCAL STATEMENT

EXPLANATION

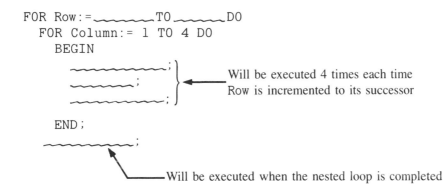

```
FOR OLoop:=_____TO_____DO
   FOR ILoop:=_____TO_____DO
      ~~~~~~~~~~~~~~~~~ ;
   ~~~~~~~~~~~~~~~~~ ;
```

Each time the outer loop, OLoop, is incremented to its successor, the inner loop, ILoop, will complete its full cycle. Assume the outer loop executes X times and the inner loop executes Y times for each outer loop cycle. The product of $X*Y$ would be the number of times that the statement in the inner loop would be executed.

——— To be executed during the looping process

——— To be executed upon completion of the looping

```
FOR Row:=_____TO_____DO
   FOR Column:= 1 TO 4 DO
      BEGIN
         ~~~~~~~~~~~~~ ;
         ~~~~~~~~~~~~ ;
         ~~~~~~~~~~~~~ ;
      END;
      ~~~~~~~~~~~~~ ;
```

Will be executed 4 times each time Row is incremented to its successor

Will be executed when the nested loop is completed

```
FOR Number:= 1 TO 5 DO
  BEGIN
      ~~~~~~~~~;
      ~~~~~~~~;
    FOR Alpha:= 'A' TO 'C' DO
      BEGIN
          ~~~~~~;  ⎫
          ~~~~;    ⎬  Will be executed (3 * 5) or 15 times
          ~~~~~~;  ⎭
          ~~~~~~~
        END;
  END;
~~~~~~~~~~~~~~~~;
```

Will be executed when the outer
loop, Number, is completed

## 13.3 DEMONSTRATION PROBLEM

1. Generate a multiplication table for the natural numbers 1 to 10.

Print Sample

| | | | | | | | | | |
|---|---|---|---|---|---|---|---|---|---|
| 1 | 2 | 3 | 4 | 5 | 6 | 7 | 8 | 9 | 10 |
| 2 | 4 | 6 | 8 | 10 | 12 | 14 | 16 | 18 | 20 |
| 3 | 6 | 9 | 12 | 15 | 18 | 21 | 24 | 27 | 30 |
| 4 | 8 | 12 | 16 | 20 | 24 | 28 | 32 | 36 | 40 |
| 5 | 10 | 15 | 20 | 25 | 30 | 35 | 40 | 45 | 50 |
| 6 | 12 | 18 | 24 | 30 | 36 | 42 | 48 | 54 | 60 |
| 7 | 14 | 21 | 28 | 35 | 42 | 49 | 56 | 63 | 70 |
| 8 | 16 | 24 | 32 | 40 | 48 | 56 | 64 | 72 | 80 |
| 9 | 18 | 27 | 36 | 45 | 54 | 63 | 72 | 81 | 90 |
| 10 | 20 | 30 | 40 | 50 | 60 | 70 | 80 | 90 | 100 |

ALGORITHM

1. Set up for printer (APPLE & IBM)
2. FOR Row = 1 to 10
   2.1 FOR Column = 1 to 10
       2.1.1 Print Row * Column
   2.2 Return carriage and print blank line

```
PROGRAM MultTable;
  VAR Row,Column: INTEGER;
      Lp: TEXT;        (*APPLE & IBM*)
BEGIN
  REWRITE(Lp,'PRINTER:');    (*APPLE & IBM*)
  FOR Row:= 1 to 10 DO
    BEGIN
      FOR Column:= 1 TO 10 DO
        WRITE(Lp,Row * Column:5);
      WRITELN(Lp);
      WRITELN(Lp);
    END;
END.
```

## 13.4 SKILL DEVELOPMENT EXERCISES

1. Write a program that will print out tickets for a school play to be held in the auditorium. The auditorium has M rows with N seats in each row. (Note: Input M and N as small numbers if you are making a hard copy run of this program.)

Print Sample

```
GENERAL ADMISSION $ 2

ROW 1

SEAT 1

_____
GENERAL ADMISSION $ 2

ROW 1

SEAT 2

_____
GENERAL ADMISSION $ 2

ROW 1

etc.
```

2. The data to be processed contains groups of five numbers. Write a program that uses a READLN statement to specify the number of groups of five numbers to be processed. Use nested FOR–TO loops to input and calculate the average of the consecutive groups of five numbers. Study the data sample and Print Sample for further clarification.

Data Sample:

```
 5, 81, 90, 65, 57     (1st group)
45, 98, 76, 20, 89     (2nd group)
 2,  6, 70, 87, 94     (3rd group)
43, 20, 55, 46, 50     (4th group)
```

Print Sample

```
ITEM NUMBERS        AVERAGE
   1 TO  5           59.6
   6 TO 10           65.6
  11 TO 15           51.8
  16 TO 20           42.8
```

# Lesson 14
# ADDITIONAL PASCAL STATEMENTS

## 14.1 OBJECTIVES

Objectives: 1. To be able to use CASE-OF statements in place of multiple decision.
2. To be able to use REPEAT-UNTIL statements to control looping.

## 14.2 CASE-OF AND REPEAT-UNTIL STATEMENTS

CASE-OF Statements

PASCAL STATEMENT                              EXPLANATION

```
                  ──── Expression or variable
CASE      OF
    4:   (1)  ;
  5,6:   (2)  ;
    9:   (3)  ;
   10:   (4)  ;
END;
        (5)   ;
```

The case expression or variable must be of the ordinal type (an integer in this example). The values do not have to be listed in sequence and not all values have to be included. If the expression represents a value not in the case list, the statement following the END statement will be executed on the APPLE, IBM, and TRS-80. However, on some computers an expression that produces a value that is not listed as one of the case values will produce a fatal error.

*Summary*

| Expression value | Executed statements |
|---|---|
| 4 | (1) (5) |
| 5 | (2) (5) |
| 6 | (2) (5) |
| 9 | (3) (5) |
| 10 | (4) (5) |
| A number not listed | (5) only |

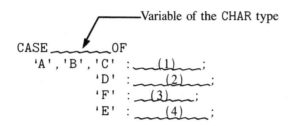

——Variable of the CHAR type

```
CASE _____ OF
    'A','B','C' : ___(1)___ ;
           'D' : ___(2)___ ;
           'F' : __(3)__ ;
           'E' : ___(4)___ ;

END;
    ____(5)____ ;
```

The case variable can be of the CHAR type. The values do not have to be listed alphabetically and not all values have to be included.

*Summary*

| Variable Value | Executed Statements |
|----------------|---------------------|
| 'A' | (1) (5) |
| 'B' | (1) (5) |
| 'C' | (1) (5) |
| 'D' | (2) (5) |
| 'E' | (4) (5) |
| A letter not listed | (5) |

——Expression or variable

```
CASE __ OF
   1,2,3:BEGIN
           ___(1)___ ;
           ___(2)___ ;
        END;
   4,5:BEGIN
           ___(3)___ ;
           ___(4)___ ;
           ___(5)___ ;
        END;
     6: ___(6)___ ;
END;
    ___(7)___ ;
```

Multiple statements can be executed for any case value if a BEGIN and END are used.

*Summary*

| Expression Value | Executed Statement |
|------------------|--------------------|
| 1 | (1)(2)(7) |
| 2 | (1)(2)(7) |
| 3 | (1)(2)(7) |
| 4 | (3)(4)(5)(7) |
| 5 | (3)(4)(5)(7) |
| 6 | (6)(7) |
| Number not listed | (7) |

(Not an option on most computers)

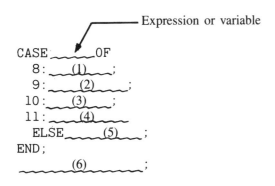

CASE ____ OF
  8: ___(1)___ ;
  9: ___(2)___ ;
10: ___(3)___ ;
11: ___(4)___
  ELSE ____(5)____ ;
END;
_____(6)_____ ;

An ELSE clause may be included on some computers and will be executed if no other case is satisfied. On computers with this capability, if the ELSE clause is omitted, and no case is satisfied, control will pass to the next statement without an error.

*Summary*

| Expression Value | Executed Statement |
|---|---|
| 8 | (1)(6) |
| 9 | (2)(6) |
| 10 | (3)(6) |
| 11 | (4)(6) |
| A number not listed | (5)(6) |

REPEAT-UNTIL Statement

PASCAL STATEMENT

EXPLANATION

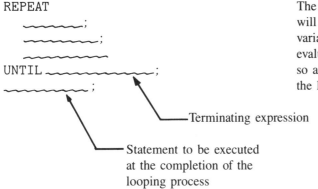

REPEAT
  _____;
  _____;
  _____
UNTIL _____ ;
_____ ;

The statements between the REPEAT and UNTIL will be executed until the terminating expression or variable is evaluated as true. The expression is evaluated after the statements have been executed so any stopping signal value will be processed in the looping procedure.

——Terminating expression

——Statement to be executed at the completion of the looping process

REPEAT-UNTIL and WHILE-DO Comparison

REPEAT-UNTIL

1. REPEAT executes at least one time.

2. Does not need BEGIN and END.

3. *Exits* when BOOLEAN is true.

WHILE-DO

1. WHILE executes zero or more times.

2. Needs BEGIN and END when it contains more than one statement.

3. *Exits* when BOOLEAN is false.

### 14.3 DEMONSTRATION PROBLEM

1. Write a program to average test scores and determine a letter grade. The input is to consist of an ID number and 4 test scores with a stopping signal of −99 for one of the scores. Print out the ID number, average, and letter grade. The following scale is to be used:

| | |
|---|---|
| 90–100 | A |
| 80–89 | B |
| 70–79 | C |
| 60–69 | D |
| 0 –59 | F |

Display Sample

```
ENTER ID, 4 GRADES (0 -99 0 0 0 TO QUIT)
1000 94 85 100 92
ENTER ID, 4 GRADES (0 -99 0 0 0 TO QUIT)
1001 65 72 71 78
ENTER ID, 4 GRADES (0 -99 0 0 0 TO QUIT)
1003 71 62 50 57
ENTER ID, 4 GRADES (0 -99 0 0 0 TO QUIT)
1004 45 59 48 51
ENTER ID, 4 GRADES (0 -99 0 0 0 TO QUIT)
0 -99 0 0 0
PROGRAM COMPLETE
```

Print Sample

| ID | AVERAGE | GRADE |
|---|---|---|
| 1000 | 93 | A |
| 1001 | 72 | C |
| 1003 | 60 | D |
| 1004 | 51 | F |

ALGORITHM

1. Set up printer (APPLE & IBM)
2. Print heading
3. REPEAT until average is negative
   3.1 Read ID and 4 grades
   3.2 Calculate average and number of tens
   3.3 CASE–OF
       3.3.1 Print ID, average, letter grade

```
PROGRAM L14Demo1;
   VAR Id, Ave, NoOfTens: INTEGER;
       G1, G2, G3, G4: REAL;
       Lp: TEXT;          (*APPLE & IBM*)
BEGIN
   REWRITE (Lp, 'PRINTER:'); (*APPLE & IBM*)
   WRITELN (Lp, 'ID':4,'AVERAGE':11,'GRADE':8);
   REPEAT
     WRITELN ('ENTER ID, 4 GRADES (0 -99 0 0 0 TO QUIT)');
     READLN (Id, G1, G2, G3, G4);
     Ave:= TRUNC ((G1+G2+G3+G4)/4+0.5);
     NoOfTens:= Ave DIV 10;
     CASE NoOfTens OF
               10,9: WRITELN (Lp,Id:5,Ave:7,'A':9);
                  8: WRITELN (Lp,Id:5,Ave:7,'B':9);
                  7: WRITELN (Lp,Id:5,Ave:7,'C':9);
                  6: WRITELN (Lp,Id:5,Ave:7,'D':9);
       0,1,2,3,4,5: WRITELN (Lp,Id:5,Ave:7,'F':9);
                 -2: WRITELN ('PROGRAM COMPLETE');
                     (* AVERAGE OF -99,0,0,0 IS -24.75 *)
                     (* AND DIVIDED BY 10 EQUAL -2 *)
     END;
   UNTIL Ave < 0;
END.
```

The above program when written as a procedure could be used as part of a larger program. It receives a student's Id number and average as value parameters (Technique 2 of Lesson 10) from the main program and prints out the Id, Average, and letter grade.

```
                                   ┌──────────────Value parameters
                            ┌──────┘          │
                            ↓                 ↓
PROCEDURE L14Demo1 (Id: INTEGER; Ave: REAL);
   VAR NoOfTens: INTEGER;
       Lp: TEXT;        (*APPLE & IBM*)
   BEGIN
     REWRITE (Lp,'PRINTER:');   (*APPLE & IBM*)
     NoOfTens:= ROUND(Ave) DIV 10;
     CASE NoOfTens OF
               10,9: WRITELN (Lp,Id:5,Ave:7,'A':9);
                  8: WRITELN (Lp,Id:5,Ave:7,'B':9);
                  7: WRITELN (Lp,Id:5,Ave:7,'C':9);
                  6: WRITELN (Lp,Id:5,Ave:7,'D':9);
       0,1,2,3,4,5: WRITELN (Lp,Id:5,Ave:7,'F':9);
     END;
   END;
```

## 14.4 SKILL DEVELOPMENT EXERCISES

1. Following are the quoted rates for renting an automobile from a car rental agency:

| | |
|---|---|
| 1(Compact) | $12 per day |
| | $.14 per mile |
| 2(Standard) | $16 per day |
| | $.16 per mile |
| 3(Luxury) | $20 per day |
| | $.18 per mile |
| Insurance | Collision $1.20 |
| | Liability $1.45 |

Write a program that allows the customer service clerk to enter the automobile class, number of days, and miles driven in the company computer and get a display of the charges. Because the insurance charges are subject to change, assign them to constants so the program can be easily adjusted when necessary.

Charges = Daily Rate * No. of Days + Rate per Mile * Miles + Collision Insurance + Liability Insurance

Display Sample

```
PLEASE ENTER
AUTO CLASS, # OF DAYS, MILES DRIVEN (0 0 0 STOP)

CLASS-DAYS-MILES     CHARGES
1  3  420
                       97.45
3  5  624
                      214.97
2  1  180
                       47.45
0  0  0
PROGRAM TERMINATED
```

2. Write a program to convert measurements from US units to metric units. Conversions involving the following units should be written into the program:

| 1 inch | = 2.54 cm (centimeters) |
|--------|-------------------------|
| 1 foot | = 30.48 cm (centimeters) |
| 1 yard | = 0.9 m (meters) |
| 1 mile | = 1.6 km (kilometers) |
| 1 pound | = 0.45 kg (kilograms) |
| 1 quart | = 0.95 l (liters) |
| 1 gallon | = 3.8 l (liters) |

The operator will enter the measure to be converted followed by one of the codes (I-inches), (F-Feet), (Y-Yards), (M-Miles), (P-Pounds), (Q-Quarts), and (G-Gallons), and the computer will print out the conversion table. A code of "S" will end the program.

Display Sample (TRS-80)

```
PLEASE ENTER
QUANTITY, UNIT TO CONVERT
(0  S TO STOP)

124 P
15 F
12.3 I
250 M
5 Y
0 S
```

[1]Display Sample (APPLE & IBM PC)

```
PLEASE ENTER
QUANTITY, UNIT TO CONVERT
(OS TO STOP)

124P
15F
12.3I
250M
5Y
0S
```

Print Sample

```
    US        METRIC
124.0  POUND   55.8 KG
 15.0   FOOT  457.2 CM
 12.3   INCH   31.2 CM
250.0   MILE  400.0 KM
  5.0   YARD    4.5  M
```

## 14.5 REVIEW EXERCISES (LESSONS 1–14)

1. Dollar amounts, shown in the data sample, are invested in 2-year certificates, compounded monthly. At the end of each 2-year period the accumulated amount is again invested for two years, but at a higher interest rate (old rate + 2.5%). Write a program that uses the simple interest formula to determine the accumulated amount after eight years. Use the interest rates shown below.

| 5% | first 2-year period | Simple Interest Formula |
|----|---------------------|-------------------------|
| 7.5% | second 2-year period | $i = prt$ |
| 10% | third 2-year period | |
| 12.5% | fourth 2-year period | |

Data Sample

1000, 10500, 25000, 800

---

[1] When an INTEGER or REAL type is follow by a CHAR type variable in a READLN statement, no delimiter (blank) is used.

Print Sample

```
┌─────────────────────────────────────────────┐
│  INVESTMENT        ACCUMULATED VALUE          │
│    1000.00             2008.13                │
│   10500.00            21085.36                │
│   25000.00            50203.23                │
│     800.00             1606.50                │
│                                               │
└───────────────────────────────────────────────
```

2. Write a program that will request the operator to input a whole number and then will print out the number and all factors as shown in the Print Sample. Do not print a set of factors twice (for example, do not print both 4 × 5 and 5 × 4).

Data Sample

12, 13, 21, 18, 100

Print Sample

```
┌─────────────────────────────────────────────────────────────────┐
│ NUMBERS  FACTORS                                                  │
│    12     1 x  12    2 x  6    3 x  4                              │
│    13     1 x  13                                                 │
│    21     1 x  21    3 x  7                                       │
│    18     1 x  18    2 x  9    3 x  6                             │
│   100     1 x 100    2 x  50   4 x  25   5 x  20   10 x  10        │
│                                                                   │
└───────────────────────────────────────────────────────────────────
```

3. State board exams are to be given to 24 students. Because no error in assigning time and place is acceptable, a computer is to be used to make assignment notices. Four rooms are to be used with two stations per room for the three morning periods. The printout is to be as shown below.

Print Sample

```
┌─────────────────────────────────────────────────────┐
│ STUDENT #  1 ROOM 1 PERIOD 1 STATION 1                │
│ ─ ─ ─ ─ ─ ─ ─ ─ ─ ─ ─ ─ ─ ─ ─ ─ ─ ─ ─                │
│ STUDENT #  2 ROOM 1 PERIOD 1 STATION 2                │
│ ─ ─ ─ ─ ─ ─ ─ ─ ─ ─ ─ ─ ─ ─ ─ ─ ─ ─ ─                │
│ STUDENT #  3 ROOM 1 PERIOD 2 STATION 1                │
│ ─ ─ ─ ─ ─ ─ ─ ─ ─ ─ ─ ─ ─ ─ ─ ─ ─ ─ ─                │
│ STUDENT #  4 ROOM 1 PERIOD 2 STATION 2                │
│ ─ ─ ─ ─ ─ ─ ─ ─ ─ ─ ─ ─ ─ ─ ─ ─ ─ ─ ─                │
│ STUDENT #  5 ROOM 1 PERIOD 3 STATION 1                │
│ ─ ─ ─ ─ ─ ─ ─ ─ ─ ─ ─ ─ ─ ─ ─ ─ ─ ─ ─                │
│ STUDENT #  6 ROOM 1 PERIOD 3 STATION 2                │
│ ─ ─ ─ ─ ─ ─ ─ ─ ─ ─ ─ ─ ─ ─ ─ ─ ─ ─ ─                │
│ STUDENT #  7 ROOM 2 PERIOD 1 STATION 1                │
│ ─ ─ ─ ─ ─ ─ ─ ─ ─ ─ ─ ─ ─ ─ ─ ─ ─ ─ ─                │
│ STUDENT #  8 ROOM 2 PERIOD 1 STATION 2                │
│                 .                                     │
│                 .                                     │
│                 .                                     │
│ ─ ─ ─ ─ ─ ─ ─ ─ ─ ─ ─ ─ ─ ─ ─ ─ ─ ─ ─                │
│ STUDENT #23 ROOM 4 PERIOD 3 STATION 1                 │
│ ─ ─ ─ ─ ─ ─ ─ ─ ─ ─ ─ ─ ─ ─ ─ ─ ─ ─ ─                │
│ STUDENT #24 ROOM 4 PERIOD 3 STATION 2                 │
│ ─ ─ ─ ─ ─ ─ ─ ─ ─ ─ ─ ─ ─ ─ ─ ─ ─ ─ ─                │
└───────────────────────────────────────────────────────
```

4. Write a Pascal program to find and print all three-digit numbers which are equal to the sum of the cubes of their digits. (4 answers)

Example:      $153 = 1^3 + 5^3 + 3^3$

Print Sample

```
153
370
371
407
```

# Lesson 15
# ARRAYS

## 15.1 OBJECTIVES

Objectives: 1. To learn to define an array (subscripted variable).
2. To use arrays in programming.
3. To generate random numbers.

## 15.2 ARRAYS (SUBSCRIPTED VARIABLES)

Defining a variable as an array.

STATEMENT                                          EXPLANATION

Establishes limits for Array. Must be separated by 2 periods and of the INTEGER, CHAR, or BOOLEAN type.

VAR Numbers: ARRAY [1..5] OF INTEGER;    Declares the variable Numbers as an array. The array has the size of 5. That is, it has five locations (Numbers [1], Numbers [2], up to Numbers [5]) that may be used. The limits must be ordinal and of the same type.

Specifies that the numbers assigned to the array are to be from the set of integers.

Must be within limits of 1–5.

Must be an integer.

*Examples*
Numbers [1]:= 135;
Numbers [2]:= 64 DIV 3;
Numbers [5]:= Count;

Assigns the value on the right of the : = to the array variable which is determined by the number in the brackets.

Establishes limits for Array. Must be separated by 2 periods and of the INTEGER, CHAR, or BOOLEAN type.

VAR Num: ARRAY ['A'..'E'] OF REAL;    Defines the variable Num as an array with limits from A to E. That is Num [A], Num [B], to Num [E]. The first limit must be a predecessor of the second limit.

Specifies that the numbers assigned to the array are chosen from the set of reals.

—Must be a real.

*Examples*

```
Num [C]:= 1.358;
Num [A]:= SQRT (10);
Num [D]:= 1 / 5;
```

—Must be within the limits of A–E.

*Example 1* (Example of loading an array)

```
PROGRAM Example;
  VAR Item: ARRAY [1..6] OF INTEGER; (*Declares the array*)
                                     (*Global*)
PROCEDURE Assign;
  VAR Count: INTEGER; (*Local variables*)
  BEGIN
    FOR Count:= 1 TO 6 DO
      Item [Count]:= SQR (Count);
    WRITELN ('ARRAY ITEMS HAVE BEEN ASSIGNED');
  END;
```

The following assignments have been made by procedure `Assign`.

| 1 | 4 | 9 | 16 | 25 | 36 |
|---|---|---|----|----|----|
| ↓ | ↓ | ↓ | ↓ | ↓ | ↓ |
| Item [1] | Item [2] | Item [3] | Item [4] | Item [5] | Item [6] |

*Example 2* (Assume procedure `Assign` has been executed)

```
PROCEDURE Print;
  VAR PerfectSq: INTEGER;
  BEGIN
    FOR PerfectSq:= 5 DOWNTO 2 DO
      WRITELN (Item [PerfectSq]:5);
    WRITELN;
    WRITELN ('LIST COMPLETE');
  END;
```

Display Sample

```
   25  16  9  4

LIST COMPLETE
```

Note: 1. The brackets must be used around the subscript number (that is, Num[3]).
2. No specific limit other than the storage capacity of the computer is set on the number of storage locations to use when establishing limits using the INTEGER ordinal.
```
VAR Number[1..1000] OF ~~~~;
```
   (1000 storage locations)
```
VAR Number[1000..5000] OF ~~~~;
```
   (4000 storage locations)

3. The maximum number of storage locations is limited by the number of letters in the alphabet when using the CHAR ordinal.

   ```
   VAR Num['A'..'Z'] OF CHAR;
   ```
         (26 storage locations)
   ```
   VAR Num['c'..'f'] OF CHAR;
   ```
         (4 storage locations)

4. Defining the array is not limited to just integers and reals as indicated in this lesson. More about defining arrays will be discussed in upcoming lessons.

**APPLE**

Random Numbers

| PASCAL STATEMENT | EXPLANATION |
| --- | --- |
| `USES   APPLESTUFF;` | APPLESTUFF is a collection of procedures that are needed to compile a program containing the RANDOM function. APPLESTUFF must be declared before the variable declaration and the disk containing APPLESTUFF must be in one of the drives when compiling. |
| `X1:= RANDOM;` | A randomly selected integer between zero and 32,767 will be assigned to X1. Each time the statement containing RANDOM is executed a new integer is assigned to X1; however, the same sequence of random numbers will be produced each time the program is run. |
| `Aran:= RANDOM MOD 5` | A randomly selected number is divided by 5, and the remainder assigned to Aran. Because the remainder is an integer (0, 1, 2, 3, or 4) the statement effectively selects a random integer between 0 and 4 inclusive. |
| `UpLimit:= 10;`<br>`Bran:= 1 + RANDOM MOD UpLimit;` | A random integer from 1 to 10 will be assigned to Bran. The same logic is used as in the previous example. |
| `RANDOMIZE;` | In the previous examples, each time the program ran, the same sequence of random numbers would have been generated. If the RANDOMIZED statement is placed in the program and is executed before the RANDOM function is used, a different sequence of random numbers is generated each time the program is executed. In computer jargon, when a RANDOMIZE statement is executed a different seed is used for each running of the program. RANDOMIZE needs to be executed only once in a program. |

**TRS-80**

Random Numbers

| STATEMENT | EXPLANATION |
|---|---|
| `RandomNum:= RND(5);` | A random integer between 1 and 5 will be assigned to `RandomNum`. `RandomNum` is an integer type variable. Any integer between 1 and 32,767 can be used in the argument of the `RND( )` statement. |
| `RandomNumber:= RND(N);` | An integer type variable may be used as the argument of the `RND( )` statement. In the sample on the left a random integer between 1 and N will be assigned to `RandomNumber`. The value assigned to the variable used as the argument must be a positive integer. The variable `RandomNumber` may be an `INTEGER` or a `REAL`. |
| `RanNum:= RND(11) - 1;` | A random number between 0 and 10 inclusive will be assigned to `RanNum`. |
| `NumRandom:= RNDR;` | A real number between 0 and 1 will be assigned to `NumRandom`. The variable, in this case `NumRandom`, must be declared as a `REAL`. |

Note: Each time a program is run, the TRS-80 will select a new sequence of random numbers.

**IBM PC**

Random Numbers

| PASCAL STATEMENT | EXPLANATION |
|---|---|
| `Seed:= Seed*233+113;`<br>`RandomNum:= Seed MOD 5;` | A randomly selected integer is divided by 5, and the remainder assigned to `RandomNum`. Because the remainder is an integer (0, 1, 2, 3, or 4) the statement effectively selects a random integer between 0 and 4 inclusive. Each time the statements are executed a new integer is assigned to `RandomNum`; however, the same set of random numbers will be produced each time the program is run. |
| `UpLimit:= 10;`<br>〜〜〜〜<br>`Seed:= Seed*233+113;`<br>`RandomInt:= 1 + Seed MOD UpLimit;` | A random integer from 1 to 10 inclusive will be assigned to `RandomInt`. The same logic is used as in the previous example. |

```
READLN (Seed);
```

~~~~~~~~

~~~~~~~~

```
Seed:= Seed*233+133;
RanElement:= Seed MOD 23767;
```

Different sets of random numbers can be obtained for each running of the program by assigning a different integer to Seed. The method of assigning an initial value to the seed variable is immaterial.

## 15.3 DEMONSTRATION PROBLEMS

1. Write a program that will, for a set of eight data values, average the first and eighth, second and seventh, third and sixth, and fourth and fifth.

Display Sample

```
ENTER 8 NUMBERS ONE AT A TIME
5
8
11
14
16
20
35
18
```

Print Sample

```
11.50
21.50
15.50
15.00
```

ALGORITHM (Not using procedures)

1. Set up for printer (APPLE & IBM)
2. Prompt for entering numbers
3. For eight loops
   3.1 Assign number to array Element[ ]
4. For four loops
   4.1 Calculate averages (Element[1] + Element[8])/2, etc.)
   4.2 Print average

```
PROGRAM L15Demo1;
   VAR Num, NoOfAve: INTEGER;
       Ave: REAL;
       Element: ARRAY[1..8] OF REAL;
       Lp: TEXT;                               (*APPLE & IBM*)
BEGIN
   REWRITE (Lp,'PRINTER:');                    (*APPLE & IBM*)
   WRITELN('ENTER 8 NUMBERS ONE AT A TIME');
   FOR Num:= 1 TO 8 DO
     READLN(Element[Num]);
   FOR NoOfAve:= 1 TO 4 DO
     BEGIN
       Ave:= (Element[NoOfAve] + Element[9-NoOfAve])/2;
       WRITELN(Lp,Ave:5:2);
     END;
END.
```

2. Generalize Problem 1 so that it will handle a positive even number of data values. In the declaration allow for as many as 100 data values.

Display Sample

```
HOW MANY NUMBERS? 6
ENTER 6 NUMBERS ONE AT A TIME
12.4
10
8.8
6.2
18.3
7
```

Print Sample

```
9.70
14.15
7.50
```

ALGORITHM CHANGES (Not using procedures)

1.  (No change)
2. Prompt and enter HowMany numbers
3. For HowMany loop
   3.1  (No change)
4. For HowMany / 2 loops
   4.1 Calculate average( (Element[1] + Element[last element])/2), etc.
   4.2  (No change)

```
PROGRAM L15Demo2;
   VAR Num, NoOfAve, HowMany: INTEGER;
       Ave: REAL;
       Element: ARRAY[1..100] OF REAL;
       Lp: TEXT;          (*APPLE & IBM*)
BEGIN
   REWRITE (Lp,'PRINTER:');     (*APPLE & IBM*)
   WRITE('HOW MANY NUMBERS? ');
   READLN(HowMany);
   WRITELN('ENTER ' ,HowMany,' NUMBERS ONE AT A TIME');
   FOR Num:= 1 TO HowMany DO
     READLN(Element[Num]);
   FOR NoOfAve:= 1 TO HowMany DIV 2 DO
     BEGIN
       Ave:= (Element[NoOfAve] + Element[HowMany + 1 - NoOfAve])/2;
       WRITELN(Lp,Ave:5:2);
     END;
END.
```

3. Write a program that requests the user to enter UpperLim (the largest random number to be generated), and have the computer display ten random integers between 1 and UpperLim. Run the program several times to make sure a new sequence of numbers is generated each time and that they are within the input limit.

Display Sample (1st run)

```
ENTER UPPER LIMIT
6
    1  3  5  6  1  4   2  1  2  6
LIST COMPLETE
```

Display Sample (2nd run)

```
ENTER UPPER LIMIT
40
    17  13  2  36  35   31  3  27  2  28
LIST COMPLETE
```

**APPLE**

```
PROGRAM L15Demo3;
  USES APPLESTUFF;
  VAR RNumber,UpperLim,Count: INTEGER;
BEGIN
  RANDOMIZE;
  WRITELN ('ENTER UPPER LIMIT');
  READLN (UpperLim);
  FOR Count:= 1 TO 10 DO
    BEGIN
      RNumber:= 1 + RANDOM MOD UpperLim;
      WRITE (RNumber:5);
    END;
  WRITELN;
  WRITELN ('LIST COMPLETE');
END.
```

**TRS-80**

```
PROGRAM L15Demo3;
  VAR RNumber,UpperLim,Count: INTEGER;
BEGIN
  WRITELN ('ENTER UPPER LIMIT');
  READLN (UpperLim);
  FOR Count:= 1 TO 10 DO
    BEGIN
      RNumber:= RND (UpperLim);
      WRITE (RNumber:5);
    END;
  WRITELN;
  WRITELN ('LIST COMPLETE');
END.
```

**IBM PC**

```
PROGRAM L15Demo3;
  VAR RNumber,UpperLim,Count,Seed: INTEGER;
BEGIN
  WRITE ('SEED? '); READLN (Seed);
  WRITELN ('ENTER UPPER LIMIT');
  READLN (UpperLim);
  FOR Count:= 1 TO 10 DO
    BEGIN
      Seed:= Seed*233+113;
      RNumber:= 1 + Seed MOD UpperLim;
      WRITE (RNumber:5);
    END;
  WRITELN;
  WRITELN ('LIST COMPLETE');
END.
```

## 15.4 SKILL DEVELOPMENT EXERCISES

Note: The intent of this lesson is to use arrays without passing an array as a parameter to procedures. Passing arrays as parameters to procedures is presented in Lesson 16 and will then be used in the programs.

1. Write a program that asks for input of nine numbers and begins by averaging the first through the third, then the first through sixth, and finally the first through the ninth. Print the answers as shown in the Print Sample. Use only two FOR—DO loops.

Display Sample

```
ENTER 9 NUMBERS

23.4
10.5
6.6
12.3
9.0
18.9
6.7
9.9
10.2
```

Print Sample

```
   23.4  10.5  6.6  12.3  9.0  18.9  6.7  9.9  10.2

THE AVERAGE OF
1 TO 3 = 13.50
1 TO 6 = 13.45
1 TO 9 = 11.94
```

2. Write a program that will generate worksheets to practice the multiplication of two numbers. Limit the numbers to randomly selected reals between 0 and 10 with one digit to the right of the decimal. Label the problems using the letters A through E and follow them with answers also labeled A through E. Each time the program is run, a worksheet with different numbers would be produced.

Print Sample

```
A. 5.6 X 6.5 =_____

B. 8.2 X 7.7 =_____

C. 0.8 X 1.3 =_____

D. 2.4 X 9.5 =_____

E. 5.6 X 0.4 =_____

        _____

ANSWERS
A.    36.40
B.    63.14
C.     1.04
D.    22.80
E.     2.24
```

3. Write a program which prints a cost table for an indefinite number of items. The computer operator should enter the number of different types of items and the price for each type of item. The computer will assign the prices to an array and then print out a table showing the cost of each type of item in quantities from 1 to 5.

Cost = No. of Items * Price

Subdivide the problem so that it lends itself to using two procedures. One procedure to enter the data and a second procedure to complete the cost table.

Display Sample (1st Run)

```
HOW MANY ITEMS? 3
ENTER ITEM PRICES ONE AT A TIME
13.25
10
5.95
```

Print Sample (1st Run)

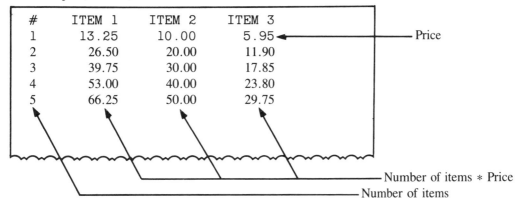

Display Sample (2nd Run)

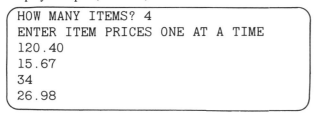

Print Sample (2nd Run)

```
#    ITEM 1    ITEM 2    ITEM 3    ITEM 4
1    120.40     15.67     34.00     26.98
2    240.80     31.34     68.00     53.96
3    361.20     47.01    102.00     80.94
4    481.60     62.68    136.00    107.92
5    602.00     78.35    170.00    134.90
```

4. Using data containing a set of eight integers followed by a second set of eight integers, write a program that assigns all sixteen integers into a subscripted array. Process the array by printing the two sets of eight numbers and the difference of the corresponding elements below each of the two elements. Study the print sample for clarification.

Data Sample

85, 40, 71, 36, 51, 42, 81, 92 (1st Set)
31, 11, 14, 18, 12, 31, 25, 14 (2nd Set)

Print Sample

```
1ST SET: 85 40 71 36 51 42 81 92
2ND SET: 31 11 14 18 12 31 25 14
DIFF   : 54 29 57 18 39 11 56 78
```

# Lesson 16
# MANIPULATING ARRAYS

## 16.1 OBJECTIVES

Objectives: 1. To learn to manipulate arrays by (a) interchanging elements of an array, (b) comparing elements of an array, and (c) calculating with arrays.
2. To pass arrays as parameters to procedures.
3. To develop a method of generalizing programs.

## 16.2 MANIPULATING ARRAYS AND PASSING PARAMETERS

*Comparing Numbers Stored In An Array*

```
IF A[I] = A[I+1] THEN
            ~~~~~~~~~~~~;
```

When I = 1, the Pascal statement on the left will compare the value stored in A[1] with the value stored in A[2]. When I = 4, the value in A[4] will be compared to the value A[5]. When I = 10, the value in A[10] will be compared to the value in A[11], etc.

*Calculating With Two Arrays*

```
S := A[I] + B[I]
```

The Pascal statement at the left shows how to add corresponding elements of array A and array B. (For example, when I = 6, the value stored in A[6] will be added to the value stored in B[6] and the result will be stored in S.)

*Interchanging Two Elements Of An Array*

Interchanging two values stored in an array requires the creation of a third storage location. Follow the procedure shown below.

Assume we want to interchange the values stored in A[4] and A[7] where A[4] = 12 and A[7] = −7.

| | | |
|---|---|---|
| W := A[4] | First: | Create a third storage location, say W, and store one of the values in that location. |
| A[4] := A[7] | Second: | Take the other value and assign it to the array location used in the first step. |
| A[7] := W | Third: | Take the value stored in the (temporarily) created location and assign it to the array location *not* used in the first step. |

| | Original | first step | second step | third step |
|---|---|---|---|---|
| A[4] | 12 | 12 | −7 | −7 |
| A[7] | −7 | −7 | −7 | 12 |
| W | | 12 | 12 | 12 |

Transferring elements from one array to another

*Example 1*

```
PROGRAM _____;
   VAR DataA: ARRAY [1..20] OF REAL;
       DataB: ARRAY [1..15] OF REAL;
BEGIN
   ~~~~~
   ~~~~~
   DataB [3]:= DataA [5];
   ~~~~~
   ~~~~~
   ~~~~~
   DataB [7]:= DataA [2] + DataA [3];
   ~~~~~
   ~~~~~
END.
```

{ Transfers element 5 of array DataA to element 3 of array DataB.

{ Transfers the sum of element 2 and element 3 of array DataA to element 7 of array DataB.

*Example 2*

```
PROGRAM _____;
   VAR IdGroup1: ARRAY [1..10] OF INTEGER;
       IdGroup2: ARRAY [1..10] OF INTEGER;
BEGIN
   ~~~~~
   ~~~~~
   IdGroup1:= IdGroup2
   ~~~~~
   ~~~~~
END.
```

{ All elements of array IdGroup2 are transferred to the corresponding elements of array IdGroup1. The arrays must be of the same type and size.

*Passing Arrays To A Procedure*

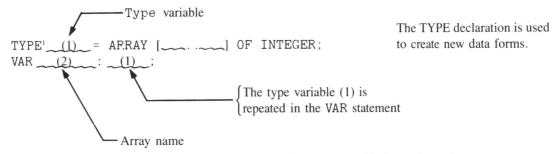

The TYPE declaration is used to create new data forms.

{ The type variable (1) is repeated in the VAR statement

The type variable is used to allow an array to be passed as a parameter to a procedure. The type variable name will be placed after the colon in the parameter list of a procedure using any array from the main program.

---

[1] A more thorough explanation and use of the TYPE declaration will be presented in a later lesson.

Procedure Pass (VAR_____:_____(1)____);

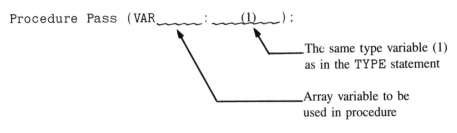

The same type variable (1) as in the TYPE statement

Array variable to be used in procedure

When arrays are passed to procedures they should be passed as VAR parameters to save memory.

(*MAIN PROGRAM*)

Procedure name

Array variable

Pass (____(2)____);

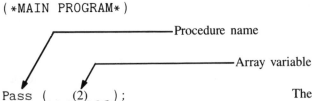

The array variable (2) contains the information that is to be passed to the procedure.

*Example 1*

```
TYPE TypArray = ARRAY [1..5] OF INTEGER;
VAR NumberSet: TypArray;
(***)
PROCEDURE Load (VAR OrigSet: TypArray);
  BEGIN
      ~~~~~~;
      ~~~~~~~;
      ~~~~~~;
  END;
(***)
PROCEDURE Print (VAR PSet: TypArray);
  BEGIN
      ~~~~~~;
      ~~~~~~~;
  END;
(************)
(*MAIN PROGRAM*)
(************)
~~~~~~~~~~;
~~~~~~~~;
Load (NumberSet); (*Procedure call*)
~~~~~~~~;
~~~~~~~~;
~~~~~~~~~;
Print (NumberSet); (*Procedure call*)
~~~~~~~;
~~~~~~~~~;
```

The variable NumberSet in the procedure call is being passed to the variable OrigSet in the procedure Load. When the procedure is completed any changes that have been made to the variable OrigSet will be passed back to NumberSet in the main program. The same is true with PSet in the procedure Print.

## 16.3 DEMONSTRATION PROBLEMS

1. Write a program that:

   a. Generates 20 random integers between 0 and 19 and assigns them to a subscripted variable A.
   b. Prints the array in the order they were assigned (that is A[1], A[2], A[3], . . . , A[20]).
   c. Prints a list the same as in part (b) but skips any number that appears previously in the list. That is, no number appears more than one time.

   Run the program several times and check the printed data to ensure it is correct.

   The problem is stated in such a way that it is already subdivided and leads to three procedures. Each procedure completes the action called for in parts (a), (b), or (c) of the original problem and are as follows:

   *RandomNum*

   Generates 20 random integers and assigns them to elements A[1], A[2], . . . , A[20] of array A respectively.

   *PrintArray*

   Displays heading and the complete array A in the order that the numbers were assigned in procedure RandomNum.

   *AmedList*

   Displays a heading and array A where each number is printed only once. That is, before an element of the array is printed a check is made to see if that same number has already been printed. If it has already been printed, it will not be printed a second time.

   PROCEDURE ALGORITHMS

   1. RandomNum (VAR Array ↑²)
      1.1 Set up for 20 loops
          1.1.1 Generate a random number
          1.1.2 Assign number to successive elements of array A
   2. PrintArray (VAR¹ Array ↓³)
      2.1 Set up for 20 loops
          2.1.1 Display an element of array A
      2.2 Return after last and leave blank line
   3. AmedList (VAR¹Array ↓)
      3.1 Set up for 20 loops
          3.1.1 Assign Print: = TRUE
          3.1.2 Look at each element from 1 to one less than the element under consideration. (If equal (that is, it has already been printed) assign Print: = FALSE)
          3.1.3 If Print = TRUE then print element

---

¹ VARiable parameters are used to save memory even though some procedures do not need to send information back to the main program.

² The ↑ implies that an array will be passed from the procedure to the main program.

³ The ↓ implies that an array will be passed from the main program to the procedure.

APPLE

```
PROGRAM L16Demol;
  USES APPLESTUFF;
  TYPE List = ARRAY [1..20] OF INTEGER;
  VAR Numbers: List;
(*** )
PROCEDURE RandomNum (VAR OrigList: List);
  VAR Count: INTEGER;
  BEGIN
    RANDOMIZE;
    FOR Count:=1 TO 20 DO
      OrigList [Count]:= RANDOM MOD 20
  END;
(***)
PROCEDURE PrintArray (VAR Prtlist: List);
  VAR Index: INTEGER;
  BEGIN
    WRITELN('TWENTY RANDOM NUMBERS');
    FOR Index:=1 TO 20 DO
      WRITE(PrtList [Index]:4);
    WRITELN;
    WRITELN;
  END;
(***)
PROCEDURE AmedList (VAR ShortList: List);
  VAR Count, Check: INTEGER;
      Print: BOOLEAN;
BEGIN
  WRITELN('AMENDED LIST');
  FOR Count:= 1 TO 20 DO
    BEGIN
      Print:= TRUE;
      FOR Check:=  1   TO   Count- 1   DO¹
        IF ShortList[Check] = ShortList[Count] THEN
          Print:= FALSE;
      IF Print = TRUE THEN
        WRITE(ShortList[Count]:4);
    END;
END;
(************)
(*MAIN PROGRAM*)
(************)
BEGIN
  RandomNum (Numbers);     (*PROCEDURE CALL*)
  PrintArray (Numbers);    (*PROCEDURE CALL*)
  AmedList (Numbers);      (*PROCEDURE CALL*)
END.
```

The procedure RandomNum generates 20 random numbers and assigns them to array OrigList. OrigList is passed back to the main program into the array Numbers.

Array Numbers is passed to the procedure into the array PrtList and each element of PrtList is printed.

Array Numbers is passed to the procedure into the array ShortList. Before each number is printed, a check is made to see if it has already been printed.

---

¹ When Count=1 (Count-1 = 0) the FOR-TO-DO loop wil not be executed. See rules page 94.

**TRS-80**

```
PROGRAM Ll6Demol;
  TYPE List= ARRAY[l..20] OF INTEGER;
  VAR Numbers:List;
(***)
PROCEDURE RandomNum (VAR OrigList: List);
  VAR Count: INTEGER;
  BEGIN
    FOR Count:= 1 TO 20 DO
      OrigList[Count]:= RND(20) - l;
  END;
(***)
PROCEDURE PrintArray (VAR PrtList: List);
  VAR Index: INTEGER;
  BEGIN
    WRITELN('TWENTY RANDOM NUMBERS');
    FOR Index:= 1 TO 20 DO
      WRITE(PrtList[Index]:4);
    WRITELN;
    WRITELN;
  END;
(***)
PROCEDURE AmedList (VAR ShortList: List);
  VAR Count, Check: INTEGER;
      Print: BOOLEAN;
  BEGIN
    WRITELN('AMENDED LIST');
    FOR Count:= 1 TO 20 DO
      BEGIN
        Print:= TRUE;
        FOR Check:= 1 TO Count-1 DO
          IF ShortList[Check] = ShortList[Count] THEN
            Print:= FALSE;
          IF Print = TRUE THEN
            WRITE (ShortList[Count]:4);
      END;
  END;
(*************)
(*MAIN PROGRAM*)
(*************)
BEGIN
  RandomNum (Numbers);     (*PROCEDURE CALL*)
  PrintArray (Numbers);    (*PROCEDURE CALL*)
  AmedList (Numbers);      (*PROCEDURE CALL*)
END.
```

The procedure RandomNum generates 20 random numbers and assigns them to array OrigList. OrigList is passed to the main program into the array Numbers.

Array Numbers is passed to the procedure into the array PrtList and each element of PrtList is printed.

Array Numbers is passed to the procedure into the array ShortList. Before each number is printed, a check is made to see if it has already been printed.

**IBM PC**

```
PROGRAM Ll6Demol;
  TYPE List ARRAY [1..20] OF INTEGER;
  VAR Numbers: List;
(***)
PROCEDURE Randomize (VAR OrigList: List);
  VAR Count,UpLimit, RandomNum,Seed: INTEGER;
BEGIN
  FOR Count:= 1 TO 20 DO
    BEGIN
      UpLimit:= 20;
      Seed:= Seed*233+113;
      RandomNum:= 1+Seed MOD UpLimit;
      OrigList [Count]:= RandomNum;
    END;
END;
(***)
PROCEDURE PrintArray (VAR PrtList: List);
  VAR Index: INTEGER;
BEGIN
  WRITELN ('TWENTY RANDOM NUMBERS');
  FOR Index:= 1 TO 20 DO
    WRITE (PrtList [Index]:4);
  WRITELN;
  WRITELN;
END;
(***)
PROCEDURE AmedList (VAR ShortList: List);
  VAR Count,Check: INTEGER;
      Print: BOOLEAN;
BEGIN
  WRITELN ('AMENDED LIST');
  FOR Count:= 1 TO 20 DO
    BEGIN
      Print:= TRUE;
      FOR Check:=1 TO Count-1 DO¹
        IF ShortList [Check] = ShortList [Count] THEN
          Print:= FALSE;
        IF Print = TRUE THEN
          WRITE (ShortList [Count]:4);
    END;
END;
(*************)
(*MAIN PROGRAM*)
(*************)
BEGIN
  Randomize (Numbers);     (*PROCEDURE CALL*)
  PrintArray (Numbers);    (*PROCEDURE CALL*)
  AmedList (Numbers);      (*PROCEDURE CALL*)
END.
```

The procedure Randomize generates 20 random numbers and assigns them to array OrigList. OrigList is passed to the main program into the array Numbers.

Array Numbers is passed to the procedure into the array PrtList and each element of PrtList is printed.

Array Numbers is passed to the procedure into the array ShortList. Before each number is printed, a check is made to see if it has already been printed.

---

¹ When Count = 1 (Count − 1 = 0) the FOR−TO−DO loop will not be executed. See rules page 94.

2. Generalize the program written for Demonstration Problem 1 so it will generate M random integers between 1 and M. Display the numbers exactly as described in Demonstration Problem 1. Allow for up to 200 numbers to be loaded into the array(s).

**APPLE**

```
PROGRAM Ll6Demo2;
  USES APPLESTUFF;
  TYPE List = ARRAY [1..200] OF INTEGER;
  VAR Numbers: List;
      NumOf: INTEGER;
(***)
PROCEDURE RandomNum (HowMany: INTEGER; VAR OrigList: List);
  VAR Count: INTEGER;
  BEGIN
    RANDOMIZE;
    FOR Count:= 1 TO HowMany DO
      OrigList [Count]:= RANDOM MOD HowMany + 1
  END;
(***)
PROCEDURE PrintArray (HowMany: INTEGER; PrtList: List);
  VAR Index: INTEGER;
BEGIN
  WRITELN(HowMany,' RANDOM NUMBER');
  FOR Index:= 1 TO HowMany DO
    WRITE(PrtList [Index]:4);
  WRITELN;
  WRITELN;
END;
(***)
PROCEDURE AmedList (HowMany: INTEGER; ShortList: List);
  VAR Count, Check: INTEGER;
      Print: BOOLEAN;
BEGIN
  WRITELN('AMENDED LIST');
  FOR Count:= 1 TO HowMany DO
    BEGIN
      Print:= TRUE;
      FOR Check:= 1 TO Count-1 DO
        IF ShortList [Check] = ShortList [Count] THEN
          Print:= FALSE;
      IF Print = TRUE THEN
        WRITE(ShortList[Count]:4);
    END;
END;
(*************)
(*MAIN PROGRAM*)
(*************)
BEGIN
  WRITELN ('HOW MANY RANDOM NUMBERS? ');
  READLN (NumOf);
  RandomNum (NumOf,Numbers);    (*PROCEDURE CALL*)
  PrintArray (NumOf,Numbers);   (*PROCEDURE CALL*)
  AmedList (NumOf,Numbers);     (*PROCEDURE CALL*)
END.
```

**TRS-80**

```
PROGRAM L16Demo2;
  TYPE List= ARRAY[1..200] OF INTEGER:
  VAR Numbers: List;
      NumOf: INTEGER;
(***)
PROCEDURE RandomNum (HowMany: INTEGER; VAR OrigList: List);
  VAR Count: INTEGER;
  BEGIN
    FOR Count:= 1 TO HowMany DO
      OrigList[Count]:= RND(HowMany);
  END;
(***)
PROCEDURE PrintArray (Howmany: INTEGER; PrtList: List);
  VAR Index: INTEGER;
  BEGIN
    WRITELN(HowMany,' RANDOM NUMBERS');
    FOR Index:= 1 TO HowMany DO
      WRITE(PrtList[Index]:4);
    WRITELN;
    WRITELN;
  END;
(***)
PROCEDURE AmedList (HowMany: INTEGER; ShortList: List);
  VAR Count, Check: INTEGER;
      Print: BOOLEAN;
  BEGIN
    WRITELN('AMENDED LIST');
    FOR Count:= 1 TO HowMany DO
      BEGIN
        Print:= TRUE;
        FOR Check:= 1 TO Count-1 DO
          IF ShortList[Check] = ShortList[Count] THEN
            Print:= FALSE;
          IF Print = TRUE THEN
            WRITE (ShortList[Count]:4);
      END;
  END;
(*************)
(*MAIN PROGRAM*)
(*************)
BEGIN
  WRITELN ('NUMBER OF TERMS');
  READLN (NumOf);
  RandomNum (NumOf, Numbers);    (*PROCEDURE CALL*)
  PrintArray (NumOf, Numbers);    (*PROCEDURE CALL*)
  AmedList (NumOf, Numbers);    (*PROCEDURE CALL*)
END.
```

**IBM PC**

```
PROGRAM L16Demo2;
  TYPE List = ARRAY [1..200] OF INTEGER;
  VAR Numbers: List;
      NumOf: INTEGER;
(***)
PROCEDURE Randomize (HowMany: INTEGER; VAR OrigList: List);
  VAR Count,UpLimit,RandomNum,Seed: INTEGER;
BEGIN
  FOR Count:= 1 TO HowMany DO
    BEGIN
      Seed:= Seed*233+113;
      RandomNum:= 1+Seed MOD HowMany;
      OrigList [Count]:= RandomNum;
    END;
END;
(***)
PROCEDURE PrintArray (Howmany: INTEGER; PrtList: List);
  VAR Index: INTEGER;
  BEGIN
    WRITELN(HowMany,' RANDOM NUMBERS');
    FOR Index:= 1 TO HowMany DO
      WRITE(PrtList[Index]:4);
    WRITELN;
    WRITELN;
  END;
(***)
PROCEDURE AmedList (HowMany: INTEGER; ShortList: List);
  VAR Count,Check: INTEGER;
      Print: BOOLEAN;
  BEGIN
    WRITELN('AMENDED LIST');
    FOR Count:= 1 TO HowMany DO
      BEGIN
        Print:= TRUE;
        FOR Check:= 1 TO Count-1 DO
          IF ShortList[Check] = ShortList[Count] THEN
            Print:= FALSE;
          IF Print = TRUE THEN
            WRITE (ShortList[Count]:4);
      END;
  END;
(*************)
(*MAIN PROGRAM*)
(*************)
BEGIN
  WRITELN ('HOW MANY RANDOM NUMBERS? ');
  READLN (NumOf);
  Randomize (NumOf, Numbers);     (*PROCEDURE CALL*)
  PrintArray (NumOf, Numbers);    (*PROCEDURE CALL*)
  AmedList (NumOf, Numbers);      (*PROCEDURE CALL*)
END.
```

## 16.4 SKILL DEVELOPMENT EXERCISES

Reading and modifying programs is much easier when parameters are passed to procedures rather than using global variables. Therefore, it is recommended that parameters be passed when procedures are used from this lesson on.

1. The data contains the ID number and the number of correct responses made on the given test for each student in a class. Write a program that will ask the user to input the percent to be assigned to each number of correct responses (see the Display Sample below). Process the data by printing out the student's ID number and the percentage to be assigned for his test. Use a zero for an ID number to terminate the keying in of data. Study the Display and Print Samples below for further clarification.

Display Sample

```
HOW MANY QUESTIONS? 12
INPUT THE PERCENTAGE TO BE
ASSIGNED FOR THE INDICATED
NUMBER OF CORRECT RESPONSES

 0    ?   0
 1    ?   8
 2    ?   17
 3    ?   25
 4    ?   33
 5    ?   42
 6    ?   50
 7    ?   58
 8    ?   67
 9    ?   75
10    ?   83
11    ?   92
12    ?   100

ENTER
ID, # CORRECT RESPONSES (0 0 TO STOP)
1000   5
1001   7
1004   2
1005   10
1006   12
1010   8
0   0
```

Print Sample

```
  ID      PERCENT
 1000       42
 1001       58
 1004       17
 1005       83
 1006       100
 1010       67
```

2. Write a program to input M, the number of elements in set A, and N, the number of elements in set B. Then load the elements of set A and set B into arrays. Print out the elements in set A and set B and the elements of the intersection of sets A and B. Provide appropriate headings. Allow sets as large as 25 elements each to be used.

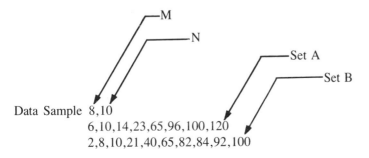

Data Sample  8,10
6,10,14,23,65,96,100,120
2,8,10,21,40,65,82,84,92,100

Print Sample

```
SET A
   6  10  14  23  65    96 100 120
SET B
   2   8  10  21  46  65  82   84  92 100
A INTERSECT B
  10  65  100
```

3. Write a program that:

a. Accepts an input M.
b. Generates M random integers between 1 and 500 and assigns them to a subscripted variable (array).
c. Prints the elements of the array in ascending order.

Run the program several times and check the printed data to insure it is correct.

Note: Appendix VII illustrates the logic involved in a bubble sort and may be referred to if necessary.

4. Write a program that will illustrate how two different arrays can be passed to the same procedure. Complete the following steps.

a. Generate an array of 10 random numbers.
b. Print this array (referred to as the original).
c. Set the first element to zero and print the new array.
d. Set the second element of the original array to zero and print the new array.
e. Set the third element of the original array to zero and print the new array.
f. And so forth until all ten have been printed.

See the Display Sample below for more information.

Display Sample

```
ORIGINAL NUMBERS
  2     7     6     8    10     1     5    10    10     8
ALTERED NUMBERS
  0     7     6     8    10     1     5    10    10     8
  2     0     6     8    10     1     5    10    10     8
  2     7     0     8    10     1     5    10    10     8
  2     7     6     0    10     1     5    10    10     8
  2     7     6     8     0     1     5    10    10     8
  2     7     6     8    10     0     5    10    10     8
  2     7     6     8    10     1     0    10    10     8
  2     7     6     8    10     1     5     0    10     8
  2     7     6     8    10     1     5    10     0     8
  2     7     6     8    10     1     5    10    10     0
```

Note that the diagonal will be zeros

5. A bicycle shop needs a program to calculate new prices on items that are carried in inventory. The program should allow for increasing and decreasing prices.

   Note: Until files are introduced in later lessons, it is not practical to work with large numbers of items. For this reason only 4 sizes are used in this program.

   The first set of calculations are to decrease all prices by 10% for a sale. To do this the operator should have to enter only a negative (percent) value. The second set of calculations are to increase the original prices by 1% to keep up with inflation. This is accomplished by entering a positive (percent) number. The original data should not have to be reentered for each calculation.

| Data   | SIZE |       |      |       |
|--------|------|-------|------|-------|
|        | 1    | 2     | 3    | 4     |
| Tubes  | 3.40 | 8.50  | 4.75 | 6.95  |
| Tires  | 7.95 | 10.45 | 5.95 | 12.00 |
| Spokes | 0.50 | 0.75  | 1.00 | 1.25  |

See the following Display and Print Samples for more information.

ALGORITHM

1. Set up TYPE and VAR declarations
2. Load data procedure
   2.1 Set up VAR declaration
   2.2 Set up FOR–TO loop
       2.2.1 Read each item
3. Read percentage
   3.1 Give prompt
   3.2 Read number
4. Print headings
5. Calculate and print result
   5.1 Set up VAR declaration
   5.2 Set up FOR–TO for calculating and printing
       5.2.1 Calculate and print resulting price
6. Again?
   6.1 Give prompt
   6.2 Get answer

Display Sample

```
ENTER PRICES FOR INNER TUBES
ENTER VALUES ONE AT A TIME
?3.40
?8.50
?4.75
?6.95
ENTER PRICES FOR TIRES
ENTER VALUES ONE AT A TIME
?7.95
?10.45
?5.95
?12.00
ENTER PRICES FOR SPOKES
ENTER VALUES ONE AT A TIME
?0.50
?0.75
?1.00
?1.25
ENTER PERCENTAGE FOR CALCULATIONS
?-10

DO YOU WANT ANOTHER PERCENTAGE Y/N
?Y
ENTER PERCENTAGE FOR CALCULATIONS
?1

DO YOU WANT ANOTHER PERCENTAGE Y/N
?N
```

Print Sample

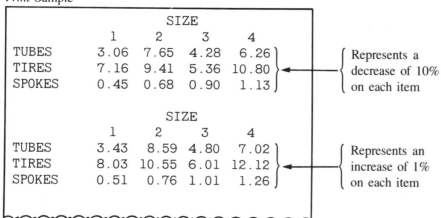

```
                   SIZE
           1     2     3     4
TUBES    3.06  7.65  4.28   6.26
TIRES    7.16  9.41  5.36  10.80
SPOKES   0.45  0.68  0.90   1.13
```
Represents a decrease of 10% on each item

```
                   SIZE
           1     2     3     4
TUBES    3.43  8.59  4.80   7.02
TIRES    8.03 10.55  6.01  12.12
SPOKES   0.51  0.76  1.01   1.26
```
Represents an increase of 1% on each item

# Lesson 17
# STRING VARIABLES (Not available on the TRS-80)

## 17.1 OBJECTIVES

Objectives: 1. To understand and be able to use string variables.
2. To be able to determine the length of strings.
3. To be able to concatenate strings.

## 17.2 ASSIGNMENT, LENGTH, and CONCATENATE

STRING DECLARATION

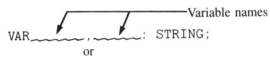

```
VAR_____,_____: STRING;
         or
VAR_____,_____: STRING[10];
```

EXPLANATION

Permits the use of string variables. While the CHAR type variable contains only one character, a STRING type variable can contain up to 80 characters. Using the [] with the STRING declaration saves memory but puts a maximum limit on the number of characters that can be placed in the string.

*Examples*

```
VAR Address,Description: STRING;
    Name,Word1,Word2,Word3: STRING[20];
```

STRING ASSIGNMENT

```
WordStr:= '_____';
```

*Examples*

```
Word1:= 'MICRO';
WordStr:= 'WOULDN"T';
```

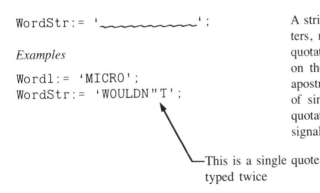

This is a single quote typed twice

EXPLANATION

A string constant consisting of the characters (letters, numbers, characters, or blanks) between the quotation marks is assigned to the string variable on the left of the assignment symbol. When an apostrophe is desired in a string, a consecutive pair of single quotation marks is treated as a single quotation mark and not as a delimiter which would signal the end of the string.

STRING FUNCTIONS                                    EXPLANATION

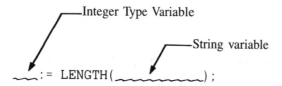

The number of characters in the string (stored in the string variable) will be determined and that number will be assigned to the variable on the left of the assignment symbol.

*Examples*

```
Wordl:= 'MICRO';
NoOfChar:=LENGTH(Wordl);
```
NoOfChar contains the value 5.

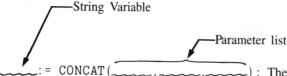

The string variables or string constants in the parameter list will be concatenated in the order they appear.

*Examples*

```
Wordl:= 'MICRO';
Word2:= 'COMPUTER';
Word3:= 'IS';
LongStr:= CONCAT (Wordl,Word2);
Combine:= CONCAT (Word2,' LANGUAGE ',WORD3);
Line:= CONCAT (Word3,'N"T');
```

The example on the left results in the following assignments:

LongStr contains  MICROCOMPUTER
Combine contains
COMPUTER LANGUAGE IS
Line contains  ISN'T

## 17.3 DEMONSTRATION PROBLEMS

1. Write a program so the operator can enter a series of verbs and the computer will respond by printing a table of those verbs and their negative contracted forms.

Display Sample

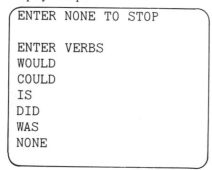

Print Sample

```
VERB     CONTRACTION
WOULD      WOULDN'T
COULD      COULDN'T
  IS          ISN'T
 DID         DIDN'T
 WAS         WASN'T
```

```
PROGRAM L17Demo1;
  CONST Contraction = 'N"T';
  VAR Lp: TEXT;            (*APPLE & IBM*)
      Verb, ConVerb: STRING;
BEGIN
  REWRITE(Lp,'PRINTER:');        (*APPLE & IBM*)
  WRITELN(Lp,'VERB':7,'CONTRACTION':15);
  READLN(Verb);
  WHILE Verb <> 'NONE' DO
    BEGIN
      ConVerb:= CONCAT(Verb,Contraction);
      WRITELN(Lp,Verb:8,ConVerb:13);
      READLN(Verb);
    END;
END.
```

2. It is desired to have a program to make worksheets to be used for a scramble word game. Write the program that allows the user to indicate how many words he would like on the worksheet and enter that many words with the letters in mixed order. The computer will print the number of the word, the word as it was entered, and the appropriate number of blanks to the right of the word. See the Display and Print Samples below for further clarification.

Display Sample

```
HOW MANY WORDS? 4
ENTER WORDS ONE AT A TIME
CPUTREOM
NDE
PECMOIL
CALASP
```

Answers

1. COMPUTER
2. END
3. COMPILE
4. PASCAL

Print Sample

```
1. CPUTREOM        _ _ _ _ _ _ _ _

2. NDE             _ _ _

3. PECMOIL         _ _ _ _ _ _ _

4. CALASP          _ _ _ _ _ _
```

```
PROGRAM L17Demo2;
  VAR Number,LineNo,Blanks,UnderLines: INTEGER;
      MixedWord: STRING;
      Lp: TEXT;
BEGIN
  REWRITE (Lp,'PRINTER:');
  WRITE('HOW MANY WORDS? ');
  READLN(Number);
  WRITELN('ENTER WORDS ONE AT A TIME');
  FOR LineNo:= 1 TO Number DO
    BEGIN
      READLN(MixedWord);
      WRITE(Lp,LineNo:2,'.   ');
      WRITE(Lp,MixedWord);
      FOR Blanks:= 1 TO 10-LENGTH(MixedWord) DO
        WRITE(Lp,' ');
      WRITE(Lp,'           ');
      FOR Underlines:= 1 TO LENGTH(MixedWord) DO
        WRITE(Lp,'- ');
      WRITELN(Lp);
      WRITELN(LP);
    END;
END.
```

## 17.4 SKILL DEVELOPMENT EXERCISE

1. A high school counselor needs a program that will print out a list of students, a code for the classes passed, and the overall average. The input should consist of the student's name and his/her percentages for each class (Mathematics, Science, Language, English, and Social Studies). A passing grade is 60% or higher. Study the Display and Print Samples below for further clarification.

    Code: M = Mathematics
          S = Science
          L = Foreign Language
          E = English
          O = Social Studies

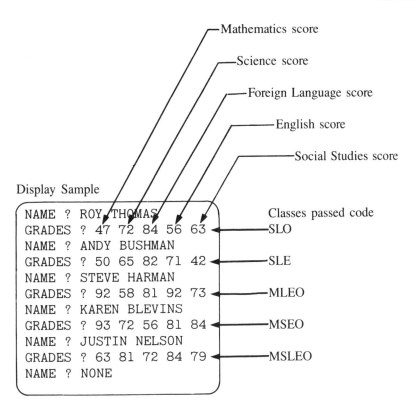

Display Sample

```
NAME  ?  ROY THOMAS
GRADES  ?  47 72 84 56 63 ◄——— SLO
NAME  ?  ANDY BUSHMAN
GRADES  ?  50 65 82 71 42 ◄——— SLE
NAME  ?  STEVE HARMAN
GRADES  ?  92 58 81 92 73 ◄——— MLEO
NAME  ?  KAREN BLEVINS
GRADES  ?  93 72 56 81 84 ◄——— MSEO
NAME  ?  JUSTIN NELSON
GRADES  ?  63 81 72 84 79 ◄——— MSLEO
NAME  ?  NONE
```

—Mathematics score
—Science score
—Foreign Language score
—English score
—Social Studies score
Classes passed code

Print Sample

```
   NAME              PASSED        AVERAGE

ROY THOMAS           SLO            64.4
ANDY BUSHMAN         SLE            62.0
STEVE HARMAN         MLEO           79.2
KAREN BLEVINS        MSEO           77.2
JUSTIN NELSON        MSLEO          75.8
```

Left
justified

Right
justified

# Lesson 18
# PACKED ARRAYS

## 18.1 OBJECTIVES

Objectives: 1. To be able to load and print packed arrays.
2. To be able to manipulate packed arrays.
3. To be able to pass arrays as parameters.
4. To be able to use SUCCessor and PREDecessor functions.

## 18.2 LOADING, PRINTING, MANIPULATING, AND COMPARING PACKED ARRAYS

Packed arrays are used much more extensively in Standard Pascal because the string variable or string type is not available. Even if UCSD or another version of Pascal, where the string variables are available, is being used, packed arrays can still be quite useful. It is therefore recommended that the lesson on packed arrays be covered even if string variables are available in order to provide a more complete knowledge of Pascal.

*Packed Array Declaration*

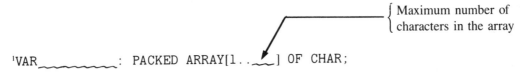

Packed arrays of CHAR can be handled in exactly the same way as ordinary arrays. The advantages of the packed array are:

1. Less storage space is needed.
2. The output of the array can be completed as a single unit of characters rather than one character at a time.
3. Assignment statements can assign an entire packed array as a single unit (but not with a READLN statement).
4. Comparisons can be made with packed arrays.

*Initializing Packed Arrays*

*Examples*

```
VAR Word1,Word2,Word3: PACKED ARRAY [1..9] OF CHAR;

Word1:= '         ';

Word2:= 'AAAAAAAAA';

Word3:= 'START    ';
```

Since Word1, Word2, and Word3 are packed arrays their lengths are fixed in the declaration statement. The string on the right must contain exactly 9 characters to coordinate with the VAR statement. Blanks may be used as valid characters.

---

[1] Although arrays of reals or integers can also be packed in order to save storage, this book will deal only with packed arrays of characters.

144

*Assignment to Elements of Packed Arrays*

*Examples*

```
VAR RoomNo: PACKED ARRAY [1..10] OF CHAR;

BEGIN

  RoomNo:= 'ROOM # ---';



  RoomNo[8]:= '2';
  RoomNo[9]:= '0';
  RoomNo[10]:= '5';

END.
```

After the three assignments RoomNo contains
ROOM # 205

*Loading Packed Arrays* (From the KEYBOARD)

*Example 1(Fixed number of characters)*

```
PROGRAM Example1;
VAR CharSet: PACKED ARRAY [1..10] OF CHAR;
    Count: INTEGER;
    Letter: CHAR;
BEGIN


  FOR Count:= 1 TO 10 DO
    BEGIN
      READ (Letter);
      CharSet [Count]:= Letter;
    END;
   ' WRITELN;

END.
```

On the APPLE a single component of a packed array cannot be set as a variable parameter; therefore, the READ ( ) and assignment to the packed array must be completed in separate statements. On the TRS–80 and IBM PC, READ (CharSet [Count]) is allowed. In the example, ten characters must be keyed in before the loop is completed and execution continues to the next statement.

*Example 2 (Variable number of characters)*

```
PROCEDURE Example2 (VAR Address: PackedArrayVarOf20Letters);
  VAR Count: INTEGER;
      SingleCh: CHAR;                        Initializing blanks(20)
  BEGIN
    Address:= '            ';
    Count:= 0;
    REPEAT
      READ (SingleCh);
     ² Count:= Count + 1;
      Address[Count]:= SingleCh;
    UNTIL EOLN;
  END;
```

After the entire line is entered and the return key is pressed, the computer will read each character, one at a time, and load the packed array until the EOLN (END-OF-LINE) is encountered. The return key puts a special EOLN character at the end of the line, and when this character is read, the EOLN, which is a Boolean expression, will become TRUE.

---

¹ The WRITELN is necessary so that the subsequent display will not appear on the same line as the input.

² When all characters have been read and the EOLN encountered, Count will contain one more than the number of letters that were entered.

*Comparing Packed Arrays*

*Example*

```
PROGRAM _____ ;
  VAR InilSet,InputSet: PACKED ARRAY [1..15] OF CHAR;
  ~~~~~~

  ~~~~~~
  IF InilSet = InputSet THEN
     ~~~~~~~~~~~~~~
  ELSE _____ ;
```

Comparisons can be made between packed arrays of the same length. The comparison is made one character at a time until a mismatch is found. A < Z, 0 < 9, and A < a are a few key relations.

Examples:  SET < ZOO
            ADAM < ANDY
            TRY1 < TRY5
            SECOND < second

More explanation is given in Appendix IV.

*Printing Packed Arrays*

```
VAR Master: PACKED ARRAY [1..20] OF CHAR;
~~~~~

~~~~~
WRITELN (Master);
~~~~~

~~~~~
```

Unlike loading packed arrays a packed array can be printed as a single unit.

*Components of Packed Arrays*

```
VAR Orig,Middle: PACKED ARRAY [1..20] OF CHAR;
    Count: INTEGER;
~~~~~~

~~~~~~
FOR Count:= 4 TO 8 DO
  Middle [Count - 3]:= Orig [Count];
~~~~~~

~~~~~~
```

Individual elements of a packed array can be accessed by using the subscript numbers. In the example, the 4th through the 8th character of the array `Orig` will be assigned to locations 1–5 of array `Middle`.

*Using Successor and Predecessor*

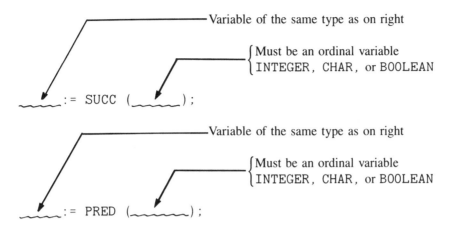

The successor (number or character that follows) or predecessor (number or character that comes before) of the argument will be assigned to the variable on the left. Both variables must be of the same ordinal type which will normally be of the IN-TEGER or CHAR type. BOOLEAN would be acceptable but has no practical application.

*Example 1*

```
VAR Count: INTEGER;

~~~

~~~
Count:= 1

~~~

~~~
WHILE Count <= 10 DO
  BEGIN

    ~~~
    ~~~
    ~~~
    Count:= SUCC (Count);
    ~~~
    ~~~

  END;
```

The statements between the BEGIN and END will be executed exactly 10 times. Count will take on the values of 1,2,3,4, . . . ,10 during the looping process.

*Example 2*

```
VAR Alph: CHAR;
    LoopCount: INTEGER;

~~~

~~~
Alph:='Z';
FOR LoopCount:= 1 TO 6 DO
  BEGIN
    WRITELN (Alph);
    Alph:= PRED (PRED (Alph));
  END;
```

From the characters "ABCD . . . PQRSTUVWX YZ" the characters, Z,X,V,T,R, and P will be displayed in that order one below the other. The characters Y,W,U,S, and Q are skipped because one PRED function is immediately followed by a second PRED function.

*Example 3*

```
PROGRAM EXAMPLE3;
  TYPE DaysOfWeek = (Mon,Tues,Wed,Thur,Fri,Sat,Sun);
    VAR Today,Tomorrow: DaysOfWeek;
        Month: INTEGER;
BEGIN
  Today:= Wed;
  For Month:= 1 TO 31 DO
    BEGIN
      IF Today = Sun THEN Tomorrow:= Mon
        ELSE Tomorrow:= SUCC (Today);
      CASE Tomorrow OF
        Mon: WRITELN ('Mon');
        Tues: WRITELN ('Tues');
        Wed: WRITELN('Wed');
        Thur; WRITELN ('Thur');
        Fri: WRITELN('Fri');
        Sat,Sun: WRITELN ('Weekend');
      END;
      Today:= Tomorrow;
    END;
END.
```

The program prints the abbreviation for the days of the week starting with Thursday and continuing for 31 days as shown in the print sample. Note that variables which are of a user defined type cannot be printed directly.

Display Sample

```
Thur
Fri
Weekend
Weekend
Mon
Tues
Wed
Thur
Fri
Weekend
Weekend
Mon
etc.
```

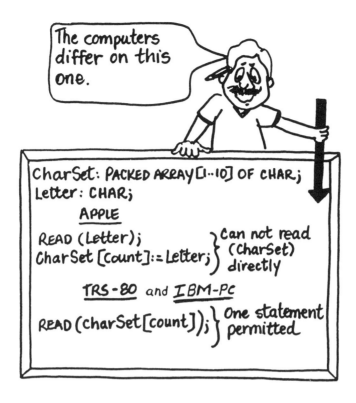

## 18.3 DEMONSTRATION PROBLEM

1. Write a program that will print 3 identical mailing labels across a sheet of paper. The name, address, city, state, and zip code should have to be entered only once. The prompt and response to quit processing should have to be executed only once rather than after each set of labels is printed. See the following Display and Print Samples for more information.

*continued on next page*

Display Sample

```
ENTER NAME:
?JOHN DOE
ENTER ADDRESS:
?1234 ANY STREET
ENTER CITY, STATE, ZIP
?YOUR TOWN, NY 10000

CORRECT=Y INCORRECT=N
?Y
ENTER NAME:
?CHARLES WAGNER
ENTER ADDRESS:
?1436 ELM DRIVE
ENTER CITY, STATE, ZIP
?BLOOMS, CA 90233

CORRECT=Y INCORRECT=N
?Y
ENTER NAME:
?NONE
ENTER ADDRESS:
?NONE
ENTER CITY, STATE, ZIP
?NONE

CORRECT=Y INCORRECT=N
?N
DO YOU WANT TO CONTINUE Y/N
N
```

Note: In order to save the user time, the prompt to stop is executed only after an incorrect entry response has been made. See the solution program for further clarification.

Print Sample

```
JOHN DOE             JOHN DOE             JOHN DOE
1234 ANY STREET      1234 ANY STREET      1234 ANY STREET
YOUR TOWN, NY 10000  YOUR TOWN, NY 10000  YOUR TOWN, NY 10000
- - - -

CHARLES WAGNER       CHARLES WAGNER       CHARLES WAGNER
1436 ELM DRIVE       1436 ELM DRIVE       1436 ELM DRIVE
BLOOMS, CA 90233     BLOOMS, CA 90233     BLOOMS, CA 90233

- - - -
```

ALGORITHM (Procedures)

1. Set up a procedure to read a packed array
   1.1 Set up loop and loop until EOLN
      1.1.1 Loop and read characters into array
2. Print a packed array
   2.1 Set up to do 3 loops
      2.1.1 Write array of characters
   2.2 Writeln to return carriage

ALGORITHM (Main Program)

1. Set up "do you want to continue" loop
2. Give prompts and read information
    2.1 Name
    2.2 Address
    2.3 City, State, and Zip
3. Correct?
    3.1 Prompt
    3.2 Readln Response
    3.3 Check Response
        3.3.1 If Y
                3.3.1.1 Print label
        3.3.2 If N
                3.3.2.1 Continue?

```
PROGRAM L18N2;
   TYPE StrVar= PACKED ARRAY [1..20] OF CHAR;
   VAR Name, Address, CityStZip: StrVar;
       Response, Letter, Continue: CHAR;
       LP: TEXT; (*APPLE & IBM*)
(***)
PROCEDURE ReadLine (VAR Temp: StrVar);
   VAR Count: INTEGER;
   BEGIN
     Temp:= '                    ';
     Count:=1;
     REPEAT
       READ (Letter);
       Temp[Count]:= Letter;
       Count:= Count + 1;
     UNTIL EOLN;
   END;
(***)
PROCEDURE Print (Temp: StrVar);
   VAR Count: INTEGER;
   BEGIN
     FOR Count:= 1 TO 3 DO
       WRITE (LP, Temp, '    ');
     WRITELN (LP);
   END;
```

Loads packed array, Temp. Padded blanks complete the array when the number of characters entered is less than 20.

Prints the packed arrays Name, Address, and CityStZip, which are passed to it from the main program.

```
(*************)
(*MAIN PROGRAM*)
(*************)
BEGIN
  Continue:= 'Y';
  REWRITE (LP,'PRINTER:'); (*APPLE & IBM*)
  WHILE Continue= 'Y' DO
    BEGIN
      WRITELN ('ENTER NAME: ');
      ReadLine (Name);        (*PROCEDURE CALL*)
      WRITELN ('ENTER ADDRESS: ');
      ReadLine (Address);     (*PROCEDURE CALL*)
      WRITELN ('ENTER CITY, STATE, ZIP: ');
      ReadLine (CityStZip); (*PROCEDURE CALL*)
      WRITELN;
      WRITELN ('CORRECT=Y INCORRECT=N');
      READLN (Response);
      IF Response= 'Y' THEN
        BEGIN
          Print (Name);        (*PROCEDURE CALL*)
          Print (Address);     (*PROCEDURE CALL*)
          Print (CityStZip); (*PROCEDURE CALL*)
          WRITELN (LP);
          WRITELN (LP,'- - - - ');
        END
      ELSE
        BEGIN
          WRITELN ('DO YOU WANT TO CONTINUE Y/N');
          READLN (Continue);
        END;
    END;
END.
```

Loads 3 packed arrays.

Will print labels only when response is 'Y'.

Will execute terminating prompt only when (CORRECT= Y INCORRECT= N) response is 'N'.

## 18.4 SKILL DEVELOPMENT EXERCISES

1. Write a program that requests the user to input a person's name, code, and place of citizenship. The code consists of three letters that represent the person's grade, sex, and ethnic code. The program should then print out the information in expanded form. See the Print and Display samples below for more information.

Code Key

| *Grade* | *Sex* | *Ethnic Group* |
|---|---|---|
| F—FRESHMAN | M—MALE | B—BLACK |
| S—SOPHOMORE | F—FEMALE | H—HISPANIC |
| J—JUNIOR | | I—INDIAN |
| E—SENIOR | | O—ORIENTAL |
| | | W—WHITE |

Display Sample

```
ENTER 0 FOR NAME TO STOP
ENTER NAME: ?HAROLD REID
ENTER CODE: ?EMB
ENTER CITIZENSHIP: ?UNITED STATES

ENTER NAME: ?FRAN BUTLER
ENTER CODE: ?JFW
ENTER CITIZENSHIP: ?UNITED STATES

ENTER NAME: ?JEAN ROBERTS
ENTER CODE: ?SFW
ENTER CITIZENSHIP: ?UNITED KINGDOM

ENTER NAME: ?0
```

Print Sample

```
     NAME        CLASS      SEX    RACE    CITIZENSHIP
HAROLD REID     SENIOR     MALE   BLACK   UNITED STATES
FRAN BUTLER     JUNIOR     FEMALE WHITE   UNITED STATES
JEAN ROBERTS    SOPHOMORE  FEMALE WHITE   UNITED KINGDOM
```

2. Write a program that will print a list of the merchandise in inventory, the stock code, total value of each item, and the total value of all inventory. The program should generate the stock code using the first four letters of the description, the first three letters of the manufacturer, and a letter, A–Z chosen in sequence[1]. The information entered should consist of the description, manufacturer, quantity in stock, and the price for one. See Display and Print samples below for more information.

---

[1] The purpose for using the A-Z in the problem is to encourage the student to use the SUCC function. This use of a letter would be impractical in an application that requires more than 26 items.

Display Sample

```
DESCRIPTION: ?COMPUTER
MANUFACTURER: ?IBM
PRICE-# IN STOCK?1200.00 4
DESCRIPTION: ?COMPUTER
MANUFACTURER: ?APPLE
PRICE-# IN STOCK?1195.00 3
DESCRIPTION: ?PRINTER
MANUFACTURER: ?EPSON
PRICE-# IN STOCK?560.00 5
DESCRIPTION: ?NONE
MANUFACTURER: ?NONE
PRICE-# IN STOCK?0 0
```

Print Sample

```
DESCRIPTION      STOCK CODE      VALUE
COMPUTER         COMP-IBM-A      4800.00
COMPUTER         COMP-APP-B      3585.00
PRINTER          PRIN-EPS-C      2800.00


TOTAL VALUE $  11185.00
```

3. You have been contracted to write a program for a teacher in your school that will take a list of words and print out a sheet of the words in scrambled form and in the original form. The original form should be to the right of the scrambled form so the teacher can block it out for copying. Number each word starting at 1.

Display Sample

```
ENTER WORD TO BE SCRAMBLED
(0 TO STOP)
COMPUTER
NOW SCRAMBLING WORD

ENTER WORD TO BE SCRAMBLED
MICRO
NOW SCRAMBLING WORD

ENTER WORD TO BE SCRAMBLED
INTERFACE
NOW SCRAMBLING WORD

ENTER WORD TO BE SCRAMBLED
0
```

Print Sample

```
1. EOCMTRUP      1. COMPUTER
2. ROIMC         2. MICRO
3. RCTFEAINE     3. INTERFACE
```

MOD is executed before any arithmetic operation unless parenthesis are used.

APPLE ONLY

COUNT: =5;

~

~

X:= RANDOM MOD COUNT-1;
　(-1,0,1,2,3)← possible x values

~

~

X:= RANDOM MOD (COUNT-1);
　(0,1,2,3)← possible x values

# Lesson 19
# RECORDS

## 19.1 OBJECTIVES

Objectives: 1. To be able to declare and use the record type.
2. To work with individual fields of a record.
3. To be able to declare and use arrays of records.
4. To pass arrays of records to procedures.

## 19.2 RECORDS and ARRAY OF RECORDS

*Record Structure Declaration*

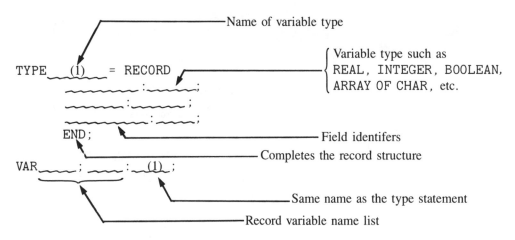

or

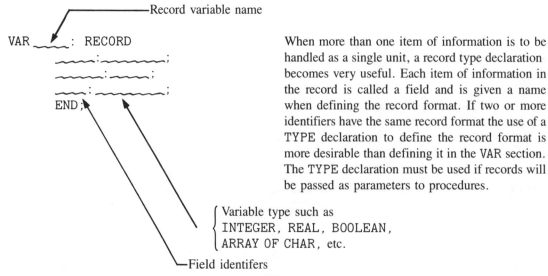

When more than one item of information is to be handled as a single unit, a record type declaration becomes very useful. Each item of information in the record is called a field and is given a name when defining the record format. If two or more identifiers have the same record format the use of a TYPE declaration to define the record format is more desirable than defining it in the VAR section. The TYPE declaration must be used if records will be passed as parameters to procedures.

156

*Examples*

```
PROGRAM Example1;
  TYPE Date = RECORD
         Day: (1..31);
         Month: ARRAY [1..3] OF CHAR;
         Year: (1900..2000);
       END;
  VAR MemorialDay,FourthJul,ThanksGiv,Xmas: Date;
```

{ Each variable has the same record format

This example shows an advantage of using the TYPE declaration because more than one record variable has the same record structure. The record structure is declared as TYPE (Date) and all the holiday variables are defined as having the Date structure.

```
PROGRAM Example2;
  VAR InvItem: RECORD
         Disc: PACKED ARRAY [1..15] OF CHAR;
         CatalogNum: PACKED ARRAY [1..7] OF CHAR;
         NumOnHand: INTEGER;
         Price: REAL;
         MonthPur: (Jan,Feb,Mar,Apr,May,Jun,Jul,Aug,Sep,Oct,Nov,Dec);
       END;
```

When only one identifier is to have a given record structure it may be desirable to declare the record structure in VAR section of the declaration block.

*Array of Records Declaration*

```
TYPE StudentRec = RECORD
         Name: PACKED ARRAY [1..20] OF CHAR;
         Level: (Freshman,Sophomore,Junior,Senior);
         TimesAbs: INTEGER;
         TimesTardy: INTEGER;
         Grade: REAL;
         END;
     Class = ARRAY [1..30] OF StudentRec;
```

Class is an array of 30 records with each record consisting of five fields as declared in the record declaration.

or

```
TYPE StudentRec = ARRAY [1..30] OF RECORD
        Name: PACKED ARRAY [1..20] OF CHAR;
        Level: (Freshman,Sophomore,Junior,Senior);
        TimesAbs: INTEGER;
        TimesTardy: INTEGER;
        Grade: REAL;
     END;
VAR Class: StudentRec;




PROCEDURE          (WorkClass: StudentRec);
```

*Transferring Records*

```
TYPE CharStrg = PACKED ARRAY [1..20] OF CHAR;
     Layout = RECORD
        Name: CharStrg;
        Address: CharStrg;
        TownState: CharStrg;
        AccountBal: REAL;
        Delinquent: BOOLEAN;
     END;
VAR Customer,Overdue: Layout;
```

*Example 1* (Complete record)

When records have the same structure a transfer of the complete record can be made with a single assignment statement.

```
BEGIN




    Overdue:= Customer;



END.
```

*Example 2* (Specific record fields)

```
BEGIN




    Overdue.Name:= Customer.Name;
    Overdue.AccountBal:= Customer.AccountBal;
    Overdue.Delinquent:= TRUE;



END.
```

The value TRUE is assigned to a field of the record.

*Transferring Array of Records*

```
TYPE Label = RECORD
        Name: PACKED ARRAY [1..20] OF CHAR;
        Street: PACKED ARRAY [1..15] OF CHAR;
        Town: PACKED ARRAY [1..15] OF CHAR;
        Zip: PACKED ARRAY [1..5] OF CHAR;
      END;
VAR Repub,Demo,Active,NameList: ARRAY [1..100] OF Label;
    Count,NumberTrans: INTEGER;
```

*Example 1* (complete record)

```
BEGIN
    〰〰〰
    〰〰〰
    NumberTrans:= 0;
    FOR Count:= 1 TO 100 DO
      IF Demo [Count].Zip = '59102' THEN
        BEGIN
          NumberTrans:= NumberTrans + 1;
          Active[NumberTrans]:= Demo[Count];
        END;
    〰〰〰
    〰〰〰
    〰〰〰
END.
```

All records of array Demo with a zip code of 59102 will be transferred to the array `Active`. NumberTrans will contain the number of records in array `Active`.

A complete record of Demo will be transferred

*Example 2* (Specified fields)

```
BEGIN
    〰〰〰
    FOR Count:= 1 TO 100 DO
      NameList [Count].Name:= Repub [Count].Name;
    〰〰〰
    〰〰〰
END.
```

Only one field Name, of each record of Repub will be transferred during each loop.

WITH–DO Statement (Not on TRS–80)

*Example 1*

```
PROGRAM Example1;
TYPE PackChar = PACKED ARRAY [1..10] OF CHAR;
VAR Auto = RECORD
        Make: PackChar;
        Model: PackChar;
        Color: PackChar;
        License: PackChar;
        Price: REAL;
    〰〰
    〰〰
    Auto.Make:= 'FORD      ';
    Auto.Model:= 'SEDAN     ';
    Auto.Color:= 'GREEN     ';
    Auto.License:= '3-12245   ';
    Auto.Price:= 12000.0;
```

Loading a record can be accomplished two ways on the APPLE and IBM.

Long method

On the APPLE and IBM the previous stated example can be replaced by:

```
With Auto DO
  BEGIN
    Make:= 'FORD      ';
    Model:= 'SEDAN     ';         ⎫
    Color:= 'GREEN     ';         ⎬  Short method
    License:= '3-12245   ';       ⎭
    Price:= 12000.0
  END;
```

*Example 2*

```
PROGRAM Example2;
TYPE Employee = ARRAY [1..100] OF RECORD
        Name: PACKED ARRAY [1..20];
        Address: PACKED ARRAY [1..30];
        SocialSec: PACKED ARRAY [1..12];
        WageRate: REAL;
        NumberDep: INTEGER;
VAR Instructor,Secretarys,Custodial: Employee;

PROCEDURE Load (VAR Staff: Employee);
  WITH Staff DO
    BEGIN                    ──────── Prompt
                                            ──────A procedure call to load a packed array
      ~~~~~                                      ──────Number of characters in packed array
      ~~~~~                                          ──────Record field identifier
      ~~~~~
      ~~~~~
      ~~~~~
      WRITE ('NAME: '); LRoutine (20,Name);
      WRITE ('ADDRESS: '); LRoutine (30,Address);
      WRITE ('SOCIAL SECURITY: '); LRoutine (12,SocialSec);
      WRITE ('WAGE RATE: '); READLN (WageRate);
      WRITE ('NUMBER OF DEPENDENTS: '); READLN (NumberDep);
    END;
(*MAIN PROGRAM*)

Load (Instructors); (*Procedure will load Instructors*);

Load (Secretaries); (*Frocedure will load Secretaries*);
```

## 19.3 DEMONSTRATION PROBLEM

1. Demonstrate how to load and print an array of records. Pass arrays of records to procedures and work with single fields of a record by completing the following program:

A diet center has records containing each member's name, desired weight, current weight, and three sets of weights taken at one-month intervals. The problem is to print their original record twice, then enter the current weight for the 1st month, and print the original and altered record. Then enter current weights for each person for the 2nd month, print the records, and then do the same for the 3rd month. Study the Display and Print Samples for further clarification.

Note: In order to keep the problem as simple as possible and yet make use of arrays of records the printout is not practical. Files would lend themselves to a more useful problem but will not be used until they are introduced in later lessons.

Display Sample

```
ENTER NAME :MARY PHILLIPS
ENTER DESIRED WEIGHT :115
ENTER CURRENT WEIGHT :138

ENTER NAME :RICHARD WARD
ENTER DESIRED WEIGHT :185
ENTER CURRENT WEIGHT :207

ENTER NAME :RICK NORMAN
ENTER DESIRED WEIGHT :175
ENTER CURRENT WEIGHT :192

ENTER NAME :JUNE MORGAN
DESIRED WEIGHT :120
CURRENT WEIGHT :141

NAME :MIKE DENNY
DESIRED WEIGHT :175
CURRENT WEIGHT :194


* * * * * * * * * * * * * * * * * * * * * * * * * * * *

ENTER CURRENT WEIGHTS FOR THESE PEOPLE
MARY PHILLIPS :132
RICHARD WARD :201
RICK NORMAN :187
JUNE MORGAN :138
MIKE DENNY :184
ENTER CURRENT WEIGHTS FOR THESE PEOPLE
MARY PHILLIPS :130
RICHARD WARD :200
etc.
```

Entering original record information

Entering 1st month's current weights

Entering 2nd month's current weights

Print Sample

```
NAME: MARY PHILLIPS        NAME: MARY PHILLIPS
DESIRED WEIGHT:    115     DESIRED WEIGHT:    115
STARTING WEIGHT:   138     CURRENT WEIGHT:    138

NAME: RICHARD WARD         NAME: RICHARD WARD
DESIRED WEIGHT:    185     DESIRED WEIGHT:    185
STARTING WEIGHT:   207     CURRENT WEIGHT:    207

NAME: RICK NORMAN          NAME: RICK NORMAN
DESIRED WEIGHT:    175     DESIRED WEIGHT:    175
STARTING WEIGHT:   192     CURRENT WEIGHT:    192

NAME: JUNE MORGAN          NAME: JUNE MORGAN
DESIRED WEIGHT:    120     DESIRED WEIGHT:    120
STARTING WEIGHT:   141     CURRENT WEIGHT:    141

NAME: MIKE DENNY           NAME: MIKE DENNY
DESIRED WEIGHT:    175     DESIRED WEIGHT:    175
STARTING WEIGHT:   194     CURRENT WEIGHT:    194

*********************************************************

NAME: MARY PHILLIPS        NAME: MARY PHILLIPS
DESIRED WEIGHT:    115     DESIRED WEIGHT:    115
STARTING WEIGHT:   138     CURRENT WEIGHT:    132

NAME: RICHARD WARD         NAME: RICHARD WARD
DESIRED WEIGHT:    185     DESIRED WEIGHT:    185
STARTING WEIGHT:   207     CURRENT WEIGHT:    201

NAME: RICK NORMAN          NAME: RICK NORMAN
DESIRED WEIGHT:    175     DESIRED WEIGHT:    175
STARTING WEIGHT:   192     CURRENT WEIGHT:    187

NAME: JUNE MORGAN          NAME: JUNE MORGAN
DESIRED WEIGHT:    120     DESIRED WEIGHT:    120
STARTING WEIGHT:   141     CURRENT WEIGHT:    138

NAME: MIKE DENNY           NAME: MIKE DENNY
DESIRED WEIGHT:    175     DESIRED WEIGHT:    175
STARTING WEIGHT:   194     CURRENT WEIGHT:    184

*********************************************************

NAME: MARY PHILLIPS        NAME: MARY PHILLIPS
DESIRED WEIGHT:    115     DESIRED WEIGHT:    115
STARTING WEIGHT:   138     CURRENT WEIGHT:    130

NAME: RICHARD WARD         NAME: RICHARD WARD
DESIRED WEIGHT:    185     DESIRED WEIGHT:    185
STARTING WEIGHT:   207     CURRENT WEIGHT:    200
```

Original records

Records after 1st month

Records after 2nd month

Original record information

Current record information

ALGORITHM

1. Procedure ReadLine (VAR packed array ⬆)
   1.1 Loads a name
2. Procedure ReadOrig (VAR array of records ⬆)
   2.1 For 5 loops
       2.1.1 ReadLine (Name)(*PROCEDURE CALL*)
       2.1.2 Read desired weight
       2.1.3 Read current weight
3. Procedure Print (VAR original array of records, new array of records ⬇)
   3.1 Loop 5 times
       3.1.1 Print (original array name, new array name)
       3.1.2 Print (desired weight, desired weight)
       3.1.3 Print (starting weight, current weight)
4. Procedure Update (VAR altered array of records ⬆⬇)
   4.1 For 5 loops
       4.1.1 Display name
       4.1.2 Leave name as is
       4.1.3 Leave desired weight as is
       4.1.4 Read new current weight


MAIN PROGRAM

1. ReadOrig (original array)(*PROCEDURE CALL*)
2. Current array:= original array
3. Print (original array, current array)(*PROCEDURE CALL*)
4. Loop for 3 weight changes
   4.1 Update (current array)(*PROCEDURE CALL*)
   4.2 Print (original array, current array)(*PROCEDURE CALL*)


```
PROGRAM Ll9Demo;
   TYPE Measure= ARRAY [l..5] OF RECORD
       Name: PACKED ARRAY [l..15] OF CHAR;
       DesiredWeight: INTEGER;
       Actual: INTEGER;
     END;
     StrVar= PACKED ARRAY [l..15] OF CHAR;
   VAR Orig, Current: Measure;
       Count: INTEGER;
(***)
PROCEDURE ReadLine (VAR TempStr: StrVar);
 VAR Count: INTEGER;
       TempChar: CHAR;
   BEGIN
     Count:= 0;
     TempStr:= '               ';
     REPEAT
       Count:= Count + 1;
       READ (TempChar);
       TempStr[Count]:= TempChar;
     UNTIL EOLN OR (Count >= 15);
   END;
(***)
```

Loads a packed array
(used to load names)

```
PROCEDURE ReadOrig (VAR Who: Measure);
  VAR Count: INTEGER;
  BEGIN
    FOR Count:= 1 TO 5 DO
      BEGIN
        WRITE ('ENTER NAME :');
        ReadLine (Who[Count].Name);      (*PROCEDURE CALL*)
        WRITE ('ENTER DESIRED WEIGHT :');
        READLN (Who[Count].DesiredWeight);
        WRITE ('ENTER CURRENT WEIGHT :');
        READLN(Who[Count].Actual);
        WRITELN;
      END;
  END;
(***)
PROCEDURE Print (VAR Before,Now: Measure);
 VAR Count: INTEGER;
     LP: TEXT;      (*APPLE-IBM ONLY*)
  BEGIN
    REWRITE (LP, 'PRINTER:');      (*APPLE-IBM ONLY*)
    FOR Count:= 1 TO 5 DO
      BEGIN
        WRITELN (LP,'NAME: ',Before[Count].Name,
                 '      NAME: ',Now[Count].Name);
        WRITE (LP,'DESIRED WEIGHT: ',Before[Count].DesiredWeight:5);
        WRITELN (LP,'    DESIRED WEIGHT: ',Now[Count].DesiredWeight:5);
        WRITE (LP,'STARTING WEIGHT:',Before[Count].Actual:5);
        WRITELN (LP,'    CURRENT WEIGHT: ',Now[Count].Actual:5);
        WRITELN (LP);
      END;
      WRITELN (LP,'  ********************************************** ');
      WRITELN (LP);
  END;
(***)
PROCEDURE Update (VAR Now: Measure);
  VAR Count: INTEGER;
  BEGIN
    WRITELN('ENTER CURRENT WEIGHTS FOR THESE PEOPLE');
    FOR Count:= 1 TO 5 DO
      BEGIN
        WRITE (Now[Count].Name,': ');
        READLN (Now[Count].Actual);
      END;
  END;
(*************)
(*MAIN PROGRAM*)
(*************)
BEGIN
  ReadOrig (Orig);          (*PROCEDURE CALL*)
  Current:= Orig;
  Print (Orig,Current);      (*PROCEDURE CALL*)
  FOR Count:= 1 TO 3 DO
    BEGIN
      Update (Current);      (*PROCEDURE CALL*)
      Print (Orig,Current);  (*PROCEDURE CALL*)
    END;
END.
```

Loads 5 records into array Who

Prints the original record Before on the left and record with the current weight, Now, on the right

Places current weight in array Now. Only one field, Actual, is changed.

## 19.4 SKILL DEVELOPMENT EXERCISE

The concept of records has the most direct application when using files. Therefore, only one exercise using a limited number of records will be presented in this lesson. After Lesson 24: File Applications is introduced, the use of records becomes very helpful and will be used extensively.

1. Write a program that contains two procedures as described below:

*Load Procedure*

A load procedure that receives a number from the main program that represents how many records are to be loaded and prompts for the name, hours, and rate to be entered for each record. The procedure will then calculate the wages, social security withheld, and taxes withheld according to the following equations:

Wages = Hours * Rate
Social Security = Wages * .07
Taxes = Wages * .15

Each record will consist of the following fields:

1. Name (packed array of 20 characters)
2. Wages paid (real)
3. Social Security withheld (real)
4. Taxes withheld (real)

A third or fourth procedure may be called to simplify entering the information for the records.

*Print Procedure*

A print procedure that receives the array of records and a code number 1 to 4 from the main program will print information from all records. The code number is used to determine what parts of the records are to be printed. That is:

If code = 1, print Name and Wages
If code = 2, print Name and Social Security withheld
If code = 3, print Name and Taxes withheld
If code = 4, print complete record

The main program will prompt for the number of employees and the printing code.

Display Sample

```
HOW MANY EMPLOYEES? 4

EMPLOYEE 1
NAME: BETTY MACE
HOURS: 40
RATE: 14.50

EMPLOYEE 2
NAME: LISA JUDGE
HOURS: 43
RATE: 13.85

EMPLOYEE 3
NAME: SHANNON RICKER
HOURS: 40
RATE: 11.90

EMPLOYEE 4
NAME: JOSH EARHART
HOURS: 44
RATE: 14.64

ENTER PRINT CODE (1,2,3,4 OR 5 TO STOP): 4

ENTER PRINT CODE (1,2,3,4,OR 5 TO STOP); 2

ENTER PRINT CODE (1,2,3,4 OR 5 TO STOP); 1

ENTER PRINT CODE (1,2,3,4 OR 5 TO STOP); 3

ENTER PRINT CODE (1,2,3,4 OR 5 TO STOP); 5
```

Print Sample

```
EMPLOYEE 1
NAME    : BETTY MACE
WAGES   :  580.00
SSTAXES:   40.60
TAXES   :   87.00

EMPLOYEE 2
NAME    : LISA JUDGE
WAGES   :  595.55
SSTAXES:   41.69
TAXES   :   89.33
        •
        •
        •
```
}   Code 4
    (Full records)

```
EMPLOYEE 1
NAME    : BETTY MACE
SSTAXES:   40.60

EMPLOYEE 2
NAME    : LISA JUDGE
SSTAXES:   41.69
        •
        •
        •
```
}   Code 2
    (Name & Social Sec)

```
EMPLOYEE 1
NAME    : BETTY MACE
WAGES   :  580.00

EMPLOYEE 2
NAME    : LISA JUDGE
WAGES   :  595.55
        •
        •
        •
```
}   Code 1
    (Name & Wages)

```
EMPLOYEE 1
NAME    : BETTY MACE
TAXES   :   87.00

EMPLOYEE 2
NAME    : LISA JUDGE
TAXES   :   89.33
```
}   Code 3
    (Name & Taxes)

# Lesson 20
## SETS

### 20.1 OBJECTIVES

Objectives: 1. To be able to declare and use the set type.
2. To be able to simplify problems by using sets.

### 20.2 SET DECLARATION, UNION, INTERSECTION, AND DIFFERENCE

Sets are a structured data type that is a feature of Pascal which does not appear in the other common programming languages. The concept of sets is the same as in mathematics with a set being a collection of items, numbers, letters, etc.

*Set Declaration and Assignment*

*Example 1* (Using a subset of a predefined set)

```
PROGRAM Example1;                          Predefined integers
TYPE Digits = SET OF 1..9;
VAR Odd,Even,Prime: Digits;

BEGIN


  Odd:= [1,3,5,7,9];
  Even:= [2,4,6,8];
  Prime:= [1,2,3,5,7];



END.
```

Sets must be limited (finite) in size so when working with integers a subset must be specified. In the example, the integers 1 to 9 are the only ones to be considered.

*Example 2* (Using a subset of a predefined set)

```
PROGRAM Example2;
  VAR Vowels: SET OF CHAR;
BEGIN


  Vowels:= ['A','E','I','O','U'];


END.
```

*Example 3* (Using a subset of a User Defined Set)

```
PROGRAM Example3;
  TYPE Days = (Mon,Tues,Wed,Thur,Fri,Sat,Sun);
       DaySet = SET OF Days;
  VAR WeekDay,WeekEnd: DaySet;

BEGIN



  WeekDay:= [Mon,Tues,Wed,Thur,Fri];
  WeekEnd:= [Sat,Sun];


END.
```

*Set Operations*

*Union*

```
GroupA:= [1,4,6] + [3,5,9];
```
The union of two sets is a set that contains the elements that belong to either of the two sets. `GroupA` contains the elements `[1,3,4,5, 6,9]`.

```
GroupB:= ['A','C','D'] + ['E'];
```
Group B contains the elements `['A','C', 'D','E']`.

*Intersection*

```
GroupD:= [1,6,8,9] * [1,2,8]
```
The intersection of two sets is made up of only those elements that belong to both sets. `GroupD` contains the elements `[1,8]`.

```
GroupE:= (['A'..'E'] * ['B','C','D','N']) * ['C'..'F'];
```

The intersection of the sets in parentheses will be determined first (which is `['B','C','D']`) and the intersection of that set and the last set will determine the elements in `GroupE`. `GroupE` contains the elements `['C','D']`.

*Difference*

```
GroupF:= [1,2,3,4] - [1,3,4];
```
The difference of two sets is a set containing all the elements that belong to the first set but not to the second set. `GroupF` contains the element `[2]`.

```
GroupG:= ['A','E','I','O','U'] - ['A'..'M'];
```

`GroupG` contains the elements `['O','U']`.

*Empty Set and Initializing*

GroupH:= [];

When the brackets appear with no listed elements it is an empty or null set. GroupH has been initialized and it contains no elements.

GroupI:= [Mon,Wed,Fri]*[Tues,Thur];     GroupI is an empty set.

GroupJ:= [1,2,3,4] - [1,2,3,4,5,6];     GroupJ is an empty set.

GroupK:= ['D','E','F'] - (['A'..'D'] + ['D','E','F']);

The union of the sets in parentheses is completed first; therefore, all of the elements of the first set are contained in the union and GroupK is an empty set.

*Set Relations*

*Valid relations are* <>, =, >=, <=, >, <

[1,2,3] = [2,3,1] is TRUE

A character, integer, or user defined element that belongs to a set has no special position in that set (a set is unordered). To make it less confusing for the programmer, the elements of a set are usually listed according to the position used in the type declaration statement.

['A','B','C']  =  ['A','B']  is  FALSE

['A','B','C']  <>  ['A','B']  is  TRUE

[1,4]  <  [1,2,3,4]  is  TRUE

[1,2,3,4]  <  [1,2,3,4]  is  FALSE

[]  <  ['A','B']  is  TRUE

['A','B','C']  >=  ['A','B']  is  TRUE

[]  >=  [1,2,3,]  is  FALSE

*Set Membership*

2  IN  [1,2,3]  is  TRUE

5  IN  [1,2,3]  is  FALSE

'B'  IN  ['A','B','C']  is  TRUE

*Using Variables*

```
GroupL:= ['A','B','C'];
GroupJ:= ['C','D','E'];
GroupK:= ['X','Y'];
```

| Statement | Contents of GroupM |
|---|---|
| GroupM:= GroupL * GroupJ; | ['C'] |
| GroupM:= GroupL + GroupJ; | ['A','B','C','D','E'] |
| GroupM:= GroupL * GroupK; | [] |
| GroupM:= GroupL - GroupJ; | ['A','B'] |

*Loading a Set*

```
TYPE Alphabet = SET OF CHAR;
   ~~~~~
   ~~~~~
   ~~~~~
PROCEDURE Load (VAR ChSet: Alphabet);
  VAR Letter: CHAR;
  BEGIN
    ChSet:= [];
    REPEAT
      READ (Letter);
      ChSet:= ChSet + [Letter];
    UNTIL EOLN;
  END;
```

Square brackets are needed to make the item a set before a set operation can be completed.

*Printing a Set*

```
TYPE UniversalSet = SET OF CHAR;
   ~~~~~
   ~~~~~
   ~~~~~
PROCEDURE Print (VAR GroupLetters: UniversalSet);
  VAR Count: CHAR;
  BEGIN
    FOR Count:= 'A' TO 'Z' DO
      IF Count IN GroupLetters THEN
        WRITE (Count,'   ');
    WRITELN;
  END;
```

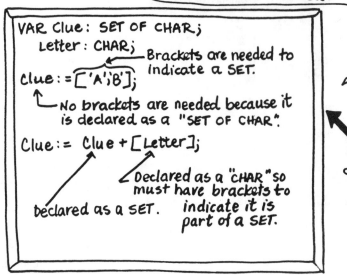

> The square brackets [ ] are used to indicate that a group of numbers, letters, or a variable is a set. If the variable has been declared as a set, no brackets are needed.

```
VAR Clue: SET OF CHAR;
    Letter: CHAR;
Clue := ['A';'B'];        Brackets are needed to
                          indicate a SET.
        No brackets are needed because it
        is declared as a "SET OF CHAR".

Clue := Clue + [Letter];
                          Declared as a "CHAR" so
                          must have brackets to
declared as a SET.        indicate it is
                          part of a SET.
```

## 20.3 DEMONSTRATION PROBLEM

1. An elementary school teacher has a display of letters on the bulletin board which are used for penmanship practice. The teacher would like a program written to complete the following steps.

   a. Enter the letters presently on the bulletin board.
   b. Enter the letters that the teacher wishes to use for the new display.
   c. Display the following information:

      1. A list of letters that are to remain on the bulletin board.
      2. A list of letters that are to be removed from the bulletin board.
      3. A list of additional letters needed to complete the new display.
      4. A list of all the letters that were not used in either group of letters.

   Study this Display Sample for further clarification.

   Display Sample

```
LETTERS IN OLD DISPLAY
PENMANSHIP
LETTERS IN NEW DISPLAY
PRACTICE


* * * * * * * * * * * * * * * * * * * * * * * * * * * * * *

LETTERS TO REMAIN
A E I P
LETTERS TO REMOVE
H M N S
ADDITIONAL LETTERS NEEDED
C R T
LETTERS OF THE ALPHABET NOT USED
B D F G J K L O Q U V W X Y Z
```

ALGORITHM

1. Procedure Load (VAR Set ↑)
   1.1 Loads a set of characters
2. Procedure Print (Set ↓)
   2.1 Prints a set of characters
3. Main Program
   3.1 Prompt for old display
       3.1.1 Call Load (OldDisplay)
   3.2 Prompt for new display
       3.2.1 Call Load (NewDisplay)
   3.3 Prompt for letters to remain
       3.3.1 Assign intersection to WorkSet
       3.3.2 Call Print (WorkSet)
   3.4 Letters to remove
       3.4.1 Assign (OldDisplay − NewDisplay) to WorkSet
       3.4.2 Call Print (WorkSet)
   3.5 Additional letters needed
       3.5.1 Assign (NewDisplay − OldDisplay) to WorkSet
       3.5.2 Call Print (WorkSet)
   3.6 Letters of the alphabet not used
       3.6.1 For Count:= 'A' TO 'Z'
           3.6.1.1 Print count when not in OldDisplay or NewDisplay

```
PROGRAM L20Demo;
  TYPE UniversalSet = SET OF CHAR;
  VAR OldDisplay,NewDisplay,WorkSet: UniversalSet;
      Count: CHAR;
(***)
PROCEDURE Load (VAR ChSet: UniversalSet);
  VAR Letter: CHAR;
  BEGIN
    ChSet:= [];
    REPEAT
      READ (Letter);
      ChSet:= ChSet + [Letter];
    UNTIL EOLN;
  END;
(***)
PROCEDURE Print (VAR GroupLetters: UniversalSet);
  VAR Count: CHAR;
  BEGIN
    FOR Count:= 'A' TO 'Z' DO
      IF Count IN GroupLetters THEN
        WRITE (Count,'   ');
    WRITELN;
  END;
(*************)
(*MAIN PROGRAM*)
(*************)
BEGIN
WRITELN ('LETTERS IN OLD DISPLAY');
  Load (OldDisplay);  (*Procedure Call*)
```

```
WRITELN ('LETTERS IN NEW DISPLAY');
  Load (NewDisplay);  (*Procedure Call*)
WRITELN;
WRITELN (' ****************************************************** ');
WRITELN;
WRITELN ('LETTERS TO REMAIN');
  WorkSet:= NewDisplay * OldDisplay;
  Print (WorkSet);  (*Procedure Call*)
WRITELN ('LETTERS TO REMOVE');
  WorkSet:= OldDisplay - NewDisplay;
  Print (WorkSet);  (*Procedure Call*)
WRITELN ('ADDITIONAL LETTERS NEEDED');
  WorkSet:= NewDisplay - OldDisplay;
  Print (WorkSet);  (*Procedure Call*)
WRITELN ('LETTERS OF THE ALPHABET NOT USED');
  FOR Count:'A' TO 'Z' DO
    IF NOT((Count IN OldDisplay) OR (Count IN NewDisplay)) THEN
      WRITE (Count,' ');
WRITELN;
END.
```

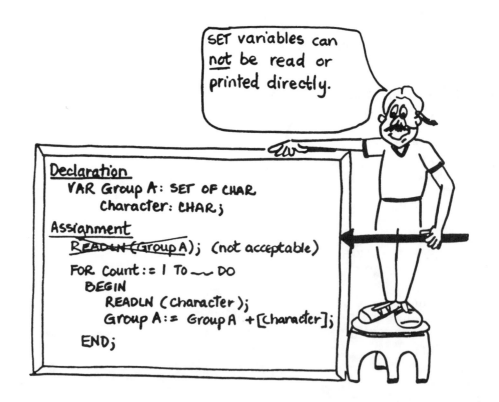

## 20.4 SKILL DEVELOPMENT EXERCISES

1. Write a program that uses sets in printing 5 groups of randomly selected numbers between 1 and 10 inclusive. Each group should contain 10 numbers with no number repeated. Use sets to check if the generated number has already been printed.

Print Sample

```
GROUP 1
   5 10  8  9  1  4  6  3  7  2
GROUP 2
   7  8  1  3  6  9  2 10  4  5
GROUP 3
   6  3 10  2  4  8  5  9  7  1
GROUP 4
   6  3  4  7 10  5  2  1  9  8
GROUP 5
   2  7  5  8  1  9  6  4 10  3
```

2. Modify the program for Problem 1 to print 5 groups of randomly selected letters. Each group should contain 10 letters with no letter repeated.

Print Sample:

```
GROUP 1
   C  M  K  Z  P  N  I  A  S  O
GROUP 2
   V  A  H  M  B  R  Y  X  I  P
GROUP 3
   Y  E  P  V  Z  I  A  G  F  M
GROUP 4
   G  N  D  B  Y  L  Q  I  M  R
GROUP 5
   M  V  D  F  T  E  B  N  A  O
```

3. Write a program to make up worksheets for an elementary teacher. The teacher should be able to enter how many words are to be on the worksheet followed by the actual words. The printout is to contain a numbered column with the words printed with underlines in place of all vowels and a second numbered column with the complete words. Make the column with the complete words far enough to the right so the teacher can have the student cover the answers while completing the worksheet.

Print Sample

```
1.C__MP__T__R          1.COMPUTER
2.T_____CH__R          2.TEACHER
3.ST__D__NT            3.STUDENT
4.TH__NKSG__V__NG      4.THANKSGIVING
5.H__LL__W____N        5.HALLOWEEN
```

4. Write a program that prompts the user to enter a choice between adding characters to a set or deleting characters from a set. The program should print out the resulting set after each alteration. Have the program check the set to determine when it is empty. When the set is empty the program should terminate. See Display Sample for more information.

Display sample

```
REMOVE ALL LETTERS FROM SET TO STOP
ENTER A-ADD OR D-DELETE
?A
ENTER "*" TO TERMINATE
ENTER EACH LETTER ON A SEPARATE LINE
?A
?K
?5
?B
?*

THE SET IS:
5 A B K

ENTER A-ADD OR D-DELETE
?D
ENTER "*" TO TERMINATE
ENTER EACH LETTER ON A SEPARATE LINE
?K
?B
?*

THE SET IS:
5 A

ENTER A-ADD OR D-DELETE
?D
ENTER "*" TO TERMINATE
ENTER EACH LETTER ON A SEPARATE LINE
?A
?5
?*
```

# Lesson 21
# DOUBLE SUBSCRIPTED VARIABLES

## 21.1 OBJECTIVES

Objectives: 1. To learn to declare a variable as a double subscripted variable (matrix).
2. To manipulate and use double subscripted variables.

## 21.2 DECLARING AND MANIPULATING DOUBLE SUBSCRIPTED VARIABLES

Declaring a double subscripted variable

```
TYPE  (1)  = ARRAY[ (2) .. (3) .. (5) ] OF ____;
VAR ____ : (1) ;
```

The only difference between a double subscripted variable and a single subscripted variable is the addition of a second range. A single subscripted variable would only have parts (2) and (3). In a double subscripted variable another range is added. See parts (4) and (5). The subscript limits (2) and (3) are referred to as the row and parts (4) and (5) are referred to as the column. Parts (2),(3),(4), and (5) have the same restrictions as the limits for a single subscripted variable (See page 114). A double subscripted variable is also called a matrix.

|   | COLUMN | | | |
|---|---|---|---|---|
|   | 1 | 2 | 3 | 4 |
| R   1 | 5 | 8 | 6 | 7 |
| O | | | | |
| W   2 | 1 | 9 | 4 | 0 |
| 3 | 2 | 7 | 8 | 6 |
| 4 | 5 | 1 | 0 | 4 |

|   | COLUMN | | | |
|---|---|---|---|---|
|   | 1 | 2 | 3 | 4 |
| R   1 | A(1,1) | A(1,2) | A(1,3) | (1,4) |
| O | | | | |
| W   2 | A(2,1) | A(2,2) | A(2,3) | A(2,4) |
| 3 | A(3,1) | A(3,2) | A(3,3) | A(3,4) |
| 4 | A(4,1) | A(4,2) | A(4,3) | A(4,4) |

Assume the numbers on the left are to be assigned to a double subscripted variable A with 4 rows and 4 columns. The variable names that would be used are illustrated on the right. For example the number 7 in column 2 at left corresponds to the variable A(3,2) in the table at right. This means that A(3,2) would have the value 7. A(2,3) would have the value of 4 and so forth.

Examples

```
TYPE List= ARRAY[1..3,1..5] OF INTEGER;
```
Designates a 3 × 5 matrix of INTEGERS.

```
TYPE Table= ARRAY[1..10,1..25] OF REAL;
```
Designates a 10 × 25 matrix of REALS.

```
TYPE General= ARRAY[1..7,1..3] OF CHAR;
```
Designates a 7 × 3 matrix of CHARacters.

Making assignments to double subscripted variables

*Loading a single element*

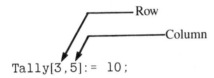

```
Tally[3,5]:= 10;
```

Only one value, 10, would be loaded into one location, row 3 column 5 of the double subscripted variable.

```
Tally[4,1]:= 81;
```

In this case, 81, would be loaded into one location, row 4 column 1 of the double subscripted variable.

*Loading an entire matrix*

```
FOR Row:= 1 TO___DO
  FOR Column:= 1 TO___DO
    READ (_____[Row,Column]);
```

A matrix of the size determined by the numbers in the FOR–TO–DO loops would be loaded in its entirety. If the matrix was 3 by 3 then the computer would load the first location (Row1, Column1), then (Row1, Column2), (Row1, Column3), then (Row2, Column1), (Row2, Column2), etc.

## 21.3 DEMONSTRATION PROBLEM

1. Write a program that completes the following steps:

   a. Loads a 3 × 5 double subscripted variable (matrix) with the following numbers:

   |    |     |   |     |    |
   |----|-----|---|-----|----|
   | 2  | 3   | 1 | −2  | 8  |
   | −1 | 5   | 0 | 6   | 10 |
   | 4  | −3  | 1 | 7   | 11 |

   b. Prints the array.
   c. Interchanges the values stored in column 4 with the values stored in column 1 and prints the resulting matrix.
   d. Multiplies the values in row 3 of the resulting matrix (of part C) by 5 and prints the resulting matrix.

Note: This problem lends itself to 4 procedures.

ALGORITHM (Procedures)

1. Load array
   1.1 Set up loops
   1.2 Read each value
2. Print array
   2.1 Set up loops
   2.2 Print each value
3. Interchange values
   3.1 Set up loop for 3 rows
   3.2 Swap column 4 with column 1
4. Multiply row 3 by 5
   4.1 Set up loop for column 1 to column 5
   4.2 Multiply each value by 5

ALGORITHM (Main Program)

1. Load array
2. Print array
3. Interchange elements
4. Print array
5. Multiply row 3 by 5
6. Print array

Display Sample

```
ENTER NUMBERS
?2 3 1 -2 8
?-1 5 0 6 10
?4 -3 1 7 11
```

Print Sample

| 2 | 3 | 1 | -2 | 8 |
|---|---|---|---|---|
| -1 | 5 | 0 | 6 | 10 |
| 4 | -3 | 1 | 7 | 11 |
| -2 | 3 | 1 | 2 | 8 |
| 6 | 5 | 0 | -1 | 10 |
| 7 | -3 | 1 | 4 | 11 |
| -2 | 3 | 1 | 2 | 8 |
| 6 | 5 | 0 | -1 | 10 |
| 35 | -15 | 5 | 20 | 55 |

```
PROGRAM L21Demo1;
  TYPE ThreeByFive = ARRAY[1..3,1..5] OF INTEGER;
  VAR OurMatrix: ThreeByFive;
      Lp: TEXT;
(***)
PROCEDURE LoadIt (VAR AnyMatrix: ThreeByFive);
  VAR Row, Column: INTEGER;
  BEGIN
    WRITELN ('ENTER NUMBERS');
      FOR Row:= 1 TO 3 DO
        FOR Column:= 1 TO 5 DO
          READ (AnyMatrix[Row,Column]);
      END;
```

Loads a 3 × 5 matrix

```
(***)
PROCEDURE PrintIt (VAR AnyMatrix: ThreeByFive);
  VAR Row, Column: INTEGER;
  BEGIN
    FOR Row:= 1 TO 3 DO
      BEGIN
        FOR Column:= 1 TO 5 DO
          WRITE (Lp,AnyMatrix[Row,Column]:5);
        WRITELN (Lp,' ');
      END;
    WRITELN (Lp, ' ');
  END;
(***)
PROCEDURE Interchange (VAR AnyMatrix: ThreeByFive);
  VAR Row,HoldOne: INTEGER;
  BEGIN
    FOR Row:= 1 TO 3 DO
      BEGIN
        HoldOne:= AnyMatrix[Row,4];
        AnyMatrix[Row,4]:= AnyMatrix[Row,1];
        AnyMatrix[Row,1]:= HoldOne;
      END;
  END;
(***)
PROCEDURE TimesFive (VAR AnyMatrix: ThreeByFive);
  VAR Column: INTEGER;
  BEGIN
    FOR Column:= 1 TO 5 DO
      AnyMatrix[3,Column]:= AnyMatrix[3,Column] * 5;
  END;
(*************)
(*MAIN PROGRAM*)
(*************)
BEGIN
  REWRITE (Lp,'PRINTER:');
  LoadIt (OurMatrix);         (*PROCEDURE CALL*)
  PrintIt (OurMatrix);        (*PROCEDURE CALL*)
  Interchange (OurMatrix);    (*PROCEDURE CALL*)
  PrintIt (OurMatrix);        (*PROCEDURE CALL*)
  TimesFive (OurMatrix);      (*PROCEDURE CALL*)
  PrintIt (OurMatrix);        (*PROCEDURE CALL*)
END.
```

Prints a 3 × 5 matrix

Interchanges column 1 with column 4

Multiplies row 3 by 5

## 21.4 SKILL DEVELOPMENT EXERCISES

1. Write a program that will complete the following steps:

a. Data is given at the right for a 5 × 5 matrix. Load the data into the computer's memory, storing it in a 5 × 5 array, and print out the matrix (array).

Data Sample

| | | | | | |
|---|---|---|---|---|---|
| Row 1 | 1, | 3, | 45, | 89, | 76 |
| Row 2 | 60, | 42, | 47, | 39, | 0 |
| Row 3 | 64, | 21, | 3, | 64, | 35 |
| Row 4 | 78, | 24, | 76, | 69, | 20 |
| Row 5 | 16, | 83, | 91, | 80, | 5 |

b. Interchange the values stored in row 1 and the values stored in row 5 and print the resulting matrix.

Print Sample (Step b)

```
16  83  91  80   5
60  42  47  39   0
64  21   3  64  35
78  24  76  69  20
 1   3  45  89  76
```

c. Print out the sum of the columns as shown in the Print Sample at the right.

Print Sample (Step c)

```
SUM OF COLUMN 1= 219
SUM OF COLUMN 2= 173
SUM OF COLUMN 3= 262
SUM OF COLUMN 4= 341
SUM OF COLUMN 5= 136
```

Print Sample (Step d)

```
 0  83  91  80   0
60   0  47   0   0
64  21   0  64  35
78   0  76   0  20
 0   3  45  89   0
```

d. Zero out both diagonals and print the resulting matrix. (Only one loop is necessary to zero out both diagonals.)

2. The following tables are given to enable you to determine the percent of an employee's gross salary that is to be deducted for federal taxes. (To shorten the practice program only four tax brackets with a maximum of five dependents will be considered.)

Tax Bracket (in percent)

|  |  | (1) | (2) | (3) | (4) |
|---|---|---|---|---|---|
| Number of | 1 | 4 | 6 | 8 | 10 |
| dependents | 2 | 3.5 | 5.5 | 7.1 | 9.2 |
|  | 3 | 3 | 5 | 6.8 | 8.5 |
|  | 4 | 2.5 | 4.5 | 6.4 | 8 |
|  | 5 | 2 | 4.1 | 6 | 7.1 |

Table 1

| Weekly Salary | Tax Bracket |
|---|---|
| 0 – (179.99) | (1) |
| 180– (259.99) | (2) |
| 260– (349.99) | (3) |
| 350– ( up ) | (4) |

Table 2

Write a program that will:

a. Assign the 20 numbers, which indicate the percent to be deducted from gross salary (Table 1 above), into a two-dimensional (5 × 4) array. That is:

```
T1(1,1):= 4;      T1(1,2):= 6;      T1(1,3):= 8;      T1(1,4):= 10;
T1(2,1):= 3.5;    T1(2,2):= 5.5;    T1(2,3):= 7.1;    T1(2,4):= 9.2;
T1(3,1):= 3;      T1(3,2):= 5;      T1(3,3):= 6.8;    T1(3,4):= 8.5;
T1(4,1):= 2.5;    T1(4,2):= 4.5;    T1(4,3):= 6.4;    T1(4,4):= 8;
T1(5,1):= 2;      T1(5,2):= 4.1;    T1(5,3):= 6;      T1(5,4):= 7.1;
```

b. Assign the four numbers that indicate the upper limit or each tax bracket (circled numbers in Table 2 shown above) into a one-dimensional array. Choose a number to replace the 'up' as the top weekly salary for the table. That is:

```
T2(1):= 179.99; T2(2):= 259.99; T2(3):= 349.99; T2(4):= 9E6;
```

c. Process additional data consisting of a person's name, number of dependents, hours worked, and rate of pay (per hour). To simplify the program assume no overtime rate is paid.

d. Print out the name, gross salary, deduction, and net wages for each employee. (Round deductions to the nearest hundredth.)

Data Sample

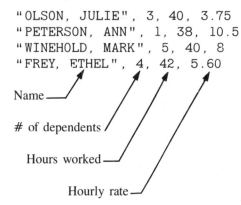

```
"OLSON, JULIE", 3, 40, 3.75
"PETERSON, ANN", 1, 38, 10.5
"WINEHOLD, MARK", 5, 40, 8
"FREY, ETHEL", 4, 42, 5.60
```

Name ———

# of dependents

Hours worked ———

Hourly rate ———

Print Sample

```
NAME                GROSS    DED      NET
OLSON, JULIE        150.00    4.50   145.50
PETERSON, ANN       399.00   39.90   359.10
WINEHOLD, MARK      320.00   19.20   300.80
FREY, ETHEL         235.20   10.58   224.64
```

# Lesson 22
# ARRAYS OF PACKED ARRAYS OF CHARACTERS

## 22.1 OBJECTIVES

Objectives: 1. To learn to declare variables as arrays of packed arrays of characters.
2. To learn to load arrays of packed arrays of characters.
3. To use arrays of packed arrays of characters in alphabetizing.

## 22.2 DECLARING AND MANIPULATING ARRAYS OF PACKED ARRAYS

Declaring a variable as an array of packed arrays

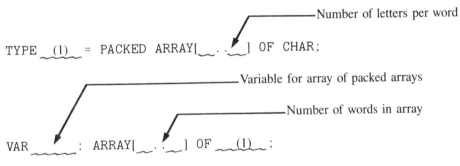

Number of letters per word

TYPE __(1)__ = PACKED ARRAY[__..__] OF CHAR;

Variable for array of packed arrays

Number of words in array

VAR _____ : ARRAY[__..__] OF __(1)__;

### EXPLANATION

A packed array of characters can be thought of as a single array where each element holds several characters. Each element is referred to as a word or string. It follows that a variable can be declared as an array of packed arrays (words).

or

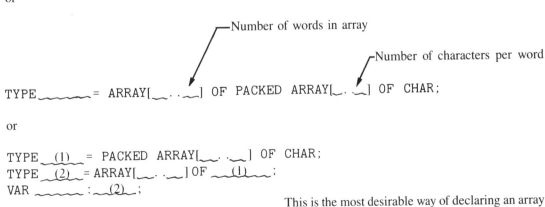

Number of words in array

Number of characters per word

TYPE_____= ARRAY[__..__] OF PACKED ARRAY[__..__] OF CHAR;

or

TYPE __(1)__ = PACKED ARRAY[__..__] OF CHAR;
TYPE __(2)__ = ARRAY[__..__] OF __(1)__;
VAR _____ : __(2)__;

This is the most desirable way of declaring an array of packed arrays when procedures will be used.

183

Assigning a complete array

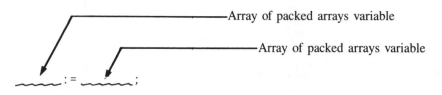

*Example 1*

OldNames:= NewNames;

All words or strings in NewName are transferred to the corresponding locations in OldNames.

Assigning one word of an array

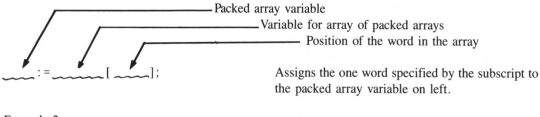

*Example 2*

ThisWord:= List [3];

All characters or letters in the third word of List are transferred to the corresponding character locations in the packed array ThisWord.

Assigning one letter of one word of an array

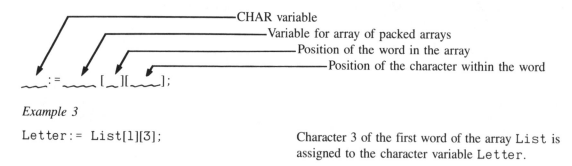

*Example 3*

Letter:= List[1][3];

Character 3 of the first word of the array List is assigned to the character variable Letter.

Other useful assignment statements

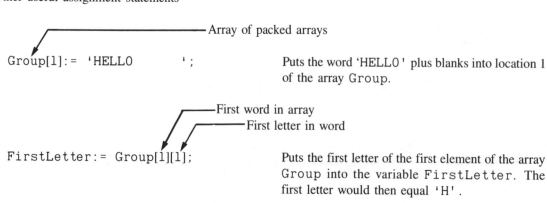

Group[1]:= 'HELLO      ';

Puts the word 'HELLO' plus blanks into location 1 of the array Group.

FirstLetter:= Group[1][1];

Puts the first letter of the first element of the array Group into the variable FirstLetter. The first letter would then equal 'H'.

USEFUL PASCAL STATEMENTS

EXPLANATION

┌─Position of the word in the array
___Group[Z]___

May be used like a regular packed array variable.

*Examples*

┌─────────Procedure to load a packed array

ReadLine (Group [Z]);

One word is passed.

┌─────────Procedure to read a character

ReadLetter (Group [2][1]);

One letter is passed.

┌─────────Procedure to load an array of packed arrays

ReadArray (Group);

Entire array is passed.

WRITELN (Group[2]);

Prints the packed array.

WRITELN (Group [2][1]);

Prints first letter of Group[2].

Note: WRITELN (Group); is not allowed.

## 22.3 DEMONSTRATION PROBLEM

1. A company has requested a program that will group employee names according to the first letter of the last name. The names will be entered with the first name first followed by a space and then the last name. For example "JOSEPH MILLS". See Display and Print Samples below.

Display Sample

Print Sample

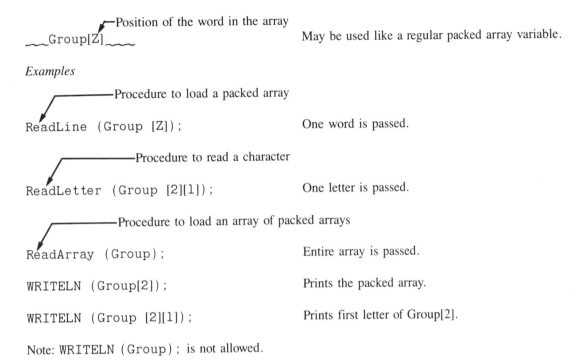

```
HOW MANY NAMES: 13
ENTER NAMES
TOM KROLL
TAMMY JONES
ED KREIGER
HARRY NICHOLS
DAVID BOWMAN
MARCUS JUVICK
BILL BLAIN
JOHN KRAFT
VICKI BRUSH
BETH KUZMA
SUZAN NAGEL
MARY BLEHM
JERROLD NYBO
```

```
DAVID BOWMAN
BILL BLAIN
VICKI BRUSH
MARY BLEHM

TAMMY JONES
MARCUS JUVICK

TOM KROLL
ED KREIGER
JOHN KRAFT
BETH KUZMA

HARRY NICHOLS
SUZAN NAGEL
JERROLD NYBO
```

ALGORITHM (Procedures)

1. Load packed array (Name)
2. Load array of names
   2.1 Count from 1 to number of names
       2.1.1 Call procedure 1
3. Print names by group
   3.1 Loop from A to Z
       3.1.1 Loop through names
               3.1.1.1 Search for blank
               3.1.1.2 Print when character after blank equals counter
       3.1.2 Print blank


ALGORITHM (Main Program)

1. Read number of names
2. Call procedure to load array of names
3. Call procedure to print names


```
PROGRAM L22Demol;
  TYPE StrVar= PACKED ARRAY[1..20] OF CHAR;
       List= ARRAY[1..50] OF StrVar;
  VAR Number: INTEGER;
      Employees: List;
(***)
PROCEDURE ReadLine (VAR Name: StrVar);
  VAR Count: INTEGER;
      Letter: CHAR;
  BEGIN
    Count:= 0;
    Name:= '                    ';
    REPEAT
      READ (Letter);
      Count:= Count + 1;
      Name[Count]:= Letter;
    UNTIL EOLN;
  END;
(***)
PROCEDURE ReadNames (Number: INTEGER; VAR Employees: List);
  VAR Count: INTEGER;
  BEGIN
    WRITELN ('ENTER NAMES');
    FOR Count:= 1 TO Number DO
      ReadLine (Employees[Count]);      (*PROCEDURE CALL*)
  END;
```

Loads a name as a packed array in Name.

Loads array Employee.

```
(***)
PROCEDURE PrintNames (Number: INTEGER; VAR Employees: List);
  VAR Count, Loop: INTEGER;
      AlphaLoop: CHAR;
      Lp: TEXT;                    (*APPLE & IBM*)
      Print: BOOLEAN;
  BEGIN
    REWRITE (Lp,'PRINTER:');   (*APPLE & IBM*)
    Print:= FALSE;
    FOR AlphaLoop:= 'A' TO 'Z' DO
      BEGIN
        FOR Count:= 1 TO Number DO
          FOR Loop:= 1 TO 19 DO
            IF Employees[Count][Loop]=' ' THEN
              IF Employees[Count][Loop+1]= AlphaLoop THEN
                BEGIN
                  WRITELN (Lp, Employees[Count]);
                  Print:= TRUE;
                END;
        IF Print= TRUE THEN
          BEGIN
            WRITELN (LP);
            Print:= FALSE;
          END;
      END;
  END;
(*************)
(*MAIN PROGRAM*)
(*************)
BEGIN
  WRITE ('HOW MANY NAMES: ');
  READLN (Number);
  ReadNames (Number, Employees);     (*PROCEDURE CALL*)
  PrintNames (Number, Employees);    (*PROCEDURE CALL*)
END.
```

Prints names by groups.

## 22.4 SKILL DEVELOPMENT EXERCISES

1. Write a program that will load an array of words and will print the words in the original order in one column and alphabetized in a second column.

Display Sample

```
ENTER WORDS (NONE TO STOP)
DISC
BYTE
PASCAL
ANALOG COMPUTER
CORE
BINARY DIGIT
MICROPROCESSOR
COBOL
CHARACTER
INTEGRATED CIRCUIT
NONE
```

Print Sample

```
DISC                  ANALOG COMPUTER
BYTE                  BINARY DIGIT
PASCAL                BYTE
ANALOG COMPUTER       CHARACTER
CORE                  COBOL
BINARY DIGIT          CORE
MICROPROCESSOR        DISC
COBOL                 INTEGRATED CIRCUIT
CHARACTER             MICROPROCESSOR
INTEGRATED CIRCUIT    PASCAL
```

Hint: Sorting packed arrays is very similar to sorting numbers except that each element of the array is a group of letters. Appendix 6 offers an illustration of how numbers are sorted in a bubble sort. The same logic can be used on packed arrays. Think of each packed array as a single unit (number).

# Lesson 23
# INTRODUCTION TO FILES

**APPLE IBM PC**

## 23.1 OBJECTIVES

Objectives: 1. To be able to store and retrieve information from the disk using data files.
2. To understand the concept of transferring information between the computer and the disk.
3. To use records in file manipulation.

## 23.2 REWRITE, RESET, PUT, GET, CLOSE AND EOF

PASCAL STATEMENT                EXPLANATION

Declaration

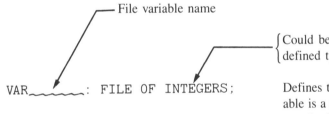

File variable name

Could be REAL, BOOLEAN, STRING, or user defined type

```
VAR        : FILE OF INTEGERS;
```

Defines the variable as a file variable. A file variable is a special type of variable that is used when transferring information between the computer and a disk file.

or, when records are used;

```
TYPE   (1)   = RECORD
          Name: PACKED ARRAY [1..20] OF CHAR;
          Number: INTEGER;
       END;
VAR      :FILE OF   (1)  ;
```

The record structure is used when more than one type of item is to be placed into the file.

File variable name

File Variable Assignment

Examples

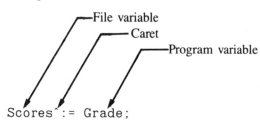

Whenever there is to be an exchange of information to or from the file variable the caret is used. In the examples, `Scores` is the file variable and the program variables are `Grade` and `Single-Grade`.

```
                        Program variable
                          File variable
                          Caret

SingleGrade:= Scores^;
```

or, when records are used:

```
                    File variable
                    The caret follows the file variable name
                    Field identifier

HomeFile^.Name:= 'KENNY BAKER      ';
```

```
      Packed array variable

WhosName:= HomeFile^.Name;
```

The first statement assigns the constant on the right to the Name field of the file variable. This file would have been declared as a file of records with `Name` as one of the field identifiers. The second statement assigns the contents of the Name field of the file variable `HomeFile` to the variable `WhosName`.

Sending Information to a File

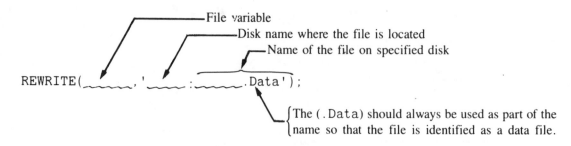

```
                    File variable
                    Disk name where the file is located
                    Name of the file on specified disk

REWRITE(_____,'_____:_____.Data');
```

The (.Data) should always be used as part of the name so that the file is identified as a data file.

*Examples*

```
REWRITE(Scores,'APPLE1:ClassRec.Data');
REWRITE(Withhold,'TaxDisk:SocialSoc.Data');
```

The REWRITE statement assigns the file variable to a specific disk file. It also clears the previous contents of the file (if any). In the first example the file ClassRec is stored on the APPLE1 disk and when the information is sent to the disk it will be accessed through the variable Scores. No data is retrieved from the disk by the REWRITE statement.

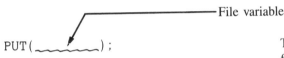 ——————File variable

```
PUT(_____);
```

The PUT statement transfers information from the file variable to the file on the disk. Subsequent PUT statements place the information at the end of the existing information in the file.

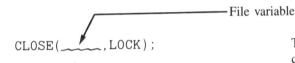 ——————File variable

```
CLOSE(_____,LOCK);
```

The word LOCK in the CLOSE statement will cause the current file name to be placed in the directory of the appropriate disk. It also places an end-of-file marker after the last data item that was placed in the file.

Sending Information to a File (Summary)

```
TYPE RecStruct = RECORD
        ID:_____;
        Ave:_____;
     END;
VAR FlVar: FILE OF RecStruct;

BEGIN

   REWRITE (FlVar,'APPLE1: DiskFlName.Data');


   FlVar^.ID:= _____;
   FlVar^.Ave:= _____;
   PUT (FlVar);

   CLOSE(FlVar,LOCK);
END.
```

These assignments can be made in many ways.

Note: This example shows how a single record would be transferred to a file. Normally more than one record is transferred, this is illustrated in the demonstration problem.

Retrieving Information from a Disk

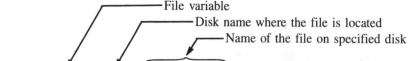

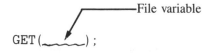

┌────────File variable
│    ┌───────Disk name where the file is located
│    │    ┌──────Name of the file on specified disk
RESET(_____,'_____:_____.Data');

The RESET statement assigns the file variable to a specific disk file. It is used when opening an existing file for the purpose of retrieving information. When executed, the RESET statement sets the pointer to the beginning of the 1st item, retrieves the 1st item in the file, and moves the pointer to the beginning of the 2nd item.

*Examples*

```
RESET(Scores,'APPLE1:ClassRec.Data');
RESET(Withhold,'TaxDisk:SocialSoc.Data');
```

In the first example data information will be retrieved from file ClassRec which is located on the APPLE1 disk. The file variable Scores will be used to transfer the information.

┌────────File variable
GET(_____);

The GET statement transfers the next data item from the disk to the file variable.

Note:  The file variables used to retrieve information must be of the same type as those used when sending the information to the file, but they do not have to be the same name.

Retrieving Information from a Disk (Summary)

```
TYPE DefRec = RECORD
        Ident:_____;
        Average:_____;
     END;

VAR WorkVar: FILE OF DefRec;

BEGIN

   RESET (WorkVar,'APPLE1.DiskFilName.Data');
                    ┌───Retrieves second item.
   GET (WorkVar);
   WRITELN (WorkVar^.Ident,WorkVar^.Average);


   CLOSE(WorkVar);
END.
```

The information in WorkVar can be handled in many ways.

Note:  This example shows how a single record would be retrieved from a file. Normally more than one record is retrieved, this is illustrated in the demonstration problem.

End of File

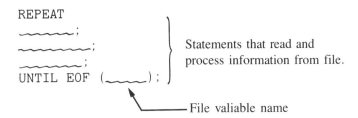

```
REPEAT
    ~~~~~;
    ~~~~~;          Statements that read and
    ~~~~~;          process information from file.
UNTIL EOF (~~~~);
```

File valiable name

The EOF (end-of-file) is used in a loop such as a REPEAT–UNTIL or a WHILE–DO loop to terminate reading from the disk. The EOF is a Boolean expression that becomes true when the end of the file is reached.

Using the WITH statement.

File Variable

```
WITH ~~~^ DO
```

The WITH statement allows the program to make use of a variable to type RECORD. It automatically attaches the record name to any field name within the body of the WITH–DO statement.

Example

```
TYPE DataStruct = RECORD
        Name:~~~~~;
        Address:~~~~~;
        SocialSec:~~~~~;
        Wages:~~~;
    END;
VAR Employee: DataStruct;
~~~~~
BEGIN
    ~~~~~

    ~~~~~
    WITH Employee^ DO
      BEGIN
        READLN (Name);
        READLN (Address);
        READLN (SocialSec);
        READLN (Wage);
        ~~~~~
      END;
    ~~~~~
    ~~~~~
END.
```

Without the WITH–DO statement the following would have to be used:
```
    READLN (Employee^.Name);
    READLN (Employee^.Address);
    etc.
```
Notice the placement of the caret.

## 23.3 DEMONSTRATION PROBLEM

1. A file is to contain records consisting of the ID number and name of students in a certain classroom. Write two programs as indicated below.

The first program should receive input for the student's ID number and name and transfer the information to a disk file. A negative ID number will signal the end of the input and should not be part of the data file.

Display Sample

```
ENTER DATA (-ID TO STOP)
ID: 1000
NAME: SARAH MANNEL
ID: 1300
NAME: CAMI BOLZ
ID: 2350
NAME: PETE BUSHMAN
ID: 3000
NAME: MARI ANDERSON
ID: 3030
NAME: BETHANY MAHONY
ID: -1
FILE HAS BEEN LOADED
```

```
PROGRAM L23LFile;
TYPE Account = RECORD
        Id: INTEGER;
        Name: STRING;
      END;
VAR FileVar: FILE OF Account;
    Count: INTEGER;
BEGIN
  REWRITE (FileVar,'Pas:DemoFile.Data');
  WRITELN ('ENTER DATA (-ID TO STOP)');
  WRITE ('ID: '); READLN (FileVar^.Id);
  WHILE FileVar^.Id >= 0 DO
    WITH FileVar^ DO
      BEGIN
        WRITE ('NAME: '); READLN(Name);
        PUT (FileVar);
        WRITE ('ID: '); READLN (Id);
      END;
  CLOSE (FileVar,LOCK);
  WRITELN ('FILE HAS BEEN LOADED');
END.
```

The second program should retrieve the information from the file created by the first program. An EOF function should be used to detect the end of the file.

Display Sample

```
  1000    SARAH MANNEL
  1300    CAMI BOLZ
  2350    PETE BUSHMAN
  3000    MARI ANDERSON
  3030    BETHANY MAHONY
LIST COMPLETE
```

```
PROGRAM L23PFile;
TYPE PrintRec = RECORD
        Ident: INTEGER;
        Name: STRING;
        END;
VAR Accounts: FILE OF PrintRec;
BEGIN
  RESET (Accounts,'Pas:DemoFile.Data');
  REPEAT
    WITH Accounts^ DO
      WRITELN (Ident:6,'       ',Name);
    GET (Accounts);
  UNTIL EOF (Accounts);
  WRITELN ('LIST COMPLETE');
  CLOSE (Accounts);
END.
```

Prints
Accounts^ .Ident
Accounts^ .Name
for each record

## 23.4 SKILL DEVELOPMENT EXERCISES

1. A bank's accounting department wants to have a program written to create a file consisting of each of the bank customers' names and the total value of three types of assets each customer has on deposit. The program should contain at least two procedures.

The first procedure should:

a. Accept data consisting of the customer's name, his balance in savings, his balance in checking, and the amount invested in certificates of deposit.

b. Create a file consisting of the customer's name and the total of the three types of savings.

| Record Sample | Name | Total assets on deposit |
|---|---|---|

The second procedure should:

a. Use the file created by the first procedure to print out a list of the names and the total savings for all the customers having total assets of over two hundred dollars on deposit.

b. Print the heading and a signal that the list is complete, as shown in the Print Sample below.

Data Sample

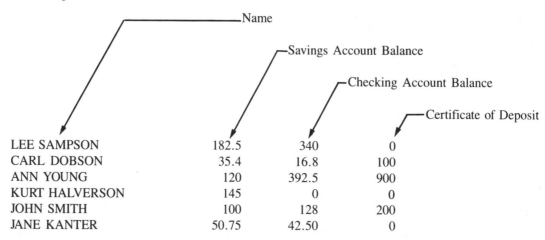

|  | Name | Savings Account Balance | Checking Account Balance | Certificate of Deposit |
|---|---|---|---|---|
| LEE SAMPSON | 182.5 | 340 | 0 | |
| CARL DOBSON | 35.4 | 16.8 | 100 | |
| ANN YOUNG | 120 | 392.5 | 900 | |
| KURT HALVERSON | 145 | 0 | 0 | |
| JOHN SMITH | 100 | 128 | 200 | |
| JANE KANTER | 50.75 | 42.50 | 0 | |

Print Sample

```
**BALANCES OVER $200**

   NAME           BALANCE

LEE SAMPSON        522.50
ANN YOUNG         1412.50
JOHN SMITH         428.00

**LIST COMPLETE**
```

2. The election officers of a certain voter registration district in Billings, Montana have contracted with you to write programs for printing mailing labels. To get the project started you are to write two programs.

a. The first program is to load the voter information into a data file. See the Record Sample.

| Record Sample | Name | Street Address | Precinct # | Party Affiliation |
|---|---|---|---|---|
| | | | | |

Data Sample

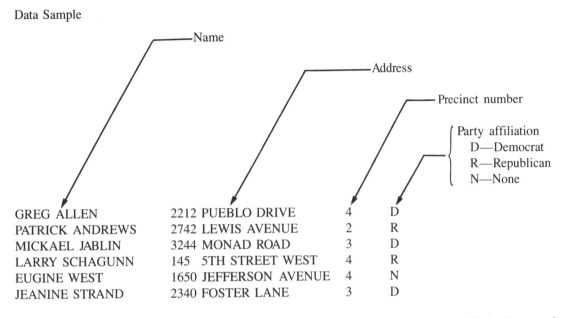

| Name | Address | Precinct number | Party affiliation<br>D—Democrat<br>R—Republican<br>N—None |

GREG ALLEN          2212 PUEBLO DRIVE         4      D
PATRICK ANDREWS     2742 LEWIS AVENUE         2      R
MICKAEL JABLIN      3244 MONAD ROAD           3      D
LARRY SCHAGUNN      145  5TH STREET WEST      4      R
EUGINE WEST         1650 JEFFERSON AVENUE     4      N
JEANINE STRAND      2340 FOSTER LANE          3      D

b. The second program is to print mailing labels for all those voters belonging to a specified subgroup of the voters in the file. This subgroup of voters could belong to a certain party or have a certain precinct number. The user is to input the desired characteristic (of the subgroup to be printed) at the beginning of the program run. See Run Samples.

*First Run Sample*

Display Sample

Print Sample

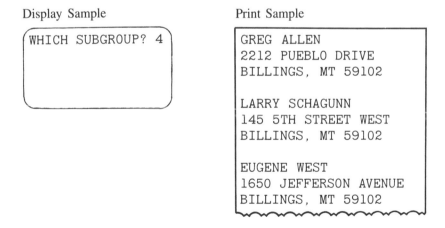

```
WHICH SUBGROUP? 4
```

```
GREG ALLEN
2212 PUEBLO DRIVE
BILLINGS, MT 59102

LARRY SCHAGUNN
145 5TH STREET WEST
BILLINGS, MT 59102

EUGENE WEST
1650 JEFFERSON AVENUE
BILLINGS, MT 59102
```

*Second Run Sample*

Display Sample

```
WHICH SUBGROUP? R
```

Print Sample

```
PATRICK ANDREWS
2742 LEWIS AVENUE
BILLINGS, MT 59102

LARRY SCHAGUNN
145 5TH STREET WEST
BILLINGS, MT 59102
```

## 23.5 REWRITE, RESET, AND CLOSE

Objectives: 1. To be able to store and retrieve information from the disk using data files.
2. To understand the concept of transferring information between the computer and the disk.
3. To use records in file manipulation.

PASCAL STATEMENTS                    EXPLANATION

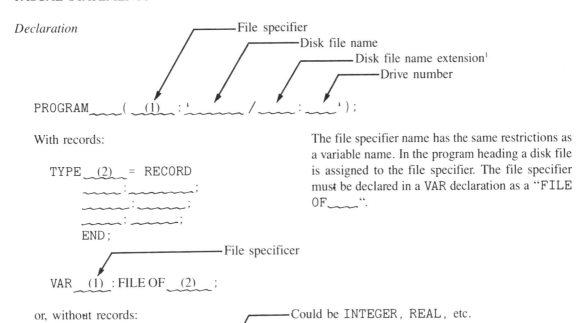

*Declaration*

File specifier
Disk file name
Disk file name extension[1]
Drive number

PROGRAM ____ ( __(1)__ : ' _____ / _____ : _____ ' ) ;

With records:

The file specifier name has the same restrictions as a variable name. In the program heading a disk file is assigned to the file specifier. The file specifier must be declared in a VAR declaration as a "FILE OF____".

TYPE __(2)__ = RECORD
_____ : _____ ;
_____ : _____ ;
_____ : _____ ;
END ;

File specificer

VAR __(1)__ : FILE OF __(2)__ ;

or, without records:                    Could be INTEGER, REAL, etc.

VAR ____ (!) ___ : FILE OF INTEGER;

Sending Information to a File

File specifier

REWRITE ( _____ ) ;

The REWRITE statement clears out any previous information in the file, designated by the file specifier, and opens it for writing.

File specifier

Variable declared as same type as file.

WRITE ( ____ , ____ ) ;

The WRITE statement sends the contents of the variable to the disk file. Subsequent WRITE statements place the information at the end of the existing information in the file.

---

[1] The extension is not required, but if 3 letters are used the directory listing is more explanatory. 'Fil' has been used as the extension in this book.

TRS–80

File specifier

CLOSE ( _____ ) ;

The CLOSE statement will close the file designated by the file specifier. If no file specifier is used then all open files are closed.

Sending Information to a File (Summary)

```
PROGRAM Example1 (FlVar:'DiskFile/Fil:1');
  TYPE RecStruct = RECORD
          ID:_____;
          Ave:_____;
      END;
  VAR FlVar: FILE OF RecStruct;
      ProgVar: RecStruct;

BEGIN

  REWRITE (FlVar);

  ProgVar.ID:=_____;
  ProgVar.Ave:=_____;
  WRITE (FlVar, ProgVar);

  CLOSE (FlVar);
END.
```

In this example the program variable ProgVar must be declared as the same type as the file specifier FlVar.

Retrieving Information from a Disk

File specifier

RESET ( _____ ) ;

The RESET statement opens the file specified by the file specifier. Reading will begin at the first record.

File specifier

Variable declared as same type as file

READ ( ____ , ____ ) ;

The READ statement will transfer the current record from the disk to the program variable. Subsequent READ statements will transfer the records from the disk in the order that they appear on the disk.

CLOSE ( ____ ) ;

A file which has been opened should be closed when the transfer of information has been completed.

Retrieving Information from a Disk (Summary)

```
PROGRAM Example2 (OurFile:'DiskFile/Fil:l');
  TYPE RecStruct = RECORD
          ID:~~~~~ ;
          AVE:~~~~;
        END;
  VAR OurFile: FILE OF RecStruct;
      ProgVar: RecStruct;

BEGIN

  RESET (OurFile);


  READ (OurFile, ProgVar);
  WRITELN (ProgVar.ID,' HAS ',ProgVar.Ave,' PERCENT');

  CLOSE (OurFile);
END.
```

Stopping Signal

Example

```
PROGRAM Example3 (TheFile:'AnyName/Fil:l');
  TYPE RecStruct = RECORD
          ID: INTEGER;
          JobCode: INTEGER;
  VAR TheFile: FILE OF RecStruct;
      Employ: RecStruct;

BEGIN

  REWRITE (TheFile);


  REPEAT
    READLN (Employ.ID,Employ.JobCode);     ⎫
    WRITE (TheFile,Employ);                ⎬ Loads file
  UNTIL Employ.ID < 0;                      ⎭



  RESET (TheFile);

  READ (TheFile,Employ);                    ⎫
  REPEAT                                    ⎪
    WRITELN (Employ.ID:5,Employ.JobCode:7);  ⎬ Reads and Prints file
    READ (TheFile,Employ);                  ⎪
  UNTIL Employ.ID < 0;                      ⎭

END.
```

## 23.6 DEMONSTRATION PROBLEM

1. A file is to contain records consisting of the ID number and name of students in a certain classroom. Write two programs as indicated below.

The first program should receive input for the student's ID number and name and transfer the information to a disk file. A negative ID number will signal the end of the input and should be used as the stopping signal in the file.

Display Sample

```
ENTER DATA (- ID TO STOP)
ID: ?1000
NAME: SARAH MANNEL
ID: ?1300
NAME: ?CAMI BOLZ
ID: ?2350
NAME: ?PETE BUSHMAN
ID: ?3000
NAME: ?MARI ANDERSON
ID: ?3030
NAME: ?BETHANY MAHONY
ID: ?-1
NAME: ?NONE
FILE HAS BEEN LOADED
```

```
PROGRAM L23Demo1L (FileVar: 'L23D1/FIL:1');
  TYPE StrVar= PACKED ARRAY[1..20] OF CHAR;
      Account = RECORD
         Id: INTEGER;
         Name: StrVar;
       END;
  VAR FileVar: FILE OF Account;
      ProgVar: Account;
      Count: INTEGER;
(***)
PROCEDURE ReadLine (VAR Name: StrVar);
  VAR Count: INTEGER;
  BEGIN
    Name:= '                    ';
    Count:= 1;
    REPEAT
      READ (Name[Count]);    (*TRS-80 ONLY*)
      Count:= Count + 1;
    UNTIL EOLN;
  END;
```

```
(*************)
(*MAIN PROGRAM*)
(*************)
BEGIN
  REWRITE (FileVar);
  WRITELN ('ENTER DATA (- ID TO STOP)');
  ProgVar.Id:= 0;
  WHILE ProgVar.Id <= 0 DO
    BEGIN
      WRITE ('ID: '); READLN (ProgVar.Id);
      WRITE ('NAME: ');
      ReadLine (ProgVar.Name);   (*PROCEDURE CALL*)
      WRITE (FileVar, ProgVar); (*SENDS RECORD TO DISK*)
    END;
  CLOSE (FileVar);
  WRITELN ('FILE HAS BEEN LOADED');
END.
```

The second program should retrieve the information from the file created by the first program. Information should be read until the stopping signal is encountered. The stopping signal should not be printed.

Display Sample

```
┌─────────────────────────────────┐
│   1000     SARAH MANNEL          │
│   1300     CAMI BOLZ             │
│   2350     PETE BUSHMAN          │
│   3000     MARI ANDERSON         │
│   3030     BETHANY MAHONY        │
│ LIST COMPLETE                    │
└─────────────────────────────────┘
```

```
PROGRAM L23Demo1P (FileVar: 'L23D1/FIL:1');
  TYPE Account= RECORD
         Id: INTEGER;
         Name: PACKED ARRAY[1..20] OF CHAR;
       END;
  VAR FileVar: FILE OF Account;
      ProgVar: Account;
BEGIN
  RESET (FileVar);
  READ (FileVar, ProgVar);
  WHILE ProgVar.Id >= 0 DO
    BEGIN
      WRITELN (ProgVar.Id:6,'    ',ProgVar.Name);
      READ (FileVar, ProgVar);
    END;
  WRITELN ('LIST COMPLETE');
  CLOSE (FileVar);
END.
```

## 23.7 SKILL DEVELOPMENT EXERCISES

1. A bank's accounting department wants to have a program written to create a file consisting of each of the bank's customers' names and the total value of three types of assets each customer has on deposit. The program should contain at least two procedures.

The first procedure should:

a. Accept data consisting of the customer's name, his balance in savings, his balance in checking, and the amount invested in certificates of deposit.
b. Create a file consisting of the customer's name and the total of the three types of savings.

| Record Sample | Name | Total assets on deposit |
|---|---|---|

The second procedure should:

a. Use the file created by the first procedure to print out a list of the names and the total savings for all the customers having total assests of over two hundred dollars on deposit.
b. Print the heading and a signal that the list is complete, as shown in the Print Sample below.

Data sample

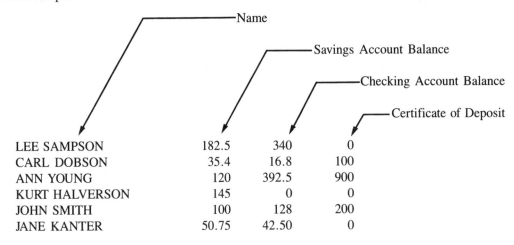

| | Name | Savings Account Balance | Checking Account Balance | Certificate of Deposit |
|---|---|---|---|---|
| LEE SAMPSON | 182.5 | 340 | 0 | |
| CARL DOBSON | 35.4 | 16.8 | 100 | |
| ANN YOUNG | 120 | 392.5 | 900 | |
| KURT HALVERSON | 145 | 0 | 0 | |
| JOHN SMITH | 100 | 128 | 200 | |
| JANE KANTER | 50.75 | 42.50 | 0 | |

Print Sample

```
**BALANCES OVER $200**

   NAME        BALANCE

LEE SAMPSON     522.50
ANN YOUNG      1412.50
JOHN SMITH      428.00

**LIST COMPLETE**
```

2. The election officers of a certain voter registration district in Billings, Montana have contracted with you to write programs for printing mailing labels. To get the project started you are to write two programs.

   a. The first program is to load the voter information into a data file. See the Record Sample.

| Record Sample | Name | Street Address | Precinct # | Party Affiliation |
|---|---|---|---|---|

Data Sample

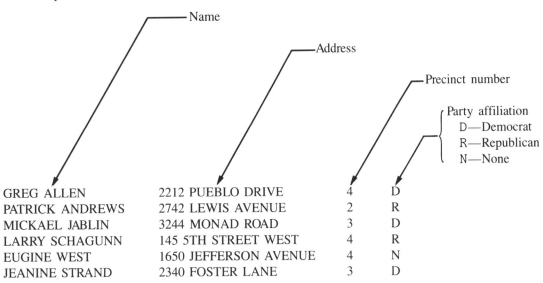

| | | | |
|---|---|---|---|
| GREG ALLEN | 2212 PUEBLO DRIVE | 4 | D |
| PATRICK ANDREWS | 2742 LEWIS AVENUE | 2 | R |
| MICKAEL JABLIN | 3244 MONAD ROAD | 3 | D |
| LARRY SCHAGUNN | 145 5TH STREET WEST | 4 | R |
| EUGINE WEST | 1650 JEFFERSON AVENUE | 4 | N |
| JEANINE STRAND | 2340 FOSTER LANE | 3 | D |

   b. The second program is to print mailing labels for all those voters belonging to a specified subgroup of the voters in the file. This subgroup of voters could belong to a certain party or have a certain precinct number. The user is to input the desired characteristic (of the subgroup to be printed) at the beginning of the program run. See Run Samples.

*First Run Sample*

Display Sample

```
WHICH SUBGROUP? 4
```

Print Sample

```
GREG ALLEN
2212 PUEBLO DRIVE
BILLINGS, MT 59102

LARRY SCHAGUNN
145 5TH STREET WEST
BILLINGS, MT 59102

EUGENE WEST
1650 JEFFERSON AVENUE
BILLINGS, MT 59102
```

*Second Run Sample*

Display Sample                    Print Sample

```
WHICH SUBGROUP? R
```

```
PATRICK ANDREWS
2742 LEWIS AVENUE
BILLINGS, MT 59102

LARRY SCHAGUNN
145 5TH STREET WEST
BILLINGS, MT 59102
```

# Lesson 24
# APPLICATIONS OF FILES

## 24.1 OBJECTIVE

Objective: 1. To gain experience in using data files.

## 24.2 SKILL DEVELOPMENT EXERCISES

1. The accounting department of the local bank wants to have a program written that will handle updating its customers' checking accounts. Only previous balance, drafts, and new balance are to be considered.

The program is to:

a. Request the user to input data containing the customer's name, previous balance, and the amount of each check written. A negative number is to signal the end of the checks listed for that account. The word NONE is to signal that all accounts have been entered.
b. Determine the new balance.
c. Print (for the customer) a form containing the customer's name, previous balance, amount of each check written, and the new balance. See the Print Sample.
d. Store in a file records containing each customer's name and new balance.
e. Read from the file created in (d) above and print, for the bank, a list of all the bank's checking account customers and their new balances. See the Print Sample.

Display Sample

```
ENTER DATA
NAME: JOHN FOSTER
BALANCE: 1285.42
CHECKS: 75.60 23.34 200 -1

NAME: ROBERT HANLEY
BALANCE: 400
CHECKS: 120.35 -1

NAME: VAUGHN THOMPSON
BALANCE: 480.92
CHECKS: 26 134.06 45 28.37 -1

NAME:NONE
BALANCE: 0
```

Print Sample

```
            **CUSTOMER INFORMATION**

JOHN FOSTER                 PREVIOUS BAL. $ 1285.42
     CHECKS $  75.60
            $  23.34
            $ 200.00
                            NEW BALANCE $  986.48
--------------------------------
ROBERT HANLEY               PREVIOUS BAL. $  400.00
     CHECKS $ 120.35
                            NEW BALANCE $  279.65
--------------------------------
VAUGHN THOMPSON             PREVIOUS BAL. $  480.92
     CHECKS $  26.00
            $ 134.06
            $  45.00
            $  28.37
                            NEW BALANCE $  247.49
--------------------------------
            **BANK INFORMATION**

NAME                 BALANCE
JOHN FOSTER          986.48
ROBERT HANLEY        279.65
VAUGHN THOMPSON      247.49
```

2. Your family has purchased a personal computer and you are to write programs to keep stock records. To get the project started, you are to write two programs. The first program is to complete the following steps:

   a. Request the user to enter data as shown in the Display Sample.
   b. Create a data file in which each record is to contain the same information as in the Display Sample. See Record Sample.
   c. Print a list of the stocks, their values, and the total value of the portfolio. See the Print Sample.

Display Sample

```
ENTER DATA
DESCRIPTION: GTIRE
# OF SHARES (SPACE) PRICE (SPACE) SELLING POINT
100   19.25   30

DESCRIPTION: TEXTRON
# OF SHARES (SPACE) PRICE (SPACE) SELLING POINT)
25   21.125   28

DESCRIPTION: IBM
# OF SHARES (SPACE) PRICE (SPACE) SELLING POINT
18   58.125   100

DESCRIPTION: AVON
# OF SHARES (SPACE) PRICE (SPACE) SELLING POINT
40   24.5   35

DESCRIPTION: BURRGH
# OF SHARES (SPACE) PRICE (SPACE) SELLING POINT
100   33.875   52

DESCRIPTION: NONE
```

Record Sample

```
TYPE _____ = RECORD
        StockAbb: PACKED ARRAY [1..15] OF CHAR;
        NumOfShares: REAL;
        PurPrice: REAL;
        SellPoint: REAL;
      END;
```

Print Sample

```
STOCK      NO.       PURCHASE  PURCHASE
ABBREV.    SHARES    PRICE     VALUE

GTIRE      100       19.250    1925.00
TEXTRON    25        21.125     528.13
IBM        18        58.125    1046.25
AVON       40        24.500     980.00
BURRGH     100       33.875    3387.50

TOTAL PURCHASED VALUE $ 7866.88
```

The second program is to complete the following steps:

a. Read the file to obtain the portfolio information.
b. Request input, as shown in the Display Sample, to obtain the most recently quoted price on each stock in the portfolio.
c. Print out a listing of the stocks, their new values using the quoted price, and a new total portfolio value. See the Print Sample.
d. Print a selling list which contains only those stocks that have exceeded the selling point. See the Print Sample to determine what information is to be included on the selling list printout.

Note: Profit = (Quoted Price − Purchase Price) * No. of Shares

Display Sample

```
ENTER STOCK QUOTES
GTIRE? 25.5
TEXTRON? 30.125
IBM? 102.75
AVON? 38
BURRGH? 41.875
```

Names are retrieved from the file and are provided as prompts.

Print Sample

```
                         **PORTFOLIO**

STOCK          NO.            QUOTED         VALUE
ABBREV.        SHARES         PRICE

GTIRE          100             25.500        2550.00
TEXTRON         25             30.125         753.13
IBM             18            102.750        1849.50
AVON            40             38.000        1520.00
BURRGH         100             41.875        4187.50

TOTAL VALUE $ 10860.13
----------------------------------------------------------
                        **SELLING LIST**

STOCK          PUR.           SELL           QUOTED        POTENTIAL
ABBREV.        PRICE          POINT          PRICE         PROFIT

TEXTRON        21.125          28             30.125        225.00
IBM            58.125         100            102.750        803.25
AVON           24.500          35             38.000        540.00

TOTAL POTENTIAL PROFIT $ 1568.25
```

# Appendix I
# APPLE OPERATING SYSTEM

**APPLE**

APPLE1 (Drive 1)
APPLE2 (Drive 2)
(APPLE2 must be in Drive 2 when compiling)

```
Command: E(dit, R(un, F(ile, C(comp, L(ink, X(ecute, A(ssem, D(ebug?
```

⟨For extended list type ?⟩

```
Command: U(ser restart, I(nitialize, H(alt, S(wap, M(ake exec
```

A brief illustration or discussion about the commands that are underlined above will be given in this appendix. These commands are the ones most commonly used and are needed to complete the assignments in this text. Consult the User's Manual for more complete explanations.

### EDITOR

Type E while at the Command level to execute the Editor program. A list of the options is then displayed. The options underlined are the ones most commonly used and will be the only ones discussed in this text.

```
)Edit: A(djust C(py D(lete F(ind I(nsrt J(mp R(place Q(uit X(chng Z(ap
```

*Adjust Alignment* (Adjust)

When a line is to move left or right to obtain a new alignment the A(djst option may be used.

```
    E(dit ◀──── If not in Editor
        ⟨position cursor at the beginning of line to move⟩
        A(djst
        ⟨press (◀,▶) to adjust line⟩
        ⟨press (ctrl L) to adjust following line the same number of spaces⟩
        ⟨press (ctrl O) to adjust preceding line the same number of spaces⟩
        ⟨ctrl C⟩ to accept, ⟨Esc⟩ to reject
        May be repeated as many times as necessary
        Q(uit ◀──── When no more editing is necessary
        U(pdate
```

211

*Delete Characters* (Delete)

A program that is in the workfile may have to be altered by deleting characters.

```
E(dit ◄———— If not in the Editor
    〈position cursor (return, ◄,►)〉
    D(elete
    〈type (→) to delete characters〉
    〈ctrl C〉 to accept deletes, 〈Esc〉 to reject deletes
    May be repeated as many times as necessary
    Q(uit ◄———— When no more editing is to be completed
    U(pdate
```

*Delete a Line* (Delete)

A complete line can be deleted, when in the D(elete mode, by pressing the return key. It is not necessary to delete a single character at a time.

```
E(dit ◄———— If not in the Editor
    〈position at 1st character of line to be deleted〉
    D(elete
    〈return〉◄———— Deletes a line
    〈return〉◄———— Each return deletes an additional line
    〈ctrl C〉 to accept deletes, 〈Esc〉 to reject deletes
    May be repeated as many times as necessary
    Q(uit ◄———— When no more editing is to be completed
    U(pdate
```

*Type in a Program* (Insert)

Before a program can be typed into the computer the system workfile may have to be cleared. *Clear System Workfile* (see the Filer section of this appendix) is used to accomplish this task.

```
E(dit ◄———— If not in the Editor
    I(nsert
    〈Type program〉
    〈ctrl C〉◄———— Exits from input mode
    Q(uit ◄———— When no editing is needed
    U(pdate
```

*Insert Characters* (Insert)

A program that is in the workfile may have to be altered by inserting additional characters.

```
E(dit ◄————If not in the Editor
    〈Position cursor (return, ◄,►)〉
    I(nsert
    〈type characters〉
    〈ctrl C〉 to accept inserts, 〈Esc〉 to reject inserts
    May be repeated as many times as necessary
    Q(uit ◄———— When no more editing is to be completed
    U(pdate
```

*Exchange Characters* (Exchange)

When consecutive characters are to be changed the X(chng option can be executed. For example: Program is exchanged for PROGRAM or UNIT1 is changed to Unit2.

> E(dit ◄———— If not in Editor
> ⟨Position cursor (return, ◄-,-►)⟩
> X(chng
> ⟨the character under the cursor will be⟩
> ⟨replaced by a typed character⟩
> ⟨ctrl C⟩ to accept exchange, ⟨Esc⟩ to reject exchange
> May be repeated as many times as necessary
> Q(uit ◄———— When no more editing is to be completed
> U(pdate

*Cursor Control*

In the preceding examples only the (return, ◄-,-►) cursor controls were mentioned; however, many more are available. A few of the more useful cursor controls are mentioned below:

> E(dit ◄———— If not in the editor
> ⟨ctrl O⟩ moves cursor up one line
> ⟨5 ctrl O⟩ moves cursor up 5 lines
>
> ⟨ctrl L⟩ moves cursor down one line
> ⟨8 ctrl L⟩ moves cursor down eight lines
>
> ————represents infinite moves
>
> ⟨/ ctrl O⟩ moves cursor to beginning of program
> ⟨/ ctrl L⟩ moves cursor to end of program
>
> J(ump B moves cursor to beginning of program
> J(ump E moves cursor to end of program

**FILER**

Typing F while at the command level executes the Filer program. A list of options is then displayed. The options underlined are the ones most commonly used and will be the only ones discussed in this text.

Filer: G, S, N, L, R, C, T, D, Q
⟨G(et, S(ave, N(ew, L(dir, R(em, C(cng, T(rans, Q(uit⟩

⟨for extended list type ?⟩

Filer: W, B, E, K, M, P, V, X, Z
⟨W(hat, B(ad-blks, E(xt-dir, K(rnch, M(ake, P(refix, V(ols, X(amine, Z(ero⟩

*Retrieve a Program From a Disk* (Get)

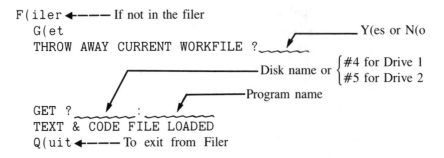

```
F(iler ◄———— If not in the filer
  G(et
  THROW AWAY CURRENT WORKFILE ?_____  ——————————— Y(es or N(o
                                              ┌ #4 for Drive 1
                        ——————— Disk name or ┤
                                              └ #5 for Drive 2
                          ——————— Program name
  GET ?_____:_____
  TEXT & CODE FILE LOADED
  Q(uit ◄———— To exit from Filer
```

*Save a Program on a Disk* (Save)

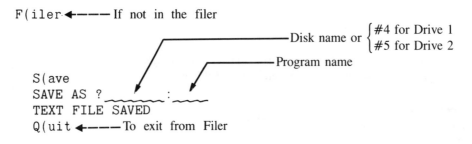

```
F(iler ◄———— If not in the filer
                                            ┌ #4 for Drive 1
                       ——————— Disk name or ┤
                                            └ #5 for Drive 2
                        ——————— Program name
  S(ave
  SAVE AS ?_____:_____
  TEXT FILE SAVED
  Q(uit ◄———— To exit from Filer
```

*Clear System Workfile* (New)

```
F(iler ◄———— If not in the Filer
  N(ew
  THROW AWAY CURRENT WORKFILE ? Y(es
  WORKFILE CLEARED
  Q(uit ◄———— To exit from Filer
```

*List Directory on Monitor* (List Directory)

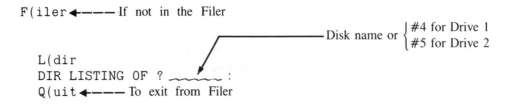

```
F(iler ◄———— If not in the Filer
                                          ┌ #4 for Drive 1
                     ——————— Disk name or ┤
                                          └ #5 for Drive 2
  L(dir
  DIR LISTING OF ?_____:
  Q(uit ◄———— To exit from Filer
```

*List Directory on Printer* (List Directory)

```
F(iler ◄———— If not in the Filer
                                          ┌ #4 for Drive 1
                     ——————— Disk name or ┤
                                          └ #5 for Drive 2
  L(dir
  DIR LISTING OF ?_____:,Printer:
  Q(uit ◄———— To exit Filer
```

*Remove a File from a Disk* (Remove)

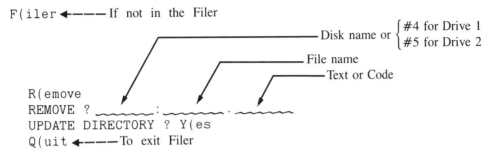

```
F(iler ◄———— If not in the Filer
                                                ———— Disk name or { #4 for Drive 1
                                                                   { #5 for Drive 2
                                      ——— File name
                                   ——— Text or Code
     R(emove
     REMOVE ? _____ : _____ . _____
     UPDATE DIRECTORY ? Y(es
     Q(uit ◄———— To exit Filer
```

*Change the Name of a Disk* (Change)

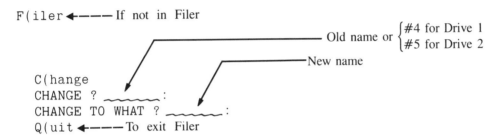

```
F(iler ◄———— If not in Filer
                                                ———— Old name or { #4 for Drive 1
                                                                 { #5 for Drive 2
                                   ——— New name
     C(hange
     CHANGE ? _____ :
     CHANGE TO WHAT ? _____ :
     Q(uit ◄———— To exit Filer
```

*List a Program on the Printer* (Transfer)

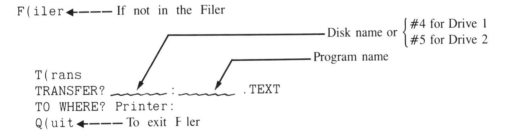

```
F(iler ◄———— If not in the Filer
                                                ———— Disk name or { #4 for Drive 1
                                                                  { #5 for Drive 2
                                   ——— Program name
     T(rans
     TRANSFER? _____ : _____ . TEXT
     TO WHERE? Printer:
     Q(uit ◄———— To exit F ler
```

*List the Program in the Workfile on the Printer* (Transfer)

```
F(iler ◄———— If not in Filer
  T(rans
  TRANSFER? System.wrk.text
  TO WHERE ? Printer:
  Q(uit ◄———— To exit Filer
```

*Krunch a Disk* (Crunch)

Moves the files on a specified diskette so that unused blocks are combined. `Krunch` is used when the disk seems to be out of space because the unused space on the disk is fragmented.

```
F(iler ◄———— If not in the Filer
                                          ┌——Disk name or number
    K(runch                               │
    CRUNCH WHAT VOL ? _____ :  ◄—────────┘
    FROM END OF DISK, BLOCK 280 ? (Y/N) Y
    ⟨do not touch any key until moving process is complete⟩
    Q(uit ◄———— To exit Filer
```

*Erase a Disk* (Zero)

Erases the directory of the specified volume. `Z(ero` is used to clear a used disk. The command does not format the disk; therefore the disk must already have been formatted by the FORMATTER utility program.

```
F(iler ◄———— If not in Filer
                                          ┌——Disk name or number
    Z(ero                                 │
    ZERO DIR OF WHAT VOL ? _____ :  ◄────┘
    DUPLICATE DIR ? N
                         └———————— Always respond with N
    Q(uit ◄———— To exit Filer
```

*Formatting (Initializing) a Disk* (Execute)

```
X(ecute ◄———— Command level
    EXECUTE WHICH FILE?
    ⟨Place the APPLE3 disk in Drive 2⟩
    ⟨Respond with ⟩ APPLE3:FORMATTER
    FORMAT WHICH DISK (4, 5, 9..12)?
    ⟨Place the disk to be formatted in Drive 2⟩
    ⟨Respond with⟩ 5
    ⟨Disk will be formatted⟩
    FORMAT WHICH DISK (4, 5, 9..12)?
    ⟨When all disks have been formatted, respond with ⟨return⟩ only⟩
```

Note: A disk formatted with APPLE3:FORMATTER will have the name (BLANK).
In most cases the name should be changed. See `Change` in the Filer section.

# Appendix II
# TRS–80 OPERATING SYSTEM

**TRS–80**

**Basic functions: Compile, Kill, Load, Run, Save, Edit**

COMPILE    To compile a program, load the program into the Editor if it is not already there, then select 'C' for Compile. The computer will then compile the program. If an error is found the computer will stop and pressing ENTER will return to the menu. After compiling is complete, ENTER must be pressed.

KILL       To erase or clear the contents of the Editor select 'K'. Respond to the prompt by pressing 'Y'.

LOAD       This command loads a program into the Editor. When 'L' is pressed the computer will prompt for the file name. If this command is not wanted it can be aborted (quit) by pressing BREAK. Enter the name that the program is stored under on the disk along with any extension and/or password and/or the drive number (see DOS manual for more information on program names). Then press ENTER. After the loading is complete, the computer will prompt to press ENTER. Doing this returns to the menu.

RUN        To Run a program select 'R' for Run. The computer will then Run the compiled program. If the program has not been compiled the computer will first compile it. After execution is complete the computer will prompt to press ENTER. Pressing ENTER returns to the menu.

SAVE       This command saves the contents of the Editor to the disk. Pressing BREAK aborts. After entering the name that the program is to be stored under (which may include an extension, password, and drive number (see DOS manual)) press ENTER. After the program is saved the computer will prompt to press ENTER. Pressing ENTER returns to the menu.

EDIT       Cursor commands: ←, ↑, ↓, →
           Control commands: C,D,E,F,N,O,P,Q,T,W

Cursor commands:

   ↓ Moves the cursor down to the next line.
   ↑ Moves the cursor up to the previous line.
   → Moves the cursor to the next position to the right on the current line.
   ← Moves the cursor to the previous position to the left on the current line.
   SHIFT ← Erases the previous character to the left of the cursor on the current line.

Control commands:

   While holding SHIFT ↓ (the control function) press:

   C  To cancel any editing that has been made on the present line. If ENTER has been pressed this will not work.

D To delete the character over the cursor and move everything on the right one space left.

```
PRROGRAM_____;   original  statement
PROGRAM _____;   pressing  control  D
PROGRAM_____;    final  statement
```

E To erase the line that the cursor is positioned on.

```
PROGRAM _____;⎫
_ VAR _____;   ⎬ original  lines
BEGIN                  ⎭

PROGRAM_____;⎫
BEGIN                 ⎬ after control E
                      ⎭
```

L To open a blank line at the current cursor position. All lines below the cursor are moved down one line.

```
PROGRAM _____;  ⎫
_ VAR _____;    ⎬ original lines
                      
PROGRAM_____;   ⎫
—                      ⎬ after control L
  VAR _____;    ⎭
```

N To display the next 15 lines of the program.

O To open a space at the current cursor position. Everything from the cursor position to the right including the character that the cursor is on moves right.

```
PRGRAM _____;   original  statement
PR_GRAM _____;  control  O
PROGRAM _____;  typing  the  missing  O
```

P To display the previous 15 lines of the program.

Q To exit the Editor and return to the menu.

T To move cursor to top of program.

```
FOR_____ TO ____ DO ⎫
_____ ⎬ original  lines
_____ ⎭

PROGRAM _____;  ⎫
  VAR _____;    ⎬ after control T
  _____;        ⎭
```

W The contents of the Editor (the program) from the current cursor position to the end of the program are sent to the printer. This is the method of listing programs on the line printer. Remember that the cursor should be at the top left of the first line of the program.

# Appendix III
# IBM OPERATING SYSTEM

**IBM PC**

SYSTEM 2: (DRIVE 4)
PASCAL: (DRIVE 5)
<PASCAL: must be in drive 5 when compiling>

Command: <u>E(dit</u>, <u>R(un</u>, <u>F(ile</u>, <u>C(omp</u>, L(ink, X(ecute, A(ssem?

<For extended list type ?>

Command: D(ebug, H(alt, I(nitialize, U(ser restart, M(onitor

A brief illustration or discussion about the commands that are underlined above will be given in this appendix. These commands are the ones most commonly used and are needed to complete the assignments in this text. Consult the User's Guide and Reference Manual for more complete explanations.


## AIII.1 EDITOR

Type E while at the Command level to execute the Editor program. A list of the options are then displayed. The options underlined are the ones most commonly used and will be the only ones discussed in this text.

>Edit: <u>A(djst</u> C(py <u>D(let</u> F(ind <u>I(nsrt</u> J(mp K(ol R(plc <u>Q(uit</u> <u>X(ch</u> Z(ap


*Adjust alignment* (Adjust)

When a line is to move left or right to obtain a new alignment the A(djst option may be used.

```
E(dit◄————If not in the Editor
    <position cursor at the beginning of line to move>
    A(djst
    <press (◄, ►)  to  adjust  line>
    <press (▼) to adjust following line the same number of spaces>
    <press (▲) to adjust preceeding line the same number of spaces>
    <ctrl C> to accept, <Esc> to reject
    May be repeated as many times as necessary
    Q(uit◄———— When no more editing is necessary
    U(pdate
```

*Delete Characters* (Delete)

A program that is in the workfile may have to be altered by deleting characters.

```
E(dit◄————If not in the Editor
    <position cursor (return, ◄, ➔)>
    D(let
    <type (➔) to delete characters>
    <ctrl C> to accept deletes, <Esc> to reject deletes
    May be repeated as many times as necessary
    Q(uit◄————When no more editing is to be completed
    U(pdate
```

*Delete a Line* (Delete)

A complete line can be deleted, when in the D(let mode, by pressing the return key. It is not necessary to delete a single character at a time.

```
E(dit◄———— If not in the Editor
    <position at 1st character of line to be deleted>
    D(let
    <return>◄———— Deletes line
    <return>◄———— Each return deletes an additional line
    <ctrl C> to accept deletes, <Esc> to reject deletes
    May be repeated as many times as necessary
    Q(uit◄———— When no more editing is to be completed
    U(pdate
```

*Type in a Program* (Insert)

Before a program can be typed into the computer the system workfile may have to be cleared. *Clearing the Workfile* (see the Filer section of this appendix) is used to accomplish this task.

```
E(dit◄———— If not in the Editor
    I(nsrt
    <Type program>
    <ctrl C>◄———— Exits from input mode
    Q(uit◄————When no editing is needed
    U(pdate
```

*Insert Characters* (Insert)

A program that is in the workfile may have to be altered by inserting additional characters.

```
E(dit◄———— If not in the Editor
    <position cursor (return, ◄, ➔)>
    I(nsrt
    <Type characters>
```

<ctrl C> to accept inserts, <Esc> to reject inserts
May be repeated as many times as necessary
Q(uit◄──── When no more editing is to be completed
U(pdate


*Exchange Characters* (Exchange)

When consecutive characters are to be changed the X(ch option can be executed. For example: Program is exchanged for PROGRAM or UNIT1 is changed to Unit2.

E(dit◄──── If not in the Editor
    <position cursor (return, ◄, ►)>
    X(ch
    <the characters under the cursor will be>
    <replaced by a typed character>
    <ctrl C> to accept exchange, <Esc> to reject exchange
    May be repeated as many times as necessary
    Q(uit◄────When no more editing is to be completed
    U(pdate


*Cursor Control*

In the preceding examples only the (return, ◄, ►) cursor controls were mentioned. More are available, however. A few of the more useful cursor controls are mentioned below:

E(dit◄──── If not in the Editor
    (↑) moves cursor up one line
    (↓) moves cursor down one line

    J(mp B moves cursor to beginning of program
    J(mp E moves cursor to end of program


## FILER

Typing F while at the command level executes the Filer program. A list of options are then listed. The options underlined are the ones most commonly used and will be the only ones discussed in this text.

Filer: G(et, S(ave, W(hat, N(ew, L(dir, R(em, C(hng, T(rans, D(ate

<For extended list type ?>
Filer: Q(uit, B(ad-blks, E(xt-dir, K(rnch, M(ake, P(refix, V(ols

<For further extended list type ?>
Filer: X(amine, Z(ero

*Retrieve a Program From a Disk* (Get)

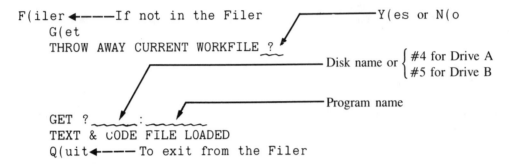

```
F(iler ◄———If not in the Filer                        ─Y(es or N(o
    G(et
    THROW AWAY CURRENT WORKFILE ?
                                                    ┌ #4 for Drive A
                                       Disk name or │
                                                    └ #5 for Drive B

                                       Program name

    GET ?_____:_____
    TEXT & CODE FILE LOADED
    Q(uit◄——— To exit from the Filer
```

*Save a Program on a Disk* (Save)

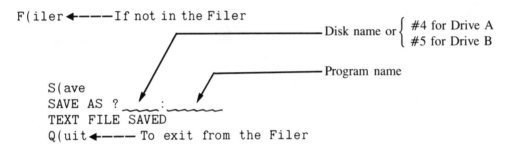

```
F(iler ◄———If not in the Filer
                                                    ┌ #4 for Drive A
                                       Disk name or │
                                                    └ #5 for Drive B

                                       Program name

    S(ave
    SAVE AS ?_____:_____
    TEXT FILE SAVED
    Q(uit◄——— To exit from the Filer
```

*Clear System Work File* (New)

```
F(iler◄——— If not in the Filer
    N(ew
    THROW AWAY CURRENT WORKFILE ? Y(es
    WORKFILE CLEARED
    Q(uit◄———To exit from the Filer
```

*List Directory on Monitor* (List Directory)

```
F(iler◄———If not in the Filer
                                                    ┌ #4 for Drive A
                                       Disk name or │
                                                    └ #5 for Drive B
    L(dir
    DIR LISTING OF ?_____:
    Q(uit◄——— To exit from the Filer
```

*List Directory on Printer* (List Directory)

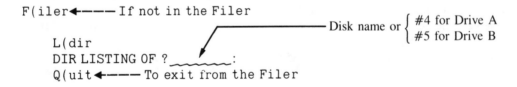

```
F(iler◄——— If not in the Filer
                                                    ┌ #4 for Drive A
                                       Disk name or │
                                                    └ #5 for Drive B
    L(dir
        DIR LISTING OF ?_____:,#6:
    Q(uit◄——— To exit Filer
```

*Remove a File From a Disk* (Remove)

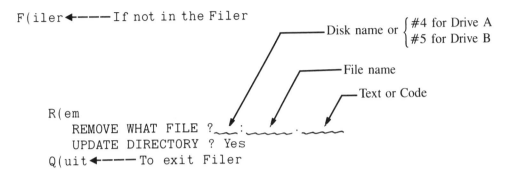

```
F(iler ◄──── If not in the Filer
                                            ┌ #4 for Drive A
                            Disk name or ┤
                                            └ #5 for Drive B

                                        File name

                                        Text or Code
    R(em
        REMOVE WHAT FILE ?___:_____._____
        UPDATE DIRECTORY ? Yes
    Q(uit ◄─── To exit Filer
```

*Change the Name of a Disk* (Change)

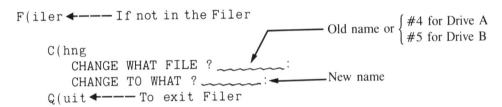

```
F(iler ◄──── If not in the Filer
                                            ┌ #4 for Drive A
                            Old name or ┤
                                            └ #5 for Drive B
        C(hng
            CHANGE WHAT FILE ? _____:
            CHANGE TO WHAT ? _____:◄─── New name
        Q(uit ◄─── To exit Filer
```

*List a Program on the Printer* (Transfer)

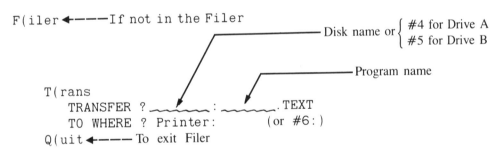

```
F(iler ◄───If not in the Filer
                                            ┌ #4 for Drive A
                            Disk name or ┤
                                            └ #5 for Drive B

                                        Program name
        T(rans
            TRANSFER ?_____:_____.TEXT
            TO WHERE ? Printer:      (or #6:)
        Q(uit ◄─── To exit Filer
```

*List the Program in the Work File on the Printer* (Transfer)

```
F(iler ◄──── If not in the Filer
    T(rans
        TRANSFER ? System.wrk.text
        TO WHERE ? Printer:
    Q(uit ◄─── To exit Filer
```

*Krunch a Disk* (Crunch)

Moves the files on a specified diskette so that unused blocks are combined. Krunch is used when the disk seems to be out of space because the unused space on the disk is fragmented.

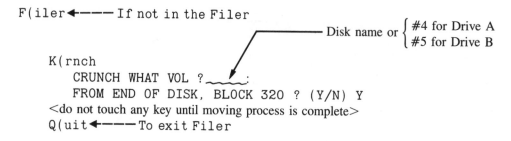

```
F(iler◄———If not in the Filer
```
Disk name or $\begin{cases} \text{\#4 for Drive A} \\ \text{\#5 for Drive B} \end{cases}$
```
    K(rnch
        CRUNCH WHAT VOL ?_____:
        FROM END OF DISK, BLOCK 320 ? (Y/N) Y
    <do not touch any key until moving process is complete>
    Q(uit◄———To exit Filer
```

*Erase a Disk* (Zero)

Erases the directory of the specified volume. Z(ero is used to clear a used disk. The command does not format the disk; therefore the disk must already have been formatted by the DISKFORMAT utility program.

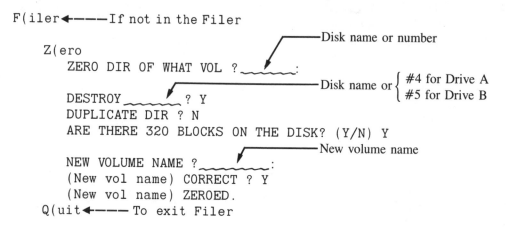

```
F(iler◄———If not in the Filer
```
Disk name or number
```
    Z(ero
        ZERO DIR OF WHAT VOL ?_____:
```
Disk name or $\begin{cases} \text{\#4 for Drive A} \\ \text{\#5 for Drive B} \end{cases}$
```
        DESTROY_____? Y
        DUPLICATE DIR ? N
        ARE THERE 320 BLOCKS ON THE DISK? (Y/N) Y
```
New volume name
```
        NEW VOLUME NAME ?_____:
        (New vol name) CORRECT ? Y
        (New vol name) ZEROED.
    Q(uit◄———To exit Filer
```

*Formatting (Initializing) a Disk* (Execute)

At the Command level, type:

```
X(ecute
    EXECUTE WHAT FILE ?
```
<Place the UTILITY disk in drive #5>
<Respond with> #5:DISKFORMAT
```
    ENTER UNIT NUMBER OF DISK TO BE FORMATTED (4..5):
```
<Remove BOTH the SYSTEM 2: disk and UTILITY: disk>
<Place the disk to be formatted in drive #5>
<Respond with> 5
```
    INSERT DISK IN UNIT 5 AND PRESS <ENTER>...
```
<Since the blank disk is already in #5, press enter>
<Disk will be formatted>
```
U(ser-restart ◄———If more disks are to be formatted
```

# Appendix IV
## ALPHABETICAL SEQUENCE

Relational operations ($>$, $<=$, etc.) in Pascal compare strings according to the following sequence of letters:

| | | | | | |
|---|---|---|---|---|---|
| space | 0 | @ | P | f | v |
| ! | 1 | A | Q | g | w |
| " | 2 | B | R | h | x |
| # | 3 | C | S | i | y |
| $ | 4 | D | T | j | z |
| % | 5 | E | U | k | |
| & | 6 | F | V | l | |
| ' | 7 | G | W | m | |
| ( | 8 | H | X | n | |
| ) | 9 | I | Y | o | |
| * | : | J | Z | p | |
| + | ; | K | a | q | |
| , | < | L | b | r | |
| − | = | M | c | s | |
| . | > | N | d | t | |
| / | ? | O | e | u | |

Examples:

CHILDREN $<$ children
Children $\quad <$ children
childreN $\quad <$ children

The computer checks each letter of the word on the left with the corresponding letter of the word on the right. When the letters are different, the computer then decides which letter comes first according to the above chart. The letter that comes first is said to be less than the other letter. The characters in the upper left of the chart are less than all letters after it. For any given character, all characters that follow are greater and all previous characters are less. If the letters are the same, the process continues until corresponding letters are not the same. If no letter is found to be different, the two strings are evaluated as equal. Notice that capital and lower case letters are not the same.

If the comparison was "america $<$ America" the computer would check each letter and determine if the comparison is true. In this case the first letter would be compared. "a" is not less than "A" according to the above list; therefore, the comparison would be evaluated as false.

| Statement | Evaluation |
|---|---|
| Hello $<$ almost | TRUE |
| good $<$ GOOD | FALSE |
| H $<$ a | TRUE |

Notice that the "H" comes before the "a" even though "A" comes before "H" in the alphabet. This is due to the different positions of the upper and lower case letters.

# Appendix V
# DATA ENTRY WITH A DATA FILE

**APPLE IBM PC**

To avoid entering the data each time a program is run Data Files may be used. A second advantage is that data is entered by using the editor so all of the editing features of the editor can be used to change, add to, or delete an entry of the data.

*Loading Data into a Data File*

```
E(dit◄──── If not in Editor
  I(nsert
  <type data>
  <control C> to accept data, <Esc> to reject
  Q(uit ◄────When no more editing is to be completed
  W(rite to a file name and return
```

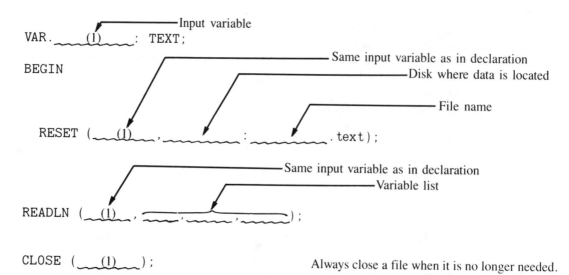

```
                                                   ┌──Disk
                                                   │        ┌──File name
Name of output file (<cr> to return) ─ ─► ____:____
```

*Using a Data File for Data Entry*

```
                    ┌──────Input variable
VAR. ____(1)____ : TEXT;
                                          ┌──Same input variable as in declaration
BEGIN                                     │  ┌──Disk where data is located
                                          │  │  ┌──File name
RESET ( ___(1)___ , _____ : _____.text);

                    ┌──Same input variable as in declaration
                    │  ┌──Variable list
READLN ( ___(1)___ , ___,___,___ );

CLOSE ( ___(1)___ );          Always close a file when it is no longer needed.
```

*Demonstration Problem*

Write a program that will read groups of five numbers from a data file and will display the sum and average. Enter a negative number for the first of the five numbers as a stopping signal.

Data File Display

```
5  8  6  4  3
16  21  43  17  82
10.1   1.6   7.5   8.3   9.3
-1  0  0  0  0
```

Entered using the editor and saved under the name DFile. To avoid problems, the data should be typed so that each line will provide the data for a single READLN statement.

Display Sample

```
   SUM     AVERAGE
  26.00       5.20
 179.00      35.80
  36.80       7.36
```

```pascal
PROGRAM Appex5Demo;
   VAR X1,X2,X3,X4,X5: REAL;
       Sum,Ave: REAL;            ──── Disk where data is located
       DFileVar: TEXT;              ──── File name
BEGIN
   RESET (DFileVar, 'Pas:DFile.text');
   WRITELN ('SUM':7,'AVERAGE':12);
   READLN (DFileVar,X1,X2,X3,X4,X5);
   WHILE X1 >= 0 DO
     BEGIN
       Sum:= X1+X2+X3+X4+X5;
       Ave:= Sum / 5;
       WRITELN (Sum:8:2,Ave:10:2);
       READLN (DFileVar,X1,X2,X3,X4,X5);
     END;
   CLOSE (DFileVar);
END.
```

Note: The program can be run several times while the data file has to be entered and stored only once.

# Appendix VI
# PRINTING TO A TEXT FILE

The technique presented in this appendix could be used when output to the printer is required and a printer is not available on the computer being used. The information is output to a text file on a specified disk and printed when a printer is available.

*Printing information to a text file*

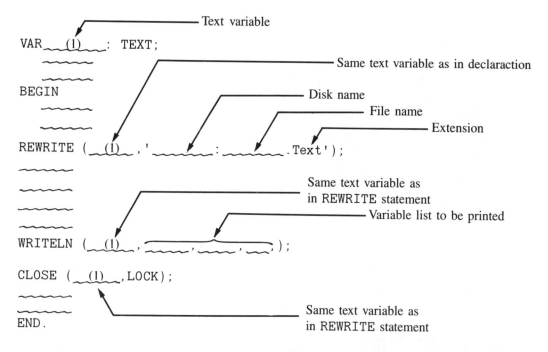

Using the REWRITE statement with a text variable permits information to be transferred to the specified disk as a text file, which can later be transferred to the printer. The WRITELN statement with the text variable being the first listed will cause the information to be sent to the specified text file. The information is transfered exactly the same as if it were going to a printer. The CLOSE—LOCK statement will cause the current file name to be placed in the directory of the appropriate disk.

**APPLE IBM PC**

*Example*

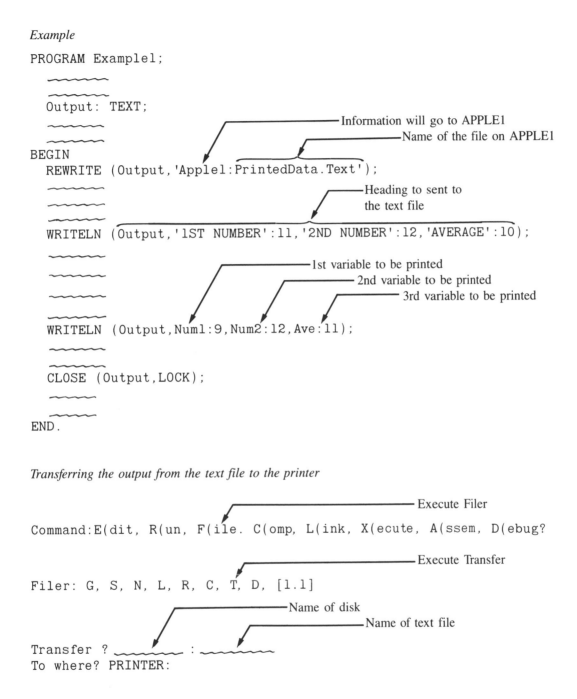

```
PROGRAM Example1;
  ~~~~~~
  ~~~~~~
  Output: TEXT;
  ~~~~~~
  ~~~~~~
BEGIN
  REWRITE (Output,'Apple1:PrintedData.Text');
  ~~~~~~
  ~~~~~~
  ~~~~~~
  WRITELN (Output,'1ST NUMBER':11,'2ND NUMBER':12,'AVERAGE':10);
  ~~~~~~
  ~~~~~~
  ~~~~~~
  ~~~~~~
  WRITELN (Output,Num1:9,Num2:12,Ave:11);
  ~~~~~~
  ~~~~~~
  CLOSE (Output,LOCK);
  ~~~~~~
  ~~~~~~
END.
```

Information will go to APPLE1

Name of the file on APPLE1

Heading to sent to the text file

1st variable to be printed

2nd variable to be printed

3rd variable to be printed

*Transferring the output from the text file to the printer*

Execute Filer

```
Command:E(dit, R(un, F(ile. C(omp, L(ink, X(ecute, A(ssem, D(ebug?
```

Execute Transfer

```
Filer: G, S, N, L, R, C, T, D, [1.1]
```

Name of disk

Name of text file

```
Transfer ? _____ : ~~~~~~~~~
To where? PRINTER:
```

*Demonstration Problem*

Write a program to determine the value of the inventory for a motorcycle shop. The operator is to enter the quantity, size in CC, and price of each type of cycle in stock. The printout should contain this information and the total value of each type of cycle. The information as shown in the print sample, including blank lines and spacing, is to be output to a text file. After the program is terminated, the Filer is then used to transfer the text file to the printer.

Display Sample

```
11   50   795.00
3    250  1295.50
2    750  1895.00
1    1100 2195.98
-1   0    0
```

Print Sample

```
QUANTITY      CC        PRICE    TOTAL AMOUNT

    11        50        795.00      8745.00
     3       250       1295.50      3886.50
     2       750       1895.00      3790.00
     1      1100       2195.98      2195.98
TOTAL VALUE  =   18617.5
```

Program (App5Demol) transfers output to a text file using:
    text variable (Table)
    disk (APPLE1)
    file name (App5Demol.Text)

```
PROGRAM App5Demol;
  VAR Quan,Size: INTEGER;
      Price,TotalAmt,TotalVal: REAL;
      Table: TEXT;
BEGIN
  REWRITE (Table,'APPLE1:App5Demol.Text');
  WRITELN (Table,'QUANTITY':9,'CC':5,'PRICE':11,'TOTAL AMOUNT':17);
  WRITELN (Table);
  TotalVal:= 0.0;
  READLN (Quan,Size,Price);
  WHILE Quan > 0 DO
    BEGIN
      TotalAmt:= Quan * Price;
      WRITELN (Table,Quan:6,Size:9,Price:11:2,TotalAmt:14:2);
      TotalVal:= TotalVal + TotalAmt;
      READLN (Quan,Size,Price);
    END;
  WRITELN (Table,'TOTAL VALUE= ',TotalVal:8:2);
  CLOSE (Table,LOCK);
END.
```

*Running the Program*

1. Have the appropriate disk (APPLE1 for the given example) in either drive.
2. Run the program the normal way.


*Print Output*

1. Execute the Filer.
2. Transfer file (App5Demo1.text for the given example) to the printer.

# Appendix VII
## SORTING

There are many ways to sort arrays of numbers; some are much more efficient than others. As a general rule, the faster a sort executes the more complicated the logic of the sort becomes. The sort presented, which is referred to as a bubble sort, is chosen for its simplicity and ease of programming. After it is mastered a student may want to go to other sources and study sorts with more involved logic.

To begin the sort procedure load the numbers into an array. The sort is then accomplished by comparing all consecutive elements and when they are out of order an interchange is completed and a Boolean variable is set to FALSE. After each pass is complete, if the Boolean variable is FALSE it is set back to TRUE and all consecutive values are again checked to see if they are in the correct order. Finally, when a pass is completed and the Boolean variable is TRUE, the sort is complete.

The same logic can be applied to alphabetizing strings or packed arrays where they are introduced in Lessons 17 and 18.

Suppose these are the data values:

|  | A[1] | A[2] | A[3] | A[5] |  |  |
|---|---|---|---|---|---|---|
|  | 7 | 10 | 3 | 6 | 1 | Start with Flag := TRUE |
| **FIRST PASS:** |  |  |  |  |  |  |
| After first | | OK | Switch | | | |
| interchange | 7 | 3 | 10 | 6 | 1 | Set Flag := FALSE |
|  |  |  | Switch | | | (Whenever an interchange |
| After second |  |  |  |  | | is completed, FLAG |
| interchange | 7 | 3 | 6 | 10 | 1 | is set to FALSE.) |
|  |  |  |  | Switch | | |
| After third |  |  |  |  |  | |
| interchange | 7 | 3 | 6 | 1 | 10 | |

Flag is FALSE so another pass is necessary. Set Flag := TRUE and start comparisons over.

| **SECOND PASS:** |  |  |  |  |  |  |
|---|---|---|---|---|---|---|
| Start with | 7 | 3 | 6 | 1 | 10 | |
|  | Switch | | | | | |
| After first |  |  |  |  |  | |
| interchange | 3 | 7 | 6 | 1 | 10 | Set Flag := FALSE |
|  |  | Switch | | | | |
| After second |  |  |  |  |  | |
| interchange | 3 | 6 | 7 | 1 | 10 | |
|  |  |  | Switch | | | |
| After third |  |  |  |  |  | |
| interchange | 3 | 6 | 1 | 7 | 10 | |
|  |  |  |  | OK | | |

Flag is FALSE so another pass is necessary. Set Flag := TRUE and start comparisons over.

THIRD PASS:
Start with

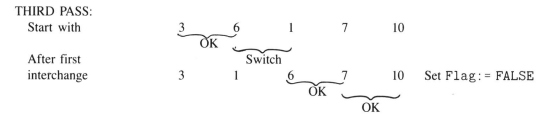

Flag is FALSE so another pass is necessary. Set Flag := TRUE and start comparisons over.

FOURTH PASS:

Start with

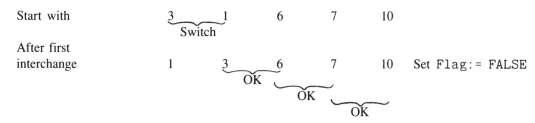

Flag is FALSE so another pass is necessary. Set Flag := TRUE and start comparisons over.

FIFTH PASS:
Start with

Flag is TRUE which means no elements were interchanged during the fifth pass through. Therefore, the numbers are sorted.